# ZADIE SMITH

PETER LANG
New York • Washington, D.C./Baltimore • Bern
Frankfurt am Main • Berlin • Brussels • Vienna • Oxford

# ZADIE SMITH
## CRITICAL ESSAYS

EDITED BY
Tracey L. Walters

PETER LANG
New York • Washington, D.C./Baltimore • Bern
Frankfurt am Main • Berlin • Brussels • Vienna • Oxford

Library of Congress Cataloging-in-Publication Data

Zadie Smith: critical essays / edited by Tracey L. Walters.
p. cm.
Includes bibliographical references.
1. Smith, Zadie—Criticism and interpretation. 2. English literature—
Black authors—History and criticism. 3. English literature—Women authors—
History and criticism. 4. Commonwealth literature (English) 5. Postcolonialism—
Commonwealth countries. 6. Identity (Philosophical concept) in literature
7. Race in literature. I. Walters, Tracey Lorraine.
PR6069.M59Z96  823'.914—dc22  2006100513
ISBN 978-0-8204-8806-6


Bibliographic information published by **Die Deutsche Bibliothek**.
**Die Deutsche Bibliothek** lists this publication in the "Deutsche
Nationalbibliografie"; detailed bibliographic data is available
on the Internet at http://dnb.ddb.de/.

Cover design by Sophie Boorsch Appel


The paper in this book meets the guidelines for permanence and durability
of the Committee on Production Guidelines for Book Longevity
of the Council of Library Resources.

*To Mummy, Bella, and Boobah*

# Contents

# Acknowledgments

First, my heartfelt gratitude goes out to Sophie Appel for patiently awaiting each chapter as I slowly learned how to format the pages (and actually never successfully learned how to format properly). Thank you for your support and gentle encouragement when production (on my part) was delayed. Thank you also to Phyllis Korper who immediately showed interest in the project and to all the staff at Peter Lang who helped make this collection possible. To my family, I have never doubted your support and appreciate your pride in my accomplishments. Thanks also to Dr. Arana, the interlibrary loan department at Stony Brook University, and the staff at London Library. Claudette, thanks for buying and mailing Smith's books. Dean, your acknowledgment and respect for my work inspires me to work harder and believe in myself. Tori and Amouri, you keep me smiling. Now, I *will* have time to play with you! I would also like to thank all the writers who contributed to this project. This collection of essays on Smith makes an important contribution to Black British literary studies.

# Introduction

*Zadie Smith: Critical Essays* is the first edited collection of essays on Zadie Smith's fiction. The decision to put together this collection was initiated in response to my inability to find adequate scholarship on Smith while researching for an assignment. In 2005 I was asked to write a biobibliographic entry on Smith. I accepted the offer assuming that a wealth of scholarship on Smith's novels was easily obtainable. As I began researching I discovered that with the exception of Claire Squires' *Zadie Smith's White Teeth: A Reader's Guide* and a handful of articles in journals, there was little criticism on Smith's work, especially her short stories. I was surprised by the lack of scholarship, especially since *White Teeth* had been highly successful and at the time Smith had published a substantial body of work. In 2006 I put out the call for papers for this collection. The response was met with enthusiasm by those equally as intrigued with Zadie Smith's narratives and Black British literature in general. The essays included in this anthology reveal the wide range of critical approaches scholars apply to Smith's novels. Within the last three years more scholars have begun building a body of scholarship devoted to Smith's work. An increasing number of articles on Smith's narratives appear in journals and at national and international conferences there have been many panels and presentations on her novels and short stories. A number of full-length studies on Smith are also soon to emerge—Phillip Tew's *Zadie Smith* is due to be published by Palgrave Macmillan in 2008. Today Smith is one of Britain's most successful, well-known Black and British writers. In addition to publishing three novels, numerous short stories, and essays, she has edited a number of anthologies. In a relatively short time Smith has earned the admiration of literary peers like Salman Rushdie, Dave Eggers, and Caryl Phillips and respect from the literary academy. Smith has received a number of Britain's prestigious literary awards including the Commonwealth Writer's Prize, the James Tait Black Memorial Prize for Fiction, and the Whitbread Award. She has also received nominations for the Man Booker Prize and the Orange Prize for Fiction.

Zadie (Sadie) was born in 1975 in Brent, North London. Smith grew up in an interracial household with her mother Yvonne Bailey-Smith, a Jamaican psychotherapist, her father Harvey Smith, a British war veteran, and her two brothers Ben and Luke. During her formative years Smith spent time alone watching black and white movies and reading. Smith was exposed to an eclectic mix of literature ranging from C.S. Lewis' *The Lion the Witch and the Wardrobe* to the Bible's *Old Testament*. Later, while a student at Cambridge University, Smith was introduced to the literature of E.M. Forster, Vladimir Nabokov, Franz Kafka, and Virginia Woolf. The influence of these writers is obvious in Smith's own writing and Smith is never bashful about admitting that she draws on the stylistic conventions of these writers. In the introduction to *On Beauty*, for example, she writes, "It should be obvious from the first line that this is a novel inspired by a love of E.M. Forster, to whom all my fiction is indebted, one way or the other. This time I wanted to repay with homage." At Cambridge Smith published a number of short stories in *The May Anthologies*, the college's literary journal which was, at the time, edited by fellow writer Nick Laird (in 2004 Smith and Laird were married). The publication of the short piece "Mrs. Begum," a story about multiculturalism and hybridity and the interplay between Whites and South Asians brought Smith to the attention of a literary agent who was impressed with the twenty-one-year-old's writing style and her approach to the subject of multiculturalism and cultural conflict. After signing with an agent from the Wylie Agency Smith was offered a £250,000 two-book deal with Hamish Hamilton. Smith's last two years at Cambridge were spent completing *White Teeth*, which was published in 2000. *White Teeth* made Smith an international phenomenon. Critics applauded Smith's ability to address a multiplicity of themes—religious fundamentalism, postcolonialism, hybridity aesthetics, and multiculturalism—in a single novel, complemented by a touch of humor. Smith's success was also partially the result of the media's interest in Smith herself. Smith's biracial heritage, age, talent, and newfound wealth made for an intriguing story about the new face and fresh voice of contemporary British literature. Quickly Smith became a representative of Britain's newfound initiative to recognize multiculturalism and diversity. Smith rejected the multicultural title ascribed to her and repeatedly in articles she expressed discontent with the label. While others praised *White Teeth* Smith was highly critical of the novel calling it "a fat and messy kid." Smith's novel was so successful that in 2002 the novel was adapted into a television mini series. In the movie Smith makes a cameo appearance. After *White Teeth* Smith published short stories in literary journals such as *The New Yorker* and *Granta*. *White Teeth* was followed by *The Autograph Man* (2002) a metafictional text about a brooding autograph man grieving the loss of his father. Similar to *White Teeth* Smith revisits themes of cultural hybridity and identity, this time from the perspective of a biracial Jewish Asian protagonist. The narrative also deals with Jewish mysticism and celebrity obsession. Critics who anticipated the clear writing style and the same heady themes broached in *White Teeth* were disappointed with Smith's disjointed narrative and experimentation with metafictional devices. Some critics accused Smith of rushing the sophomore novel and stated that the text was underdeveloped and poorly written. After the *Autograph Man* Smith took up residence as a fellow at the Radcliff School at Harvard University in Boston. In 2005 Smith published her third novel *On Beauty*, a campus novel that focuses on questions of aesthetics, politics, and identity. The narrative recounts the experiences of two competing families who allow their opposing ideological differences to obscure their ability to appreciate and recognize the beauty of humanity. In this same year Smith also published *Martha and Hanwell* a book of short stories featuring two tormented characters. The first story "Martha, Martha" features a young Black British girl who discovers that her search for an apartment is really about the search for a sense of identity. The second story, "Hanwell in Hell," is a dark tale about an emotionally traumatized man who struggles to cope with the death of his wife and estrangement from his daughters. For her next project Smith will try her hand at literary criticism. Smith intends to write a critical analysis on the works of writers like Forster and Hurston.

*Zadie Smith: Critical Essays* is divided into two sections. The first section, "Postcolonial and Postmodernist Readings of Zadie Smith's Novels" examines Smith's discussions of postmodernism, history, cultural alienation, and exile. The second section, "Race Mixing: Britishness, Blackness, and the Construction of Racial Identities," investigates Smith's exploration of nationhood, racial and gender identity, cultural nationalism, and religious fundamentalism. Smith's engagement with a broad range of themes and eclectic writing style has made it difficult for some scholars to define exactly how Smith's novels should be categorized. Critics who observe Smith's indebtedness to writers such as Forster or Woolf associate Smith's work with the British literary tradition and others who identify with her engagement of postcolonial themes of cultural alienation and exile relate her work with the Black British literary tradition.

Stylistically Smith's narratives also do not fit neatly into any literary genre for Smith's fiction shares features with the comic novel, metafictional novels, and modernist and postmodernist novels. The lead article in this anthology reveals the complexity of defining Smith's fiction. In "Contextualiz-ing Zadie Smith in a Postmodern and Postcolonial World," Matthew Pa-proth takes on to the challenge of trying to determine if Smith's novels should be read as modernist or postmodernist. Paproth maintains that Smith "positions herself firmly between modernism and postmodernism." In his investigation of *White Teeth* Paproth shows that while the novel's structure and writing style is modernist, the themes Smith interrogates—the distortion of reality and conflicts between races and classes—associate the text with postmodernism. Paproth acknowledges that the text shares qualities with both genres, but concludes that novels like *White Teeth* and *On Beauty* are modernist because despite the experimental style of the writing, the content of her narratives adheres to a structure that is modernist. In contrast to Pa-proth, Urszula Terentowicz-Fotyga's "The Impossible Self and the Poetics of the Urban Hyperreal in Zadie Smith's *The Autograph Man*" offers a post-modernist reading of Smith's fiction. Drawing upon Baudrillard's theories of "simulacrum" and Walter Benjamin's concept of "aura," Terentowicz-Fotyga employs a postmodernist reading to demonstrate that in novels like *White Teeth*, the fusion of reality and the imagined distorts the concept of the real.

While Smith's novels lend themselves structurally and thematically to postmodernist readings, the texts can also be read from a postcolonial per-spective. Rafe Dalleo's postcolonialist analysis of *White Teeth* calls for schol-ars to reassess their definition of Smith's narratives as either British or Black British. Dalleo's postcolonial approach highlights a number of qualities that relate Smith's writing with Caribbean literature. Dalleo suggests that the "Caribbeaness" of the characters, the presence and discussion of the large Caribbean immigrant population, and the transplantation of Caribbean cul-ture into British society (language and clothing) provide the novel's Carib-bean qualities. Ulka Anjaria's postcolonial analysis highlights both the political and aesthetic qualities of *White Teeth* and *On Beauty*. Anjaria dem-onstrates how *On Beauty* engages readers with both a postcolonial critique and a philosophical discussion of aesthetics. Postcolonial readings often focus on how the immigrant's experience of displacement leads to a conflict with national and ethnic identity. Maeve Tynan's reading of *On Beauty* departs from traditional postcolonial investigations of Smith's fiction. Instead of fo-cusing on the cultural alienation experienced by the immigrant population, Tynan investigates the experiences of British-born children who find the question of identity to be less complex than it is for their parents. Tynan also interrogates the significance of Smith's revision of Forster's *Howards End*, arguing that intertextuality enriches the text rather than devalues its originality. While most articles interrogate Smith's discussions of identity and marginalization from a racial and national perspective, Fischer, Walters, and Raynor address identity politics from a gendered perspective. Similar to Tynan, Fischer makes note of Smith's revision of Forster's *Howards End*. But instead of concentrating on how Smith signifies on Forster's novel, Fischer underscores the relevance of acknowledging how Smith signifies on the literature of Black female writers Zora Neale Hurston and Toni Morrison. Fischer demonstrates that the character Kiki in *On Beauty* shares a number of characteristics with Janie, the protagonist of Hurston's *Their Eyes Were Watching God*. Like Janie, Kiki struggles to escape from an oppressive relationship that denies her voice and independence. Both women find it is only after they leave the men in their lives that they are able to create their own definition of self. Typically Smith's writing is associated with a White male literary tradition. Fischer's essay offers a reading of Smith's fiction that connects her to a Black female literary tradition, an aspect that has been overlooked by most other scholars. My own essay examines Smith's portrayal of Black women as the mammy, matriarch, and jezebel stereotypes. The article tries to explain Smith's motivation for creating these kinds of derogatory images of Black women. Sharon Raynor's postcolonial comparative reading of "Hanwell in Hell" and Sam Selvon's *Lonely Londoners* also addresses the representation of women in Black literature. Raynor shows that in both novels the female characters are "silenced" and overshadowed by male characters who compensate for their own feelings of alienation by marginalizing women.

One of the distinguishing features between postmillennial Black British writers and the first generation of Black British writers is that the younger writers offer a different discussion of Britishness, identity, and cultural conflict. Lexi Stuckey's examination of "Hanwell in Hell" reveals that Smith's story exposes the failure of multiculturalism. Stuckey argues that the story stands in contrast to earlier works like *White Teeth*, which present an optimistic view of multiculturalism. Stuckey shows how in "Hanwell in Hell" the protagonist's color-blindness, his literal inability to distinguish colors and his stubborn unwillingness to acknowledge racial difference, accounts for the breakdown of his marriage and separation from his children. Kris Knauer's "The Root Canals of Zadie Smith: London's Intergenerational Adaptation" contrasts with Stuckey's reading of "Hanwell." Knauer argues that with texts like *White Teeth* Smith presents an optimistic view of contemporary multicultural, multiethnic London. Knauer explains that Smith's novels show how the influence of immigrant culture upon British culture helps redefine the notion of British cultural identity. But as Esra Mirze's essay "Fundamental Differences in Zadie Smith's *White Teeth*" demonstrates, not all of Smith's characters desire cultural assimilation or a British identity. Mirze's discussion of the relationship between religion and identity in *White Teeth* shows how some in the Asian community find it difficult to assimilate. Mirze suggests that religious differences disallow Smith's Asian characters from fully integrating into British society. She argues that Islam gives some Asians a sense of cultural identity and community that they do not wish to compromise. While these immigrants remain conflicted about Britishness and national identity, others, especially first-generation-born children either embrace or reject Islam. Like Stuckey, Knauer, and Mirze, Jakubiak also addresses questions of identity. Whereas the former scholars treat the issue from the perspective of national and cultural identity, Jakubiak's discussion centers on Smith herself and the publishing industry's marketing of *White Teeth*. Jakubiak maintains that the success of the novel is the result of an effective marketing campaign that compromised the integrity of the work and the dignity of the author. Jakubiak explores how the publishing industry promotes Smith's narrative as a "safe and easily consumable product" (202). Jakubiak notes that while many regard the novel as an "optimistic" view of multiculturalism, the narrative actually presents an "illusion" of reality.

As a Black and British writer Smith joins the ranks of other established Black writers such as Sam Selvon, Joan Riley, Beryl Gilroy, Caryl Phillips, and Andrea Levy who helped establish the Black British canon. Smith's success has contributed to the increased attention to Black British literature and allowed for recognition of underappreciated writers like Jackie Kay, Courttia Newland, Bernardine Evaristo, or Diran Adebayo. *Zadie Smith: Critical Essays* is a much-needed resource for those who study British literature, Black British literature, and diasporic literature. Hopefully this collection will inspire more scholarship devoted to Black British writing.

# SECTION I.
# Postcolonial and Postmodernist Readings of Zadie Smith's Novels

# CHAPTER I
## The Flipping Coin:
## The Modernist and Postmodernist Zadie Smith

*Matthew Paproth, Georgia Institute of Technology*

*The coin rose and flipped as a coin would rise and flip every time in a perfect world, flash-
ing its light and then revealing its dark enough times to mesmerize a man. Then, at some
point in its triumphant ascension, it began to arc, and the arc went wrong, and Archibald…turned with the others to watch it complete an elegant swoop toward the pinball
machine and somersault straight into the slot. Immediately the huge old beast lit up; the
ball shot off and began its chaotic, noisy course…until, with no one to assist it, no one to
direct it, it gave up the ghost and dropped back into the swallowing hole. (White Teeth
377)*

In *White Teeth*, Zadie Smith demonstrates the problems of living in a postmodern world, as her characters constantly collide with each other in the
pursuit of meaning and truth. Like Archie Jones, the coin-flipper of the previous passage, Smith's characters struggle to find happiness in a fractured and
chaotic world. Her characters seek answers and meanings but find themselves
caught between various binaries: the religious and the secular (Millat), Eastern and Western values (Samad), the past and the present (Irie), internal and
external history (Archie), randomness and predestination (Marcus). The chaotic, mixed-up nature of life in a postmodern society is intolerable to these
characters, a condition made evident, for example, in the rift that forms between Samad and Alsana Iqbal. When Samad sends their son Magid back to
India, Alsana responds by speaking to her husband only in half-measures,
refusing to answer definitively any of his questions: "Through the next eight
years she would determine never to say *yes* to him, never to say *no* to him, but
rather to force him to live like she did—never *knowing*….That was her
promise, that was her curse upon Samad, and it was *exquisite* revenge" (178).
When Magid returns eight years later, Samad's punishment ends: "The only
upside was the change in Alsana. The *A–Z? Yes*, Samad Miah, it is in the top
right-hand drawer, *yes*, that's where it is, *yes*. The first time she did it, he almost jumped out of his skin. The curse was lifted. No more *maybe, Samad
Miah*, no more *possibly, Samad Miah*. Yes, yes, yes. No, no, no. The fundamentals" (351). Alsana's punishment is an appropriate one in the world of

*White Teeth*, as none of its major characters is capable of dealing with the uncertainty of life.

Thus we see Smith rejecting absolutes, "the fundamentals," and embracing a postmodernist perspective, as she picks apart traditional understandings of the world by poking holes in language, religion, culture, history, and other structures through which people typically give meaning to their lives. The result of *White Teeth* is the inevitable failure of the fundamental truths that the characters pursue and the systems of order and control that underlie them. We see these failures play out in various ways throughout the novel at the expense of the majority of the characters as they follow their various extremist, fundamentalist perspectives until they inevitably crash into each other. The final scene shows the result of these clashing perspectives, each character chasing his/her own fundamental truth, leading to the escape of Marcus Chalfen's FutureMouse. Like the coin in the passage above that miraculously finds its way into the pinball machine, the mouse miraculously escapes from the crush of the various warring factions attempting to exert their influence on it, released into a life beyond their attempts to control it.

However, while Smith's outlook may be postmodernist in its rejection of absolutes, her novels are determinedly modernist in their construction. Each of her three novels relies on a stable exterior structure that governs our reading experience. *White Teeth* consists of four sections of similar length, each of which contains five chapters, begins with an epigraph, centers on a different character, and focuses on two different years. *The Autograph Man* is structured around the Kabbalah, as the chart of the novel's protagonist appears before the book and serves as a guiding presence for the movement throughout the novel. *On Beauty* contains perhaps the most binding structure, as the novel uses E.M. Forster's *Howard's End* as its palimpsest, atop which Smith presents her modern revision (updating, for example, the letters that begin Forster's novel with a series of emails). Thus it often seems as though Smith's loyalties are divided, and the structure and the content of her novels often feel at odds with one another. Compared with someone like Samuel Beckett or Salman Rushdie, whose postmodernist sensibilities permeate the structures of their works as well as the content, Smith's novels are surprisingly content to behave structurally in ways that we expect novels to behave. Unlike many postmodernist writers, she is not interested in fracturing the traditional literary experience, in playing with the narrative perspective, or in making readers question the existence of the worlds in which her novels take place.

Thus, while her narratives demonstrate that structures are an ineffective method of controlling the world or of meting out the stuff of life, Smith continually relies on such structures to give shape to her novels. Furthermore, while the novels demonstrate the failure of various characters to exert their authority and autonomy in a postmodern world, the narrators are confident, in total control of their narratives, rarely demonstrating the uncertainty or fracturedness that is common in postmodernist fiction. The traditionally modernist structures that Smith employs to present her novels are the same ones she is arguing for the impossibility of maintaining in a postmodernist, postcolonial world, where stable boundaries are constantly being obliterated and where meaning is constantly shown to be unstable. In hopes of moving us toward a better understanding of the ramifications of this rift on our understanding of Smith's fiction, I look at this disconnect between postmodernist tale and modernist telling in both *White Teeth* and *On Beauty*.

Because the words carry so much baggage, I would like to discuss briefly what I consider to be an essential difference between "modernist" and "postmodernist" writing. In his book *Postmodernist Fiction*, Brian McHale makes use of Roman Jakobson's notion of the dominant to explore the blurry line between modernism and postmodernism. McHale moves away from the traditional system of setting modernism and postmodernism in binary opposition to one another, attempting to "interrogate modernist and postmodernist texts with a view to eliciting the shifts in the hierarchy of devices," with the goal of answering the question of "what emerges as the dominant of modernist fiction [and] of postmodernist fiction?" (8). By establishing the dominants undergirding modernism and postmodernism, McHale avoids the typical problems with listing the differences between them: "such catalogues...beg important questions, such as the question of why *these* particular features should cluster in *this* particular way—in other words, the question of what *system* might underlie the catalogue" (7). Ultimately, McHale argues that "postmodernist fiction differs from modernist fiction just as a poetics dominated by ontological issues differs from one dominated by epistemological issues" (xii):

> The dominant of modernist fiction is *epistemological*. That is, modernist fiction deploys strategies which engage and foreground questions such as...What is there to be known?;

> Who knows it?; How do they know it, and with what degree of certainty?; How is
> knowledge transmitted from one knower to another, and with what degree of reli-
> ability?; How does the object of knowledge change as it passes from knower to
> knower?; What are the limits of the knowable? (9)

As he turns to postmodernist fiction, McHale discusses "postmodernism's bracketing of modernist epistemological questions and the defamiliariz-
ing effect of this move" (26):

> The dominant of postmodern fiction is *ontological*. That is, postmodernist fiction
> deploys strategies which engage and foreground questions like...Which world is
> this? What is to be done in it?...What is a world?; What kinds of world are there,
> how are they constituted, and how do they differ?; What happens when different
> kinds of world are placed in confrontation, or when boundaries between worlds are
> violated? (10)

Thus McHale concludes that, while modernist fiction focuses on epistemological questions designed to make sense of the world around us, postmodernist fiction puts these questions aside and asks ontological questions
designed to open up larger possibilities, often prompting readers to question
the very foundation of the narrative world presented in the text. The modernist aesthetic, then, is one of closure, taking place in a closed-off world and
forcing readers to work out answers that allow them to understand the characters and the themes of the work. Appropriately, given the nature of the
modernist aesthetic, McHale describes the logic governing the modernist
novel as "that of a detective story, the epistemological genre *par excel-
lence*...Characters in many classic modernist texts...sift through the evidence
of witnesses of different degrees of reliability in order to reconstruct and
solve a 'crime'" (9). The postmodernist aesthetic, however, is one of openness, in which the narrative experience is often fractured to open up possibilities and provoke further questions that are not readily answerable in the text.
McHale discusses this movement in terms of the genres of science fiction
and the fantastic; like these genres, postmodernist fiction avoids questions of
origin (why is the written world different from the real world?) and looks
instead at the possibilities offered by this bracketing of the epistemological
concerns of modernism (what freedom do I have when I stop worrying about
conveying the "real world"?). Postmodernist fiction takes the reader out of
his/her comfort zone, often subverting the traditional tropes of fiction and

asking us to reconsider the preconceptions that we bring to the act of reading and foundations upon which we build our lives.[ii]

McHale uses Beckett's trilogy as an example of the movement from a modernist to a postmodernist aesthetic. Traces of a modernist aesthetic appear in *Molloy* and can be seen in the traditional two-part structure of Molloy's and Moran's narratives, which Beckett sets beside one another, implicitly calling upon readers to compare and contrast in order to recreate some sort of meaning. However, in *Malone Dies* and especially in *The Unnamable*, Beckett sloughs off the tropes of traditional fiction, fracturing the narrative experience and constantly asking readers to ask ontological questions about the world in which the narrative is set. As each successive narrator is revealed to be the creator of all previous narrators, the trilogy moves away from the relatively stable perspective of *Molloy* and of modernist fiction. Beckett mirrors this movement in the style and perspective of each successive narrative. As we strip away each layer of the narrative onion (a metaphor Beckett famously used in his essay "Proust") on our way to its "ideal core," it becomes clear that there is no core, no answer, no culmination to our knowledge-seeking journey. Instead, we find increasingly unhinged narratives, as Beckett strips away various literary tropes with which we are familiar. By the final narrative, paragraph breaks, punctuation, and any sort of coherent narrative have been abandoned.[iii] The point here is that we see Beckett's perspective (that authority is doomed, that nothing we say or do will ever move us any closer to a true, fundamental understanding of the world) reflected in the chaotic structure of his narratives.

Rushdie's *Midnight's Children* provides an interesting comparison to Smith's novels, particularly *White Teeth*, as both explore the complicated relationship between history and the present, delving into the gaps and holes that permeate both history and any attempt to recreate it in memory or in writing. Like Smith, Rushdie presents a narrative that deals with the difficulties of adhering to a modernist paradigm (of faith in absolutes, structures, and the ability of art to uncover truth) in a postmodernist world (of mix-ups, randomness, and the failure of art to represent reality); *Midnight's Children* presents the frustrating and fractured narrative of Saleem Sinai, born at the stroke of midnight on India's first day as an independent nation. Saleem views his act of narrating as a modernist one, creating a typically modernist puzzle by dividing his story up into thirty pickle jars; however, by the end of the novel, he comes to realize that the modernist attempt to present a coherent picture of reality is doomed. Unlike the confident narrator of *White Teeth*, who manages to weave together a masterful narrative of various characters and stories, Saleem's attempts to keep his various stories separate fail utterly. Thus, by making the entire novel a failure to achieve the modernist goal of creating art that effectively mirrors reality, Rushdie demonstrates structurally the thematic concerns of the novel. This can be seen in the result of Saleem's endeavor, as, instead of thirty separate stories that add up to a faithful rendering of history, Saleem is left with chutney.

The problem with classifying Smith's fiction, then, is its determinedly straightforward, traditional presentation of narrative and its relatively uncomplicated narrative voice. Rather than presenting us with the kind of tortured, unremitting narratives that Beckett presents us with, or with the kind of mixed-up, chutnified narrative that Rushdie presents us with, Smith's narratives are leisurely paced, elegantly structured, and written from the perspective of a confident, omniscient narrator.

## Postmodernist Tales

Both *White Teeth* and *On Beauty* are populated by families of characters trying to come to terms with failing ways of interacting with the outside world. *White Teeth* revolves around members of the Jones/Bowden, the Iqbal, and the Chalfen families; *On Beauty* revolves around the Belseys and the Kippses. In both novels, Smith is concerned with the overly definitive worldviews held by her characters, demonstrating the problems caused as a result of these clashing perspectives. When neither side is willing to change or modify its viewpoint (which, the books demonstrate, it is necessary to do in a postmodern world), conflicts necessarily arise. These conflicts nearly always undo the characters who are unwilling to accommodate alternate, oppositional lifestyles. For example, the battling perspectives—both academic and social—of Howard Belsey and Monty Kipps ruin the careers of both men in the novel's final chapters, as their public and private clashing results in Kipps's falling from his pedestal of respectability and Howard's loss of both his family and his chance at tenure. Samad's unwillingness to accept the Americanizing of his sons causes him to send Magid back to India, his unwillingness to share parental responsibility with his wife leads him to eight years of her ambivalence, and his unwillingness to waver from his Muslim ideals of perfection leads him to commit adultery with his son's music teacher.

While similar in their demonstration of the importance of openness, the novels differ in the subject of their focus. In *White Teeth*, Smith demonstrates the important but fractured relationship between past and present, as her characters approach their relationship with history from various perspectives. Characters constantly attempt to control their interaction with history, viewing it either as wholly predetermined—if I understand my history, then I will understand my present and future; or as wholly arbitrary—if I ignore my past, then it will not be able to influence my present and future. However, *White Teeth* demonstrates the impossibility of escaping history or of living entirely outside of its influence. Magid, for example, is essentially uprooted from his family and from his history, and he tries to construct an identity entirely separate from it. However, he is unable to escape their influence, as the novel's final section finds him reunited with his twin brother and entangled with Irie. In the end, the interaction of the past and the present is messier and less predictable than the characters want it to be; the roots provided by history can neither be studied as a faithful forecast of our future, nor can they be entirely pruned away.

Samad views history as an accurate reflection of the present, and, accordingly, he spends much of his life trying to come to terms with the role of his family history in his own life. He feels that if he changes public perception of his traitorous great-grandfather Mangal Pande, he will become a better person. This unhealthy preoccupation with revising history can be seen in his steadfast attempts to rewrite the history of Pande: "The story of Mangal Pande…is no laughing matter. He is the tickle in the sneeze, he is why we are the way we are, the founder of modern India, the big historical cheese" (188), and in his vicious defense of Pande's legacy from contemporary historians: "Just because the word exists, it does not follow that it is a correct representation of the character of Mangal Pande. The first definition we agree on: my great-grandfather was a mutineer and I am proud to say this. I concede matters did not go quite according to plan. But traitor? Coward? The dictionary you show me is old—these definitions are now out of currency. Pande was no traitor and no coward" (209). Samad is unwilling to relinquish this history because he believes fervently that history shapes the present; if Pande is a traitor and a coward, then he, Samad, might also be: "What I have realized, is that the generations…they speak to each other, Jones. It's not a line, life is not a line—this is not palm-reading—it's a circle, and they speak to us. That is why you cannot *read* fate; you must *experience* it" (100). The narrator tersely and sympathetically summarizes Samad's position: "When a man has nothing but his blood to commend him, each drop of it matters, matters terribly; it must be jealously defended" (212).

Samad's perspective on history can also be seen in O'Connell's, the place where he and Archie meet regularly to discuss their lives: "Everything was remembered, nothing was lost. History was never revised or reinterpreted, adapted or whitewashed" (160–61). O'Connell's serves as a "neutral place" for Archie and Samad, one filled with its own shared history and one in which outside history cannot touch them:

> Simply because you could be without family in O'Connell's, without possessions or status, without past glory or future hope—you could walk through that door with nothing and be exactly the same as everybody else in there. It could be 1989 outside, or 1999, 2009, and you could still be sitting at the counter in the V-neck you wore to your wedding in 1975, 1945, 1935. Nothing changes here, things are only retold, remembered. That's why old men love it. (203)[iv]

While these "old men" want to use their relationship with the past both to blame their failures on and to attribute their successes to, the younger generation in *White Teeth* takes a much different approach to history. Living in the wreckage of her family history, Irie Jones wants to prune away the roots she feels clutching at her. Her father's willful obscurity—"I'm a Jones, you see. 'Slike a 'Smith.' We're nobody…my father used to say: 'We're the chaff, boy, we're the chaff'" (84)—and her mother's embarrassing secret—which Irie discovers upon kicking over the glass holding her false teeth—provide enough reason for Irie to want to escape the clutches of her past: "This was yet another item in a long list of parental hypocrisies and untruths, this was another example of the Jones/Bowden gift for secret history, stories you never got told, history you never entirely uncovered, rumor you never unraveled, which would be fine if every day was not littered with clues" (314). The discovery of her mother's secret prompts Irie finally to cut ties completely with her parents and move in with her grandmother.

When Irie moves in with her grandmother, who, while technically a part of her past, poses no real threat to her autonomy, she finds a "well-wooded and watered place. Where things sprang from the soil riotously and without supervision…fresh and untainted and without past or dictated future—a place where things simply *were*" (332). She goes on to imagine this place in detail: "No fictions, no myths, no lies, no tangled webs—this is how Irie imagined her homeland. Because *homeland* is one of the magical fantasy words like unicorn and soul and infinity that have now passed into the language. And the particular magic of homeland, its particular spell over Irie, was that it sounded like a beginning. The beginningest of beginnings. Like the first morning of Eden and the day after apocalypse. A blank page" (332).

Samad and Irie hold opposing viewpoints regarding the importance of history in the present, but, in the novel's final chapters, they both begin to accept reality. Samad begins to understand that history cannot alone sustain him; we see this first in his reluctant memory of a story from when he first arrived in America, as he acknowledges this embarrassing incident in which he used his bleeding thumb to write his name into the stone beneath a park bench: "A great shame washed over me the moment I finished,...because I knew what it meant, this deed. It meant *I wanted to write my name on the world*. It meant *I presumed*. Like the Englishmen who named streets in Kerala after their wives, like the Americans who shoved their flag in the moon. It was a warning from Allah. He was saying: Iqbal, you *are becoming like them*" (418–19). Rather than continuing to bury an embarrassing moment in his history, which, as we see a number of times, causes Samad problems throughout his life, here he willingly remembers it, confronts it, and, if the final scene in the novel is any indication, begins to move past it.

Samad's final act in the novel occurs during the FutureMouse demonstration, as he is sent outside to quiet the protesters. Rather than stop them, however, Samad allows them to continue: "He knows what it is to seek. He knows the dryness. He has felt the thirst you get in a strange land—horrible, persistent—the thirst that lasts your whole life" (439). Here Samad moves closer to Smith's position, which is a recognition that, although your history may be hopelessly entangled with your present-day existence, it alone does not have to constitute that existence. In other words, it is possible to move beyond it and stake out a place for yourself, outside of your individual family history. Irie has the same realization as Samad does, although she approaches it from the opposite extreme. As Irie contemplates the complicated history that her unborn child, fathered by either Magid or Millat, will be presented with, she concludes that it is impossible to escape one's history entirely: "After weeping and pacing and rolling it over and over in her mind, she thought: *whatever*, you know? What*ever*. It was always going to turn out like this, not precisely like this, but *involved* like this. This was the Iqbals we were talking about, here. This was the Joneses. How could she ever have expected anything less?" (427). Like Samad, Irie ultimately realizes the messiness of the relationship between the past and the present that, although we might wish to, we can never control the way that our roots reach into our lives.

Smith's view of the relationship between the past and the present is one facet of her postmodernist outlook, as, toward most subjects in her novels, she wants her characters to see that things are more complicated and less definitive than they would like them to be. Another subject Smith deals with in both novels is the authority of language, which she continually pokes holes in. Clara's dialect, for example, which she slips in and out of, often with little control, is one way in which this manifests itself in *White Teeth*; in addition, the symbol of the white teeth, "floating silently to the bottom of a glass" (77), suggests the importance of language as a symbol of intellect and of culture. The relationship that characters have with language is also important in *On Beauty*. Living in the isolated, academic community of Wellington, the Belseys and the Kipps continually put too much faith in the power of language until, toward the end of the novel, even Howard Belsey, for whom language is a weapon, begins to understand that words are not always the best tool for describing beauty.

In Wellington, language is a tool used to express intellect, to battle with other wielders of language, and ultimately to gain power over them. For example, when Zora Belsey meets with Dean French in an attempt to get into the class of Claire Malcolm, the woman with whom her father had an affair, it is only after she uses a certain word that she really gets his attention: "'Inappropriate,' repeated French. All he could do at this point was to aim for damage limitation. The word had been used" (146). It is the word, not what it represents, that wields the power in Wellington. Later in the same scene, as Zora continues to confront directly the reason for her inappropriate treatment, Dean French continues focusing on the language rather than the act: "Jack wished very much she would stop using that violent phrase. It was drilling into his brain: *Professor Malcolm and my father, Professor Malcolm and my father*. The very thing that was not to be spoken of this fall semester...was now being batted around his office like a pigskin filled with blood" (146).

Like his sister Zora, Levi Belsey also attempts to use language to his advantage; however, rather than using it to further infiltrate Wellington (as Zora does), Levi uses it to escape the confines of Wellington, trying out a different language instead: "This faux Brooklyn accent belonged to neither Howard nor Kiki, and had only arrived in Levi's mouth three years earlier, as he turned twelve" (11). Confident that this will effectively change his identity, Levi attempts to construct a self outside of the world of Wellington. However, Levi is never able to convince others of his identity, which is seen in his unsuccessful attempt to lead a revolt at the music mega-store where he works, where "it was immediately noticeable that only the white kids had showed up for the meeting" (186). His attempts to upset the work atmosphere lead him to be confronted by Bailey, his forty-something manager: "I *know* where you're from. Those kids don't know shit, but *I* know. They nice suburban kids. They think anyone in a pair of baggy jeans is a gangsta. But you can't fool me. I know where you *pretend to be from*...because that's where *I'm from*—but you don't see me acting like a nigger" (191–92). Bailey's confrontation of Levi results in his immediate retreat to the comforts of home.

In Wellington, language holds power even over those who attempt to live outside its realm of influence. Kiki, the character least enthralled by the power of language and most open to new ideas, disagrees strongly and loudly when Carlene Kipps suggests that "I don't ask myself *what* did I live for....I ask *whom* did I live for....I see very clearly recently that in fact I didn't live for an idea or even for God—I lived because I loved *this* person" (176). Kiki reacts violently toward this suggestion, unwilling to believe that either she or Carlene is as passive as that language suggests. However, in their fight following her discovery of Howard's lengthy affair with a colleague, Kiki recycles this phrase a number of times: "I *staked my whole life* on you. And I have no idea any more why I did that" (206). The power of this phrase—and perhaps also the frightening truth of it—results in Kiki's repeated use of it in their fight, each time in a slightly different form and with slightly different emphasis, as if she is not quite certain whether she believes it or whether she is wielding it properly: "I gave up *my life* for you. I don't even know who I am any more" (206). Finally, near the end of the fight, she resignedly repeats it: "I staked my *life* on you. I staked my *life*" (207). Kiki's repeated use of this phrase suggests that she is testing this language, trying it out, seeing how she feels about it. She is also aware of the power of language, as, seeing that her repetition of Carlene's statement is not affecting Howard in the way that she hopes, she tries a different approach, turning to the vulgar in an attempt to provoke the desired reaction from Howard: "And don't kid yourself: honey, I look at boys *all the time*—all the time. I see pretty boys every day of the week, and I think about their cocks, and what they would look like butt naked" (208). The important point here is that, like the other Wellingtonians, Kiki is exploring the power relationships attached to words and using them to exert power over Howard in their fight.

The use of language in *On Beauty* culminates in Howard's lecture on Rembrandt. Having forgotten his notes, having lost everything in his life that is important to him, and having nothing else to lose, Howard finally allows himself to appreciate silently the paintings that he has made a living criticizing. Howard's gesture, as appropriate and necessary as it appears to readers, is lost on his audience: "Howard pressed the red button. He could hear Jack French saying to his eldest son, in his characteristically loud whisper: *You see, Ralph, the order is meaningful.*...The rest of his audience were faintly frowning at the back wall" (442). When he reaches the final painting, only he and Kiki appreciate it, presumably understanding finally that sometimes it is necessary to stop talking, to stop playing the games of language. The novel moves toward an understanding of language as a flawed vessel, toward the realization that the power of language is only avoided in silence. And while there is no indication that this realization will be a lasting one for Howard and Kiki, and while his audience may stare confusedly at Howard's moment of momentary enlightenment, Smith's audience is made aware of the complicated position that language holds in our interaction with the outside world.

## Modernist Tellings

While *White Teeth* and *On Beauty* are built around demonstrating and championing a postmodernist perspective, their construction is decidedly modernist. In an essay on Forster, Smith discusses this aspect of Forster's fiction: "Forster wanted his people to be in a muddle; his was a study of the emotional, erratic and unreasonable in human life. But what interests me is that his narrative structure is muddled also; impulsive, meandering, irrational, which seeming faults lead him on to two further problematics: mawkishness and melodrama" ("Love, Actually"). Smith points to the muddled nature of Forster's narratives, which she views as commensurate with the state of his characters. However, unlike Forster's determinedly clumsy narrative structures, designed to echo the emotionally clumsy characters described within them, Smith's narratives are structurally sound and clearly marked.

Like a Joycean schema, the table of contents prefacing *White Teeth* makes visible Smith's interest in constructing a web of parallels and correspondences among the four parts of her novel. It is a carefully controlled narrative, and close analysis demonstrates the extent to which Smith uses exterior structures such as chapter titles to govern its presentation. Each of the four parts is named after a character and contains two important years in that character's life: "ARCHIE 1974, 1945," "SAMAD 1984, 1857," "IRIE 1990, 1907," and "MAGID, MILLAT, AND MARCUS 1992, 1999." Apart from the last section, which is different in a number of ways (perhaps because of its movement from present to future, rather than from present to past), there are numerous parallels among the sections devoted to Archie, Samad, and Irie. Each of the five-chapter sections begins with a similarly constructed chapter title: "The Peculiar Second Marriage of Archie Jones," "The Temptation of Samad Iqbal," and "The Miseducation of Irie Jones" (the final section shares this construction, beginning with "The Return of Magid Mahfooz Murshed Mubtasim Iqbal"); each includes a chapter title that concerns teeth: "Teething Trouble," "Molars," and "Canines: The Ripping Teeth"; and each includes a "Root Canal" chapter: "The Root Canals of Alfred Archibald Jones and Samad Miah Iqbal," "The Root Canals of Mangal Pande," and "The Root Canals of Hortense Bowden."

The complicated and comprehensive exterior structure through which Smith presents *White Teeth* encourages readers to look at the structural level to find meaning, which is a common feature of modernist novels. In order to understand fully the various parallels and connections between these sometimes disparate characters, we must connect the dots, we must become textual detectives, and we must understand the ways that their lives, perspectives, and outlooks mesh together when viewed in the way that Smith presents them to us. The narrative perspective maintains its distance, for the most part, although it has no qualms about intermittently intruding, as it does with, for example, a running joke about verb tenses ("past tense, future perfect"). The following passage is perhaps the most direct intrusion by the narrator: "Yes, Millat was stoned. And it may be absurd to us that one Iqbal can believe the breadcrumbs laid down by another Iqbal…have not yet blown away in the breeze. But it really doesn't matter what we believe" (419). Even in this minor intrusion, the most direct in the 450-page novel, the narrator is apologizing for interfering and pleading ignorance. And yet, despite this plea that what we believe "doesn't matter," the novel is carefully crafted to make us believe certain things very strongly.

If we look, for example, at the cyclical nature of the novel as a whole, it becomes clear that there is some ordering narrative force shaping and molding (in short, interfering in) our reading experience at every step. This can be seen in the novel's final chapter, as events at the launch of Marcus's Future-Mouse exhibit escalate, with each fundamentalist organization mounting an assault on the mouse. Interrupting the narrative flow in the novel's final pages is the story of Archie's mysterious encounter with Doctor Sick. Unlike the previous flashbacks (or "root canals," to use the novel's term for them), this incident is neither explained nor introduced as either a memory or as a story being told to another character. Instead, it simply appears at the most suspenseful, chaotic point in the narrative. As Archie wrestles with his mixed-up feelings about killing the Nazi, he eventually flips a coin to decide: "The coin rose and flipped as a coin would rise and flip every time in a perfect world, flashing its light and then revealing its dark enough times to mesmerize a man. Then, at some point in its triumphant ascension, it began to arc, and the arc went wrong" (447). Using the same words that he/she earlier uses to describe the coin's "elegant swoop" into a pinball machine, the narrator draws together various themes and parallels in a seemingly epiphanous moment.

This moment, as Archie leaps between Marcus and the gun pointed at him, serves as the culmination of every major character's progression throughout the book; Magid and Millat are on opposite sides of Marcus's research, Irie is pregnant with either Magid or Millat's child, Clara attempts to prevent Hortense's interference, Samad decides to allow Hortense to interfere, and Archie, of course, leaps between Millat and Marcus. But rather than allowing the moment to play out on its own, the narrator intervenes, crosscutting the scene with the narrative of Archie's war injury. It is a climactic event, one that ties together nearly every character and theme in a relatively neat and tidy bow; by harkening back to Archie's section (and the gap in which it is revealed how Archie got shot in the leg), to the other "root canals" documented in Samad's and Irie's sections, and to the earlier coin tosses (particularly the one that lands in the pinball machine). It is a typically modernist move, one intended to guide readers toward knowledge—paradoxically, we are being led toward the message that randomness and chaos prevail over resolution and closure. The point here is that the modernist structure problematizes the postmodernist message that the final scene reveals to readers. While it is perhaps an overstatement to suggest that the final chapter ties everything together in a tidy bow (many questions are left unanswered as the mouse scurries off the table and into an air vent), Smith does provide a way out for both the mouse and for Irie's unborn child. There is certainly an attempt at closure in the two "snapshots" of "Irie, Joshua, and Hortense sitting by a Caribbean Sea...while Irie's fatherless little girl...feels free as Pinocchio, a puppet clipped of paternal strings," and of "Alsana and Samad, Archie and Clara, in O'Connell's" (448), as the pieces of Smith's modernist puzzle fall together neatly in the novel's final pages.

The structure being imposed upon *On Beauty* is even more prominent than it is in *White Teeth*. Smith models the story of the Belseys and the Kipps on Forster's *Howard's End*, modernizing the narrative and the theme ("Only Connect"), including clever references, both in form and content, throughout the novel, compelling readers to "get into the research end of things" (374). In other words, the allusions throughout the novel reward the intertextual critic, both referencing and building upon the original in interesting and important ways. Smith herself comments on the importance of this connection in the afterword: "My largest structural debt should be obvious to any E.M. Forster fan; suffice it to say he gave me a classy old frame, which I covered with new material as best I could." Revision is a common trope of postmodernist fiction, as many important postmodernist novels—such as Jean Rhys's *Wide Sargasso Sea* and J.M. Coetzee's *Foe*—rewrite older novels to present different sides of the original stories or to demonstrate something lacking in them. However, Smith's treatment of *Howard's End* is more like Joyce's use of the Odyssey in *Ulysses*, as it serves primarily as a structural model and a general inspiration for *On Beauty*. The epigraph "Only Connect," for example, that precedes *Howard's End* is a serious matter in *On Beauty*, as the novel is populated with characters utterly incapable of the kind of connection that Forster values. Furthermore, although she claims that the novel is merely a "classy old frame" and in interviews plays down any attempt to adhere strictly to the plot of *Howard's End*, *On Beauty* at times suffers because of Smith's strict faithfulness to its confines. For example, the scene in which Carlene Kipps tries to convince Kiki to come with her to Amherst—"No, dear, *now*—let's go now. I have the keys—we could get the train and be there by lunch. I want you to see the pictures—they should be loved by somebody like you. We'll go right away when this is wrapped. We'll be back for tomorrow evening" (268–69)—feels forced and unnatural. This scene, if not for the link to Forster, is completely unnecessary, as neither of the characters behave similarly to how they behave in the rest of the novel. The point here is that, particularly in this awkward scene, Smith struggles to fit her narrative into

Forster's frame even when it does not seem natural to the progression of the characters or the story. This kind of moment exemplifies the difficulty of reading Smith's work in terms of the modernist/postmodernist division; one on hand, her story obviously pulls her away from the kind of straightforward, modernist relationship that she creates between her novel and Forster's, but at the same time she feels compelled to adhere to it.

The narrative perspective is another important site for analysis regarding the modernist qualities of *On Beauty*'s structure, and it is another way in which Smith models the novel on *Howard's End*. This narrator, like the narrators of both *Howard's End* and *White Teeth*, is confident and in total control of the novel's world: "We must now jump nine months forward, and back across the Atlantic Ocean" (42). The narrator maintains his/her authority over the world of the novel and is not afraid to pause the narrative flow to provide lengthy descriptions of the setting, and at times the effect of this is to make the novel feel Victorian in its attention to detail regarding setting and character. The following passage is typical of these digressions:

> A tall, garnet-coloured building in the New England style, the Belsey residence roams over four creaky floors. The date of its construction (1856) is patterned in tile above the front door, and the windows retain their mottled green glass, spreading a dreamy pasture on the floorboards whenever strong light passes through them. They are not original, these windows, but replacements, the originals being too precious to be used as windows. Heavily insured, they are kept in a large safe in the basement. A significant portion of the value of the Belsey house resides in windows that nobody may look through or open. (16)

The description, which continues for approximately three pages, is in no way disguised as part of the narrative; in other words, this information is presented plainly, in an almost journalistic style, and, at first, without value or judgment placed on it. However, as the description continues, the narrator comments ironically on the house's unused windows, allowing the audience to extend the metaphor to its occupants.

Furthermore, Smith uses free indirect discourse, a common feature of modernist fiction, throughout the novel to provide insight into various characters. Modernist fiction impels the reader to use the tools of writing to piece together its meaning, as we must essentially engage in literary interpretation in order to cobble together information about the characters. If we look, for example, at a passage from Joyce's *Dubliners*, perhaps the most famous example of free indirect discourse, we see how this process works and why it is classified as a modernist enterprise:

> Maria was a very, very small person indeed but she had a very long nose and a very long chin. She talked a little through her nose, always soothingly: "Yes, my dear," and "No, my dear." She was always sent for when the women quarreled over their tubs and always succeeded in making peace.... She had lovely ferns and wax-plants and, whenever anyone came to visit her, she always gave the visitor one or two slips from her conservatory. There was one thing she didn't like and that was the tracts on the walks; but the matron was such a nice person to deal with, so genteel. (101)

Here we see a description of Maria, a lower-class Irish maid, presented through free indirect discourse. In other words, her image of herself influences the description of that image which is presented to us. The tip of her nose does not literally touch the tip of her chin; thus we realize, either at this point or through the accumulation of evidence throughout the story, that Maria is not well educated and has an extremely negative self-image. The style of the passage both reflects and gives evidence for the facts gleaned within it; she is uneducated (the repeated use of "very," or the awkwardly constructed sentences) and unattractive, which we learn both through the narration's statement of those facts and through the ugly, unattractive style in which it is written.

The following passage, from early in *On Beauty*, describes Kiki's experience of watching Mozart with her family:

> Mozart's Requiem begins with you walking towards a huge pit. The pit is on the other side of a precipice, which you cannot see over until you are right at its edge. Your death is awaiting you in that pit. You don't know what it looks like or sounds like or smells like. You don't know whether it will be good or bad. You just walk towards it.... In the pit is a great choir, like the one you joined for two months in Wellington in which you were the only black woman.... The choir is...every person who has changed you during your time on this earth: your many lovers; your family; your enemies, the nameless, faceless woman who slept with your husband; the man you thought you were going to marry; the man you did. (69)

By allowing readers to experience this through Kiki's eyes, by essentially allowing her to assume temporary control over the narrative, Smith engages in a typical modernist exercise. We learn about a character through the act of interpreting his/her narrative, by seeing how his/her narrative ability and style compare with the narrator's. The Kiki-influenced narration is far more literate than Maria's, for example, and it is clear that she is a deep-thinking yet haunted and unhappy woman. The frightening images of the choir hidden beneath the precipice demonstrate both her feelings of uneasiness regarding her marriage and her unwillingness to confront them. The passage (which goes on for several pages) is extremely perceptive and intuitive of this new experience, which we also learn are characteristics of Kiki. If we compare it to the description of the Belsey home, the description of Mozart's Requiem is far more emotionally evocative and, although it contains little concrete external description, far more effective at conveying the experiencing of this event. Smith includes this passage of free indirect discourse essentially as an interpretive test designed to teach readers that Kiki is, although less educated, far more insightful than many of the other Wellingtonians we meet in the novel.

Finally, like *White Teeth*, *On Beauty* moves toward a moment of reconciliation and understanding for the majority of its characters. In her essay on Forster, Smith discusses his determinedly cryptic endings:

> This lack of moral enthusiasm finds an echo in every part of the structure; his endings, in particular, are diminuendos, ambivalent trailings off, that seem almost passive. This deliberate withholding of satisfaction that Forster produces has irritated many critics, Katherine Mansfield's account being as damning as any: "E.M. Forster never gets any further than warming the teapot. He's a rare fine hand at that. Feel this teapot. Is it not beautifully warm? Yes, but there ain't going to be no tea." ("Love, Actually")

Unlike Forster's "warm tea" endings, Smith sets her endings to full boil. The last chapter of *On Beauty* finds the Belsey children in good spirits despite their parents' divorce, and they each demonstrate their autonomy in their interaction with Howard; Zora reprimands him a number of times, Jerome defends his mother's love of the painting given to her by Carlene Kipps, and Levi refuses to accept his father's money. Finally, as Howard drives off to his lecture, the children collectively give him the finger. Following this scene, in which Howard appears to be turning into his father (seen in his prejudice toward a lesbian and his racist remarks about Howard's wife and biracial children), he arrives incredibly late at his lecture and forgets his notes in the car. While, as previously discussed, the point of this moment is Howard's realization that it is no longer necessary to demonstrate his intellect by criticizing Rembrandt, that he can finally admit "I—like—the—tomato" (312), nevertheless Smith presents this as an epiphany, a real true point of possible growth and change for Howard. The relationship between Howard and Kiki, certainly the central relationship of the novel, is, although recently ended and a long way from healed, momentarily rekindled: "Howard looked at Kiki. In her face, his life. Kiki looked up suddenly at Howard—not, he thought, unkindly. Howard said nothing. Another silent minute passed" (442–43). Rather than ending with the suggestion that these characters will continue their selfish ways after the novel ends, the final pages soften in their view of Howard, and we see the world through his eyes, which, as a result of losing nearly everything, finally open up to both the beauty in the Rembrandt paintings and the beauty he once saw in his wife.

The verdict is still out, the coin is still hanging in the air, regarding Smith's place in contemporary literature. Discussing Smith's fiction in terms of modernism and postmodernism demonstrates a clear division in her work between form and content, between postmodernist tales and modernist tellings. A confident, omniscient narrator relates a tale of characters who learn the necessity of relinquishing their authority in the chaotic real-world. A narrative about the messiness of the relationship between the past and the present has clear divisions between tales of the present and tales of the past. A story about the failure of art to structure life is built upon the structure of a work of high modernism. And while there are moments in the telling when the narrator winks or when the larger structure bends, and while there are moments in the tale when the characters benefit from the fundamentalist beliefs they cling to, this rift is a prominent feature of both *White Teeth* and *On Beauty*. It remains to be seen whether Smith is interested in ironing out these complexities in her future works, or whether she will reflect the fracturedness of her characters in the structure or the narrative perspective. As it is now, her fiction is like that coin tossed by Archie—landing on neither one side nor the other, rolling somewhere no one can predict, elegantly swooping and somersaulting its way into oblivion—and, like Marcus Chalfen's FutureMouse, "Archie…watched it stand very still for a second with a smug look as if it expected nothing less. He watched it scurry away, over his hand. He watched it dash along the table, and through the hands of those who wished to pin it down" (448). Smith's novels are alive and kicking, unable to be labeled either modernist or postmodernist, and rushing away from us just as we attempt to pin them down.

# Notes

[i] Although McHale discusses the detective genre as definitively modernist, it should be noted that many postmodern novels use the detective genre in order to demonstrate the failure of the modernist novel to express the true nature of mysteries. Thus, unlike the modernist mystery, which can be solved by careful textual analysis, the postmodern mystery—seen, for example, in Thomas Pynchon's *The Crying of Lot 49* or Vladimir Nabokov's *Lolita*—refuses to be solved. For a fuller discussion of this topic, see McHale (20–30).

[ii] It must be said that, while McHale provides a useful paradigm for distinguishing between the general systems underlying modernist and postmodernist fiction, his use of Jakobson's dominant does not wholly prevent him from succumbing to the problems he attempts to avoid through it. In his book, McHale too often constructs a straw modernism against which he defines postmodernist writing. In other words, the closed-off, hermetically sealed modernism that he describes sometimes seems designed solely to contrast with the openness of postmodernist writing. However, his paradigm is still more useful than most, such as Ihab Hassan's famously rigid lists of modernist and postmodernist qualities in *The Dismemberment of Orpheus*; furthermore, it is useful in this context, as it deals nicely with the aspects of authority and control that I am interested in discussing.

[iii] However, this is not meant to suggest, as a number of critics do, that in these narratives Beckett somehow moves beyond the tropes of fiction. Paul Davies, for example, concludes that in *The Unnamable* "there is a resolution of emotion and intention that we do not find earlier"(85). The point of the trilogy is that, even after they attempt to kill traditional elements of narrative (such as characters, punctuation, etc.), these narrators are bound by them because that's all they are. They exist solely in language, and they (like Beckett, and like Beckett's readers) are bound within it. By the end of the Unnamable's narrative, he has created characters, written hundreds of pages, used metaphors, and engaged in all the familiar literary tropes that he supposedly moves beyond in the opening pages. We even talk about this supposedly unnamed narrator using a name—the Unnamable.

[iv] This perspective is also championed by J.P. Hamilton, the elderly war hero for whom a young Irie, Millat, and Magid deliver groceries through a school program: "But while you're still young, the important matter is the third molars. They are more commonly referred to as the wisdom teeth, I believe.... They are the only part of the body that a man must grow into.... Have them out early.... You simply must. You can't fight against it. I wish I had. I wish I'd given up early and hedged my bets, as it were. Because they're your father's teeth, you see, wisdom teeth are passed down by the father, I'm certain of it. So you must be big enough for them"(145). Hamilton's unfounded certainty that wisdom teeth are "your father's teeth" is,

like Samad's obsession with his past, a manifestation of his desire to link concretely the present and the past.

<sup>v</sup> Irie's grandmother, Hortense Bowden, represents the opposite perspective, arguing for the necessity of keeping the boundaries in place between different races: "Black and white never come to no good. De Lord Jesus never meant us to mix it up.... 'Im want everybody to keep tings separate....When you mix It up, nuttin' good can come. It wasn't *intended*" (318).

## Works Cited

Beckett, Samuel. *Trilogy: Molloy, Malone Dies, The Unnamable*. New York: Knopf, 1997.

Joyce, James. *Dubliners: Text, Criticism, and Notes*. Ed. Robert Scholes and A. Walton Litz. New York: Penguin, 1976.

McHale, Brian. *Postmodernist Fiction*. London: Methuen, 1987.

Rushdie, Salman. *Midnight's Children*. New York: Penguin, 1980.

Smith, Zadie. *The Autograph Man*. New York: Vintage, 2003.

———. "Love, Actually." *The Guardian*, November 1, 2003. *Guardian Unlimited Books*. http://books.guardian.co.uk/review/story/0,12084,1074217,00.html.

———. *On Beauty*. New York: Penguin, 2005.

———. *White Teeth*. New York: Vintage, 2001.

# CHAPTER II

## On Beauty and Being Postcolonial: Aesthetics and Form in Zadie Smith

### Ulka Anjaria, Brandeis University

This essay attempts to understand Zadie Smith's novel *On Beauty* (2005) through the theoretical framework of postcolonial studies, despite the incomplete applicability of this framework to the issues raised in and by the novel. The term "postcolonial" has come to refer to literature that projects a *decolonized* worldview, written either in the formerly colonized world or from within metropolitan diasporas.[1] This body of literature has in the last quarter century succeeded in radically changing the world literary scene, not only through an expanding market but also through a fundamental recasting of the large literary questions of the preceding two centuries in radically decentered, democratic, and anti-canonical fashion. Such fiction has mobilized a hybrid and multivalent register to question all sorts of authoritative literary forms for their implicit and explicit associations with imperialism, nationalism, Marxism, modernism, and liberalism. The result has been heightened attention to the problem of representation, so that no aesthetic act or utterance can any longer be regarded as politically or ideologically neutral.

*On Beauty*, published a half decade after the birth of postcolonial fiction as we know it, takes such a decolonized perspective for granted. As we will see, it asks, in its wake, what might be redeemed from a deconstructed, anti-progressivist worldview in order to make life livable for the next generation, who no longer need to be convinced of the inextricability of art and politics, but take such inextricability as the precondition of their very existence. This paper follows the novel in this attempt, first tracing the postcolonial critique of form from *Midnight's Children* to *White Teeth* and then locating another problematization of aesthetics in the very different politics of *Howard's End*. The resurrection of the aesthetic in *On Beauty* can in many respects be seen as emerging out of these two very different means of grappling with the problem of art and politics. I argue that *On Beauty* revives the domestic plot to interrogate the pitfalls of both traditional aesthetics and a deconstructive, anti-aesthetic—both of which are unsuited to account for the complex experiences of post-postcolonial family life. In doing so, it presents a radically democratized critique of aesthetic norms and, at the same time, exposes the complicity of such a critique with new forms of crisis and struggle. Through a sustained conflict, and in the end a potential reconciliation, expressed in the novel's story but also apparent along its underlying structure, *On Beauty* proposes the possibility for the coexistence of beauty and being postcolonial in a world that tends to see the two as irreconcilable.

## The Postcolonial Novel and the Excess of Form

*"Whatever today's excess, tomorrow's will exceed-o it."*—Rushdie, *The Moor's Last Sigh*[2]

As many scholars have shown, the institution of a normative model of literary aesthetics was central to colonial rule, especially in the regions colonized by Britain not only through military might but through "moral and intellectual suasion" (Viswanathan, *Masks* 2).[3] Gauri Viswanathan writes, specifically of India, that "British colonial administrators, provoked by missionaries on the one hand and fears of native insubordination on the other, discovered an ally in English literature to support them in maintaining control of the natives under the guise of a liberal education" ("Beginnings" 434). Henry Schwarz traces the particular link between Romantic theories of aesthetic value and the expansion of political power in the subcontinent, arguing that "imaginative fiction played an important role as a regulator of individual conduct by bringing the subjects of the Crown more closely into line with the goals of the state. Aesthetic sensibility was cultivated in a singular relationship with official power" (566).[4]

By linking aesthetics to modern governmentality, scholars have drawn particular attention to the element of *restraint* embedded in Western notions of aesthetics—the way in which "literature disposed its reader toward a correct, controlled discipline of rules that seemed voluntary even though it was elaborately learned" (Schwarz 569). Therefore, while traditional aesthetic theory "invok[ed] a concept of man in general as producer of form, and as producer, in particular, of the forms of himself through an aesthetic labour which transcends specific economic or political determinants" (Lloyd 138–39), the assumption of universality inherent in such a conception meant that, in fact, "[t]raining in aesthetic specificity [was] a profoundly socializing practice," whose "real object [was] proper deportment, permanent disposition in a state of aesthetic readiness" (Schwarz 571–72). Moreover, "anything which deviate[d] from this central archetype [was to] be seen as incompletely developed historically rather than as radically different" (Lloyd 166).[5]

Under colonialism, regional writers and artists engaged in a complex re-signification of such aesthetic norms to contest their authority in the limited ways they were able. However, decolonization and subsequent social movements within the metropole enabled a much broader and more sustained critique of normative aesthetic value than what had previously been possible under empire. Postcolonial literature emerged from these and other related historical developments, so that, along with its theoretical counterpart, it works by rupturing the epistemic paradigms of representation in order to effect a subversion of not only the politics of colonialism but its supporting aesthetic ideologies as well. In particular, it questions the aesthetic as a criterion of literary value, in pointed refusal of the complicity of aesthetic restraint with colonial rule. As Robert Young writes,

> Postcolonial writing, together with minority writing in the west and feminist writing generally, has achieved a revolution in aesthetics and the aesthetic criteria of the literary, just at the moment when "the literary" was most under attack as an outdated category of elitist institutions. In institutional terms, the impact of feminism and postcolonialism has radically changed the criteria of what makes authentic art by challenging the cultural capital from which notions of the literary were derived. (7)

Propelled, in part, by poststructuralist theory, whose celebration of excess and "anti-foundationalist critique of the history of Western metaphysics and the 'white mythologies' that such metaphysics relied on and produced" (Israel 86) were directed at many of the same targets, postcolonial theory has encouraged the subversion of aesthetic categories and the "challenge of hegemonic forms of representation in Western models of classical realism and technologies of truth" (McCarthy and Dimitriadis 61). As Bill Ashcroft writes, "The post-colonial may successfully resist when it simply ignores, refuses, or sidesteps the system of representation which constitutes it as subject" (39). In this way, "the post-colonial subject is not only given a voice but the medium itself is changed in the process" (39). This has led, for one, to the rupture of traditional aesthetic criteria such as integrated form and narrative restraint, and to a consequent celebration of formal "excess." Ashcroft defines postcolonial excess as "quintessentially the exuberance of life which is destined to revolt" (38); "excess resists the closure of the name 'post-colonial' because it continually intimates something more; it continually offers the surplus" (40). When incorporated into the form of a text, excess subverts narrative expectations derived from traditional aesthetic norms and radically alters the nature of the text itself, let alone the story it contains. As we will see, such excess, while apparent in a novel such as *White Teeth*, is conspicuously absent in *On Beauty*, raising questions about the text's relationship to the developments of the postcolonial anti-aesthetic in the half-century following decolonization. Yet for the most part, the radical literary challenge posed by the postcolonial viewpoint is witnessed in both the form and content of the postcolonial novel. Thus when one identifies the postcolonial novel's attention to misfits, ruptures, translations, hybridity, alterity, and difference, it is a description both of its structure *and* of the content of its stories and the nature of the characters who populate them—all of which are hybrid, miscegenated, alienated, fragmented, and translated.[6] Salman Rushdie's *Midnight's Children*, widely thought to be the first exemplar of postcolonial literature (Israel 90), is thus marked not only by its explicit criticism "of colonial domination" (90) but by its "disorienting, nonlinear narrative techniques" (90)— its "re-appraisal of the emotional and ethical consequences of deconstructed realities which moves away from the rhetoric of loss towards a celebration of hybridity, plurality, inconsistency" (Schmidt 372). The "national longing for form" expressed in *Midnight's* is in this way doubly inflected as a longing not only for an ontologically stable modernity but for an irrecoverable aesthetic wholeness; unable to fully mourn, its lack is ironically productive of excess: what Timothy Brennan calls a "metafictional extravaganza" (63) and Ashcroft an "irrepressible fictional exuberance" (34).

*Midnight's Children*'s vague expression of longing is further refined in Rushdie's *The Moor's Last Sigh* by a displacement of the aesthetic into a form made up wholly of "sutures and palimpsests" (Schultheis 570). Indeed, in its explicit preoccupation with artists, *Moor's* more than *Midnight's* is concerned with the problem posed by aesthetics to a decolonized worldview. *Moor's* anti-aesthetic works as a psychoanalytic compensation, "offer[ing] the subject images with which to assuage his or her foundational desires" (Schultheis 592) and thus indexing a lack, or a formal "melancholia that can never be cured" (584).[7] In this way, even Aurora, whose "aesthetic aims are communal rather than comprehensive," whose "paintings explore the problem of imagining the nation rather than present a singular, definitive perspective of it" (Schultheis 585), can only *reflect* the condition of the postcolonial nation-state in her artwork—"her early period..., high period...and dark period" (585) reflecting fantasy, "hopefulness" (585), and apocalypse (586) respectively. Her works can only "*displace* cultures in time and in space in order to create 'in-between' spaces and times, that is, sites of contestation, where

'newness enters the world'" (Schülting 252; emphasis added); however, beyond reflection and displacement, the aesthetic here holds no redemptive
power for what is otherwise a "pessimistic" (Schultheis 573) novel.[8]

Even in a novel such as *Moor's*, therefore, which is clearly concerned with
what role aesthetics might play in coming to terms with the inherently fractured nature of postcolonial belonging, little else can be asserted besides the
residual complicity of aesthetics with the colonial—or, indeed, nationalist—
"longing for form." This impasse is more generally reflected in a critical silence in postcolonial theory surrounding issues of form and aesthetics, even
where "returns" to the aesthetic have been broached in other, traditionally
deconstructive fields.[9] As Deepika Bahri writes,

> For a long season, so great was the heft of conventional practice, so entrenched the
> fear of universalism, and so bitter the memory of battle with the tyranny of the
> canon waged precisely on the exclusive grounds of aesthetics that it would have
> seemed provocatively conservative to agitate for aesthetic considerations. Moreover,
> the rooting of most discussions on aesthetics in Western philosophy and values was,
> and is still, likely to give many a postcolonial critic pause. (15)[10]

Rather than trying to redefine an aesthetics outside of the politics of colonialism and the traditional canon, the critical and literary tendency in postcolonial studies has been to continue to disrupt aesthetic expectations and to
find additional ways in which postcolonial literature combats "the narrow
epistemic violence of imperialism" (Spivak 287), rather than to erect an alternative episteme of its own.

Zadie Smith's *White Teeth* operates in many ways along the classic principles of postcolonial literature by invoking an aesthetic of the anti-aesthetic
in the story it tells and in its formal celebration of excess.[11] For one, the novel
disavows the traditional linearity of realist narrative in order to question tem-
porality for its complicity with imperial power. In general, the movement of
narrative back and forth through time destabilizes the chronology which es-
tablishes authoritative history out of the empty, homogenous time of modernity (Stein xi); *White Teeth* takes this one step further by "repeatedly
question[ing]…the advance of history" (Procter 114), radically positing in its
stead the possibility for secular and religious time to converge in an unascer-
tained, yet apocalyptic future. At the same time, the novel explodes the nationalist, place-bound and fallacious eugenic impulses that bind so many of
its characters to their pasts (Cuder-Domínguez 184). The parallel stories of
three families; twins and other doubles; intermixing of gene pools; hybridity

and futurism all serve to project the narrative invariably in the direction of dissolution and infinite possibility, subverting the rigid determinism of all sorts of teleologies: from the Second Coming to science to the conventional narrative plotline.[12]

As if in response to this sense of dissolution, the novel's title and the chapter headings work together to promise a thematic unity through the trope of "white teeth"; however, this unity, constantly reasserted in form, is never actualized in plot. In fact, the only direct mention of the "white teeth" in the novel comes embedded in the perverse memories of an ex-military, elderly white man whom young Magid, Millat, and Irie visit to make a charity donation:

> Mr. Hamilton leaned back contemplatively in his chair. "One sometimes forgets the significance of one's teeth. We're not like the lower animals—teeth replaced regularly and all that—we're of the mammals, you see. And mammals only get two chances, with teeth. More sugar?"

The children, mindful of their two chances, declined.

> "But like all things, the business has two sides. Clean white teeth are not always wise, now are they? Par exemplum: when I was in the Congo, the only way I could identify the nigger was by the whiteness of his teeth, if you see what I mean. Horrid business. Dark as buggery, it was. And they died because of it, you see? Poor bastards. Or rather I survived, to look at it in another way, do you see?" (*White Teeth* 144)[13]

Although some scholars have argued that the novel's teeth "suggest important links between colonial and post-colonial history, through a device which reminds us, inevitably, of the theme of common humanity" (Head 118n.15), few refer to this scene.[14] Indeed, there is little in this scene that points to "common humanity"—to Mr. Hamilton white teeth are, if anything, a sign of utter difference. But any retrieval of meaning in this passage at all requires penetration of the obfuscation of Mr. Hamilton's words, raising the question of whether this quotation is inviting interpretation or, in fact, inhibiting it. Following this line of argument, one wonders whether the passage might not be satirizing the critic's impulse to identify a formal or conceptual unity through the instantly identifiable, and therefore potentially *mis*identifiable, metaphor contained within the title. Might the "white teeth," the root canals, and other "teeth" imagery operate as empty signifiers that proliferate unendingly yet remain unintelligible within a novel clearly skeptical of the political assumptions behind conventions of meaning-making?

In any case, *White Teeth*'s ending, which brings all the main characters together in the same narrative space, clearly operates on the principle of narrative excess. The scene at the FutureMouse convention is so aware of its own contrived nature that it throws into comic relief any sincere vision for apocalypse that the centripetal narrative tendency—including the very trope of the characters coming together at the end—might have suggested. As John Ball writes, "Thematically [Smith's] novel has been preoccupied with the yoking of endings to beginnings and with the inevitable (if unpredictable) ways the past erupts into the present and future" (243). Indeed, the reappearance of Doctor Sick not only links the scientific experiments of the Nazis to those of Marcus Chalfen (Head 115–17), but loops the narrative back to the incipient moment of Archie's and Samad's friendship through the additional foil of deception, whereby Samad discovers he had been lied to. Yet this revelation affects not only Samad: the reader, too, is made aware of the fallibility of even so convincing a narrative technique as the flashback, thus undercutting the entire veracity of the text-as-history. The final chapter's title, "Of Mice and Memory," indexes the impossibility of plans not only of the science-minded Chalfen, who rigorously charts the future life span of his programmed mouse, but of the novel, which has as much tendency, in the context of an excess of form, to go awry.

## I. *On Beauty* and Being Postcolonial

In contrast to the postcolonial excess of form, *On Beauty* strikes the reader as a restrained, even understated text. The long historical reach—imagined and real—of *White Teeth* provides a significant contrast to the closed temporal world within which *On Beauty*'s narrative unfolds, in which historical memory makes few claims on the present. Moreover, the exuberance of multicultural London, the ideal space for the performance and play of cultural difference, contrasts with the staid, whiteness of Wellington, *On Beauty*'s fictional New England college town,[15] and with the even more restricted chronotope of the Belsey living room. But these differences are only symptoms of a new concern that arises with *On Beauty*, absent in the excessive form and fictional world of *White Teeth*. This new concern lies beyond the negation of aesthetic value seen in postcolonial fiction and theory. It asks the question of how an individual life, with all its aesthetic needs, can unfold, justly, once the implication of art and power has been exposed.

*On Beauty* follows a short but turbulent period in the lives of its white, English protagonist, Howard Belsey, his African American wife, Kiki, and their children, Jerome, Zora, and Levi. The immediate crisis faced by the family when the novel opens has been initiated by an extramarital affair Howard had a short time before, which Kiki discovered. However, this affair is only a symptom of a deeper problem with Howard's life, which involves his inability to reconcile his theoretical skepticism of aesthetic value and beauty with his own actions in the domestic sphere. As if by osmosis, the problem of aesthetics is in varying degrees what ails all the Belseys: Kiki, unsure of how much she can demand of others when faced with her middle age and the loss of her physical beauty, and increasingly debilitated by her encroaching physical obesity; Jerome, seduced by religion and the perfect, depoliticized alignment of art and the divine; Zora, sorely needing to mitigate her sharp intellect against a mode of habitation that will allow her to live aesthetically, to fit in with the world; and Levi, unable to retain control of his individual actions in a social milieu disrupted by political oppression, where the question of aesthetics is subsumed to that of radical dissent.

Underlying these individual and often interacting strands of plot is a deeper narrative structure made up of competing terms along a series of aesthetic binaries, which gives meaning to each element of plot beyond its immediate, causal significance within the narrative. Binary pairs include white/black, thin/fat, Mozart/hip-hop, Rembrandt/Haitian art, and beautiful/ugly. This underlying structure is made intelligible both in the thematic connections between the characters' individual stories and, as will be evident below, in the constant interruption of aesthetic questions into the novel's plot. Yet in an even more profound way, this structure serves as something like a philosophical chronotope to the novel as a whole, situating it within a decolonized world in which aesthetic norms are always already problematized, but nevertheless continue to make demands on the characters' lives. In this way, the problem of aesthetics becomes an essential register along which the meaning of the novel must be understood. The conflicts between aesthetic binaries—between "high" and "low" terms—generate the diachronic plots within which each Belsey comes to terms with his or her individual aesthetic crisis. Understanding the interplay between the novel's structure and its plot is essential not only to *On Beauty*'s critical commentary on beauty, but to the novel's own beauty as well

> "Because...we're so binary, of course, in the way we think. We tend to think in opposites, in the Christian world. We're structured like that—Howard always says that's the trouble."—*On Beauty*[16]

If *White Teeth* operates on the principles of miscegenation, rupture, dissolution, and play, *On Beauty* is very differently structured over a series of carefully conceived contradictions that divide the aesthetic world into two disconcertingly neat halves. In race, music, art, body size, and other aesthetic features, the possibilities within the novelistic world are restrained by these sets of binaries dividing the traditionally beautiful from the traditionally ugly. In this way, the construction of an aesthetic universe is central to the development of the novel's plot—indeed, to what it means to be a character within this particular novelistic world. It is for this reason that the novel warrants comparison with E.M. Forster's *Howards End*, the novel to which it pays open homage (in the author's acknowledgments and in its opening line[17]) and from which obvious elements of the early plot are taken—but which is not, as some reviews have suggested, a postcolonial response in the model of Jean Rhys to Charlotte Brontë.[18] In fact, the underappreciated link between the two novels is their respective concern with the problem posed by aesthetic norms to individuals who seek human connection beyond the confines of their exclusive social milieux—be it the obviously genteel, but liberal, Schlegels or the more outwardly egalitarian but still rigidly elite academics of American liberal arts. As one critic articulates the pressing concern of *Howards End*, which is applicable to Smith's as well, "How can liberal intellectuals reconcile the private activities of aesthetic contemplation, friendships, spiritual formation, with a broader concern for the public and social interest?" (Born 142).

Indeed, a genealogical approach to *Howards End* that approaches it via the thematic concerns of *On Beauty* reveals that Forster's novel is also structured over a series of binaries from which canons of aesthetic value are questioned for their normalizing hold on the individual. These include the binaries catalogued by Björkén-Nyberg: "male/female, prose/passion, the middle class/the masses, rural/urban and English/German" (90), and by Catherine Howard: "Schlegels and Wilcoxes,...rich and poor,...masculine and feminine,...city and country" (55). The plot of *Howards End*, on one hand, emerges from the power of these binaries to dictate the terms along which an individual life unfolds, but on the other is characterized by a powerful centripetal movement toward a harmonious resolution, what Catherine Howard calls "the coming together of opposing forces" (55). Thus although the novel puts to the test an uneasy liberalism premised on the social exclusion of outcasts such as Leonard Bast and national outsiders such as the Schlegels, the ultimate goal is reconciliation, rather than radical dissolution, of its binary pairs. And indeed, this reconciliation is effected, however unsatisfactorily, in the novel's ending, and encapsulated in one of the novel's most famous lines, from which its epigraph is taken: "Only connect! That was the whole of her sermon. Only connect the prose and the passion, and both will be exalted, and human love will be seen at its highest. Live in fragments no longer. Only connect, and the beast and the monk, robbed of the isolation that is life to either, will die" (*HE* 147).

While similarly structured, *On Beauty* clearly bears the imprint of the intervening decades and the decolonization of literature by not only introducing binaries of aesthetic value which make claims on the actions of individual characters, but by allowing the suppressed terms, the devalued aesthetic categories, to index alternative aesthetic universes which make competing claims on the plot in a way not seen in *Howards End*. Blackness, fatness, middle age, and all other sorts of non-canonical, postcolonial beauty function in the novel in relative autonomy, in an alternative world engendered by the radical decolonization of the aesthetic canon. In this way, rather than working toward "the coming together of opposing forces," Smith's characters have already been forged in the wake of a rigorous critique of binary aesthetics, so that the knowledge of the impossibility of connection forms a crucial part of their individual narratives of *Bildung*. The novel therefore operates on a dynamic principle of struggle, so that, like Forster's, each character must navigate her way through the aesthetic norms that seek to determine her narrative—but at the same time, unlike Forster's, must remain aware of the conditions of radical difference under which her story is narratable in the first place. As we will see, it is only when the needs of a domestic, "novelistic" life are assimilated with the radical anti-aesthetic of the decolonized world that *On Beauty* can resolve itself with the harmony of its Forsterian predecessor.

*On Beauty*'s break from the aesthetic connectivity of Forster becomes evident in the crucial point at which the two plots achieve their most striking parallelism and then immediately diverge, following different leads out of the same narrative event. This is the scene, early on, that takes place at the public classical music concert: the Schlegels immersed in Beethoven's *Fifth* and the Belseys in Mozart's *Requiem*. From the outset, it is clear that despite the aesthetic sanctity of the concerts, there is more at stake than classical music. In both novels, the concert becomes a site of tension between the contingencies of domestic life on one hand and transcendental aesthetic appreciation on the other—a tension that sets the stage for the plots to come. Already, the idiosyncrasies of the characters and their interactions with one another within the transported domestic setting prove a significant obstacle to the aesthetic flow of the music, which seeks, like Elaine Scarry's beautiful things, to expand and to colonize indefinitely, to "bring...copies of itself into being" (3). For within the domestic tableau in both novels, each member of the family is presented as inhabiting very different positions vis-à-vis the music, unsettling the aesthetic experience with the foreshadowing of drawing-room dissent:

> All sorts and conditions are satisfied by [Beethoven's *Fifth*]. Whether you are like Mrs. Munt, and tap surreptitiously when the tunes come—of course, not so as to disturb the others; or like Helen, who can see heroes and shipwrecks in the music's flood; or like Margaret, who can only see the music; or like Tibby, who is profoundly versed in counterpoint, and holds the full score open on his knee; or like their cousin, Fräulein Mosebach, who remembers all the time that Beethoven is "echt Deutsch"; or like Fräulein Mosebach's young man, who can remember nothing but Fräulein Mosebach.... (*HE* 23)

> Somewhere around the *Confutatis*, Kiki's careful tracing of the live music with the literal programme broke down. She didn't know where she was now. In the *Lacrimosa* or miles ahead? Stuck in the middle or nearing the end? She turned to ask Howard, but he was asleep. A glimpse to her right revealed Zora concentrating on her Discman, through which a recording of the voice of a Professor N.R.A. Gould carefully guided her through each movement.... Yet surely no one among these white people could be more musical than Jerome, who, Kiki now noticed, was crying. (*OB* 70)

Within these disjointed, distinctly non-sublime responses to the aesthetic experience, it comes as no surprise that a lost domestic object of no consequence (an umbrella and a CD player, respectively) comes to dominate the narrative space following the concert, as the characters are distracted from the music by looking for it. Besides the resulting diffusion of the potential aesthetic energy into the prosaic, almost caloric, energy of the quotidian—invitations to tea, calls for lost sons, the weary exchange of things—the

lost object also results in an encounter between the family and a new character. Neither Leonard Bast nor Carl Thomas belongs in the aesthetic space of
the concert, and in their very misfits they initiate the important themes of
both novels, of the limits of traditional aesthetics to account for those marginalized from the social setting in which they are experienced. The anxieties
both new characters pose to the canonical aesthetic order, symbolized in the
juxtaposition between high art and cheap commodity, continue to surface in
the narratives to come

However, the obvious parallelism of the plots ends here.[19] For while
*Howards End* proceeds to follow the series of crises provoked among the
Schlegels by the arrival of Leonard in their lives—from the immediate questions of trust, compensation, and guilt to the revelation of Henry Wilcox's
relationship with Mrs. Bast and Helen's dramatic affair—*On Beauty* takes a
different path by dividing its narrative attention between the Belseys and
Carl, proceeding in turn to follow Carl into the alternative aesthetic universe
that the novel's decolonized politics make legible in a way unavailable to
Forster. This alternative narrative trajectory is foreshadowed by Carl's perceptive comments on Mozart, which, surprisingly, anticipate the anti-
aesthetic theories of Howard himself. In this way, unlike Leonard, Carl is
immediately resignified as more than an object of reform; his position as potential interlocutor anticipates the presentation of a radically re-aestheticized
narrative universe of his own—one that is irreducible to that of the Belseys.

The nature of this alternative narrative universe is revealed in the same
scene, by constant reference to Carl's physical beauty, which the Belseys then
proceed to take heed of in their different ways. While the narrator's descriptions—"Even so small a glimpse of his smile told you that his were perfect
white teeth, superbly arranged" (*OB* 74); "He was grinning now and the fact
that he was stupidly good-looking could no longer be ignored" (*OB* 74)—
obviously differ from Forster's of Leonard,[20] it is Kiki who is first drawn to
what she first perceives as "a tall young man with an elegant neck, sitting
next to her daughter" (*OB* 71). Then, typically, Howard's recognition of
Carl's beauty is half praising and half patronizing: "'Rubens,' said Howard
suddenly. 'Your face. From the four African heads'" (*OB* 77).[21] Already, however, we have an aesthetic revaluation, as the image of black male beauty is
contrasted with the much more pervasive association of black males with
crime—an association that surfaces later in the novel for both Carl and Levi.[22]

As if the novel, with its own aesthetic needs, must follow Carl's beauty out of the concert, the narrative here veers away from Forster's influence and from the Belseys, to introduce an alternative aesthetic world of what might be called "black beauty." This movement creates the narrative conditions for other art forms such as Spoken Word poetry, hip-hop, and Haitian music and art. All these forms are elaborated in the novel as aesthetic universes of their own, outside the centripetal pull of canon formation, but also outside the radar of Howard's anti-aesthetic theories. For example, Carl is involved in the local spoken word scene and excels at it, penning lyrics so beautiful that reluctant Wellington students dub him "Keats with a knapsack" (*OB* 230). For this he is invited to join a poetry class at Wellington, even though he is not a student there. Likewise, the world of Haitian art that Kiki is introduced to by Carlene, and Levi by Choo, gains its significance from influences as diverse as voodoo and modern art, and yet is also a valuable commodity in a poor and unstable country. It is in this aesthetic *and* political richness that the art profoundly affects the mother and son beyond its merely artistic worth. Indeed, for all those touched by this alternative aesthetic universe, the exposure is to a kind of beauty unintelligible in the binary between beautiful and ugly to which both the conservative Monty Kipps and the radical Howard Belsey end up subscribing.

Carl Thomas; black beauty; Spoken Word; Hector Hyppolite; Haitian protest music: *On Beauty* provides countless opportunities for its characters to think outside the narrow aesthetic parameters of canonical art, and all the main characters—all the Belsey clan—are, to different degrees, affected by what they discover. All, perhaps, except Howard, whose obsession with proving his own intellectual authority and reiterating his deconstructive critique of the canon causes him to miss out on the beauty of the alternative aesthetics flourishing around him. Indeed, while Carl ends up falling in the face of the more powerful, ulterior image of his black maleness, suspected as he is of stealing the Haitian Hyppolite painting that, in fact, belongs to an unknowing Kiki, his role in the novel as a radically revalued Leonard Bast raises central questions about beauty and the non-canonized Other. In many ways, Carl exists as a foil against which the primary narrative strand of the novel unfolds, which details Howard's struggle to live under the influence of a theoretical stance which, untenably, disavows aesthetics altogether.

## II. *Howards End*

> *Howard asked his students to imagine prettiness as the mask that power wears.—On Beauty*[23]

Howard Belsey is a professor of art history at Wellington College; his perpetually incomplete book on Rembrandt argues against conventional interpretive practices of art history such as the "lone genius" model and the autonomy of the aesthetic domain. Contrary to stalwarts of the aesthetic tradition, for whom "Art was a gift of God, blessing only a handful of masters" (*OB* 44), Howard believes in materialist analysis and a deconstructive, genealogical approach that is attentive to the workings of power. For instance, regarding *The Staalmeesters*, a Rembrandt conventionally seen to encapsulate the kind of "considered, rational, benign judgment" (*OB* 383) that represents the high tradition of the Enlightenment, Howard argues:

> To imagine that this painting depicts any one temporal moment is…an anachronistic, photographic fallacy. It is all so much pseudo-historical storytelling, disturbingly religious in tone. We want to believe these Staalmeesters are sages, wisely judging this imaginary audience, implicitly judging us. But none of this is truly *in* the picture. All we really see there are six rich men sitting for their portrait, expecting— *demanding*—to be collectively portrayed as wealthy, successful and morally sound. Rembrandt—paid well for his services—has merely obliged them…. The painting is an exercise in the depiction of economic power—in Howard's opinion a particularly malign and oppressive depiction. So goes Howard's spiel. (*OB* 383–84)

This skepticism toward aesthetic norms has hardened in Howard to become a principle of anti-aesthetics, so that he is critical not only of the idea of the artistic genius, but of the very project to glean meaning from texts. This is for Howard not only an abstract politics, but an attempt to break away from the kitsch aesthetics of the working class, represented by his father's love for the *Mona Lisa*,[24] and on the other side to wage a battle against the conservative forces on campus who seek to "take the liberal out of liberal arts" (*OB* 326), primarily through the revaluation of the canon against multicultural and other aesthetically "compromised" influences. Yet despite Howard's principled adherence to his theory, he has yet to attain academic success, due in part to his inability to collect his ideas together with any kind of formal coherence—in this case, the completed book manuscript required for tenure. This inability is not unrelated to Howard's disdain for form altogether.Even more fundamental to Howard's crisis, however, is his inability to distinguish between his academic theories regarding canonical art history and the principles according to which he leads his own, domestic life. In a clearly overblown response to the sheer power of aesthetics over daily life, Howard has banned representational art in his home and encourages his family to listen only to atonal music. On one level, of course, such details are narrated by the kind of delightedly ironic narrative voice we find describing the idiosyncrasies of the Chalfens in *White Teeth*. However, far from being mere descriptions of character, which often remain inert in the context of diachronic narrative developments, Howard's aesthetic dictates are productive of plot, both as they generate response from his family members, and more importantly as they impede exactly the kind of individual growth encouraged by the novel form. His children, for one, are deeply affected by the disdain toward meaning that pervades their family, although they react to it in different ways. Indeed, as we have seen, the familial dysfunction that comes in the way of the harmonious domestic plot emerges from one or another variant of the aesthetic crisis that Howard has brought upon the house.

Kiki, especially, although she does not consider herself an intellectual as it is narrowly defined in the Wellington world, is affected by Howard's refusal of canonical aesthetic categories. Initially, her husband's politics regarding art coincide with her own refusal to be defeated by the physical signs of her middle age, which are increasingly replacing the stunning physical beauty of her youth with the uncontrollable extra weight of a drastic menopause. Yet at the same time, Kiki's alienation from Howard comes exactly at those moments when, despite his stubborn adherence to theory in the domestic sphere, he is in fact unable to take his anti-aesthetic politics to their logical conclusion with regard to his wife. While this is initially a minor annoyance, it seriously threatens their marriage when Kiki discovers that Howard's affair was not an anonymous, one-night stand but a three-week stint with a close friend of them both, Claire Malcolm. This fact is not without aesthetic significance:

> "Could you have found anybody less like me if you'd *scoured* the *earth*?" [Kiki] said, thumping the table with her fist. "My *leg* weighs more than that woman. What have you made me *look like* in front of everybody in this town? You married a big black bitch and you run off with a fucking leprechaun?" (*OB* 206)

As we see, the discourse in which the couple's discord is articulated is overdetermined by the problem of aesthetics that structures the narrative as a whole. Given that their marriage was not without its own aesthetic obstacles,[25] Kiki immediately recognizes that Howard's affair with Claire entails not only a rejection of her, but an infuriating disconnect between his anti-aesthetic theories and his actions. Even Levi, generally unattuned to the subtleties by which aesthetic norms make themselves felt within the domestic sphere, senses the injury to his mother: "He felt the unfairness and illogic of the substitution. He made a decision to cut the conversation [with Claire] short as a sign of solidarity with his mother's more generous proportions" (*OB* 219–20). The whole family now knows: despite Howard's refusal of conventional aesthetic norms, he finds himself physically drawn to the most traditional, even clichéd forms of beauty. He defends himself unconvincingly:

> "Look," said Howard resolutely…. "I'm trying to be as honest as I can. If you're asking me, obviously physicality is a factor. You have…Keeks, you've changed a lot. I don't *care*, but—"
>
> . . . . . . . . . . . . . . . . . . . .
>
> "It's true that men—they respond to beauty…it doesn't end for them, this…this *concern* with beauty as a physical actuality in the world—and that's clearly imprisoning and it infantilizes…but it's *true* and…I don't know how else to explain what—." (*OB* 207)

The incongruity between Howard's sudden admission that he can and has succumbed to canonical norms of beauty and his strident theorization of the material and political conditions under which such norms are established unsettles the harmony of his character in a dramatic fashion, in what is otherwise a relatively inconspicuous domestic scene. In fact, the domesticity of the scene is very much the point: it is not that Howard is incorrect in saying that men "respond to beauty," but in asserting it as a defense against Kiki he fails to realize the hollowness of the statement in a domestic setting overdetermined by the effects of his very own anti-aesthetic theory. For Kiki, on the other hand, the hypocrisy is apparent. For all Howard's awareness of the power of aesthetic norms, he has overlooked the fact that prohibiting aesthetic valuation can perpetuate power dynamics as well, especially when the prohibition is, ultimately, an impossible one to live by.[26]

Things only deteriorate when Howard has a short and pathetic sexual encounter with Victoria Kipps, the daughter of his conservative archrival and a student in his class. Victoria's beauty, unlike Kiki's and even Carl's, is unflinchingly canonical, and in this way so overpowering, to herself and to others, that it is able to express itself only in a misguided and undiscriminating sexuality. Howard's infatuation with Victoria's beauty[27] takes full form in the very course in which he carefully unravels norms of beauty, through Rembrandt's *Seated Nude*. This painting's voluptuous nude is considered unsightly by Rembrandt's traditional critics and radically anti-aesthetic by those less so. Howard, on the other hand, has a third explanation: "Is what we see here really a *rebellion*, a turning away? We're told that this constitutes a rejection of the classical nude. OK. But. Is this nude not a *confirmation* of the ideality of the vulgar? As it is already inscribed in the idea of a specifically gendered, class debasement?" (*OB* 252). In Howard's theoretically sophisticated approach, a mere depiction of a classically unaesthetic figure does not, in itself, constitute a critique of aesthetic norms, but instead can be seen to reinforce them. In this view, even an anti-aesthetic representation is complicit with dominant norms, for the aesthetic it invokes as its assumed opposite. Yet ironically, this moment at the height of Howard's theoretical sophistication is complicit with the depth of his sexual perversity; having already violated every ethical instinct in having sex with Victoria, he is able to theorize away the guilt of doing so in language supremely alienated from the reality of his domestic existence.

Howard's short-lived affair with Victoria marks the culmination of his flawed character as it has been defined in the novel thus far. Victoria is not just a younger, still-beautiful image of Kiki, but, through her age and the fact that she has already slept with Jerome, represents the antithesis of a domestic life which the novel as a whole tends toward, in a way that *White Teeth*, for instance, does not. The incorporation of Victoria into Howard's critical apparatus for deconstructing aesthetic value marks a final recognition of the moral vacuousness, and profound unlivability, of Howard's theory. It is for this reason that unlike his affair with Claire, the discovery of Howard's affair with Victoria provokes no argument articulate enough to be represented within the domestic space of the text, but results only in unnarrated action occurring in the break between the novel's twelfth chapter and its last. In this gap, we are given to understand that Kiki has moved out of the Belsey house, leaving Howard in charge of the children and no hint as to her new location.

And unlike in *Howards End*, where the discovery of the dissimulation surrounding the inheritance is revealed without any change in the plot trajectory, in *On Beauty* Kiki gets her due, exposing and punishing not only Monty Kipps, but Howard as well, for his misguided, anti-aesthetic stance that will not recognize a thing of beauty even when it stares him in the face. Fittingly, then, in defeating both men, Kiki gains for herself Hector Hyppolite's painting of *Maîtresse Erzulie*, whose unique, non-dichotomous beauty of "jealousy, vengeance and discord, *and*, on the other hand, perpetual help, goodwill, health, beauty and fortune" (*OB* 175) is unrecognizable either to the conservative art-looter or to the radical critic.

However, all is not lost for Howard. In a twist of narrative fortune, he leaves his notes for a tenure lecture in his car and finds himself having to improvise when faced with a PowerPoint image of Rembrandt's *Hendrickje Bathing*, a young woman wading in a dark pool. It is at this moment, unable to articulate the jumble of thoughts that crowd his head, that Howard spots an estranged Kiki in the audience: the first time they have met for weeks. The possibility of forgiveness signaled in Kiki's presence intersects with his own lack of preparedness to cause him to consider the famous painting anew, to suddenly recall the "error [he has] made about beauty" (Scarry 11).[28] For the first time, Hendrickje is not only "the woman on the wall," but she is "Rembrandt's love, Hendrickje" (*OB* 443) as well. The connection between art and the domestic quality of love begins to dawn on Howard, implicating him in the painting in a new way. The *moral* element of aesthetic value— which Howard had so assiduously refused—is reanimated, constituting not only Hendrickje, but Howard himself in a new light. It is only at this point that the possibility of forgiveness arises, if not yet from Kiki, at least from a narrative whose sympathy has been progressively alienated from Howard since the very first page.

Postcolonial theory has made the argument for the inextricability of politics from the domesticated space of the novel as a partial response to the complicity of aesthetic normalization with colonial rule. While this is commonly accepted among scholars and writers alike, *On Beauty* raises a further question of how an individual life can unfold if theory, however well-intentioned, is allowed to overdetermine the domestic setting to the extent that it betrays its own politics. Without advocating a return to bourgeois literary aesthetics, Smith's novel reasserts the partial autonomy of domestic life as a counter to its unthinking politicization, suggesting that a rejection of the aesthetic can be as destructive to an individual life as a wholehearted capitulation to it. It is in this that the novel makes its most radical claim for redemption of form and aesthetic sensibility in a postcolonial world in which the complicity of aesthetic norms with power and oppression has been so thoroughly exposed. In this final, self-enclosed scene, so unlike the public showdown of *White Teeth*, the novel thus achieves its thematic and narrative closure, as the relations are resurrected between love and art, reality and image, and life and theory, to generate the will for the reunification of Kiki and Howard. Startlingly, then, *On Beauty*'s ending emerges perfectly out of *On Beauty*'s plot. Like the Rembrandt it takes pains to describe, it is one of beauty.

## Notes

[1]Postcolonial literature, like any other well-used term, has been variously defined. Some critics distinguish between an ostensibly more apolitical canon of Commonwealth literature, beginning in the 1950s, and post-1980s "postcolonial" literature, which refers specifically to a literary perspective that was "more critical of colonial domination and somewhat more sympathetic to the potentialities of political newness" (Israel 90). However, postcolonial literature is more commonly defined generally as emerging from newly decolonized nations and engaged in rupturing the assumptions of representation upon which colonial rule relied. In this context, postcolonial theory, a more expansive term, refers to a body of theory attempting to dislodge colonial hegemony by disturbing the very epistemic assumptions and norms upon which such hegemony often covertly relied.

[2] P. 124. This quotation is also cited in Weiss, "At the End."

[3] The works of Edward Said, in particular *Orientalism* and *Culture and Imperialism*, are traditionally credited with raising the question of the implication of the humanities in the production and maintenance of the colonial episteme; however, as George Levine writes, Said's work operates along a fundamental contradiction between aesthetic appreciation—Said's "humanist" side—and the project of ideological "demystification" (Levine 15).

[4] This is also discussed in Eric Stokes, *The English Utilitarians and India.*

[5] There is, of course, much more to be said about the relationship of aesthetic theory to colonialism. For my purposes, however, it is especially important to emphasize the relationship of formal restraint to the colonial project. This relationship, though well documented in studies of *colonial* discourse, has been comparatively neglected in studies of postcolonial literature, despite the fact that postcolonial literature, as we shall see, often seeks to rupture conventional aesthetic norms precisely through an affront to colonial restraint. Of course, there are other

elements of aesthetic theory that postcolonial criticism might find equally objectionable. The aesthetic theories of Kant, Hegel, and Coleridge, especially those concerning organicity and form, have been targeted in particular by poststructuralist deconstructionists (see Loesberg, *A Return to Aesthetics*) and by materialist critics (see Eagleton, *Ideology of the Aesthetic*), and thus have been critiqued by postcolonial scholars as well. Very few poststructuralists or materialists have, however, focused on the relationship between aesthetics and colonialism. Postcolonial criticism narrowly defined thus has a more specific object of critique in aesthetic theories of restraint and governmentality than other kinds of more general, anti-Enlightenment critical theory.

[6] This is true of postcolonial authors of South Asian origin as well as those, especially in England, of Afro-Caribbean origin. Stuart Hall uses the term "black" to talk about the commonalities between a number of postcolonial, diasporic identities in Great Britain. Moreover, he argues, from a black British perspective, that one cannot "resolve the questions of aesthetic value by the use of…transcendental, canonical cultural categories. I think there is another position, one which locates itself *inside* a continuous struggle and politics around black representation, but which then is able to open up a continuous critical discourse about themes, about the forms of representation, the subjects of representation, above all, the regimes of representation" (448).

[7] We see a similar concern with lack in Bahri's argument that *The Moor's Last Sigh* "struggles to retain the prospect of a utopia that never was, in an ultimate gesture of compensation that only reiterates its loss" (30).

[8] Schultheis argues that at the end of Rushdie's novel, it is "the text of *The Moor's Last Sigh* [which] retains hope in the aesthetic's capacity for imaginative renewal and vision" (591), signaling a significant collapse of content with form that is typical of the postcolonial novel. If the aesthetic promises no redemption within the novelistic world, it "plays a privileged role" as a mediating term which signals this very lack of redemption by "highlight[ing] the distance between reader and text necessary for re-vision of the nation" (591). As I hope will be evident, this is quite different from the type of aesthetic revaluation that this essay discusses regarding Zadie Smith's *On Beauty*.

[9] See, for instance, Isobel Armstrong, *The Radical Aesthetic*, in which she argues for "the project of rethinking the aesthetic" (2) in the wake of deconstruction, without "returning to a pretheoretical innocence" (2); see also Jonathan Loesberg, *A Return to Aesthetics*; George Levine, ed., *Aesthetics and Ideology*; and Tobin Siebers, "Kant and the Politics of Beauty."

[10] Although Bahri sees a resurgence in attention to aesthetics, particularly in the dialectical tradition of Eagleton and Jameson (15), she warns against the dangers "first, that this perception of aesthetics deployed without an apprehension of the historical positional status of postcolonial literature can slide into shallow politicking by other means; second and subsequent, that this will effect an even more efficient displacement of other, more compelling, and necessary forms of political representation, and indeed even of other forms of cultural expression that do not adhere to the terms of an aesthetics developed largely in Western terms" (15–16).

[11] Some critics see *White Teeth* as "post-postcolonial," as it "satirically evokes the early multi-cultural discourses of education" and "satirizes political correctness as it is enshrined within multicultural thinking" (Procter 114). However, this being the case does not preclude the novel's postcolonial critique; it merely extends the object of that critique to not merely colonialism and the nation-state, but liberal attempts at reforming the nation-state as well.

[12] Or, as Ball puts it, "Smith's densely intricate narrative interconnections work feverishly to simultaneously reinforce and ironically complicate the relations between history and destiny, choice and consequence, accident and design" (241).

[13] Quotations from *White Teeth* are hereafter referenced as *WT*.

[14] Exceptions include Cuder-Domínguez, who describes and interprets the scene in the following way: "Eventually convinced [the children] are harmless, [Mr. Hamilton] tells them stories of the Congo War, where the black men were targeted by the whiteness of their teeth. That this episode has bestowed the novel's title cannot fail to be significant, Smith's own way to point at how entrenched these values continue to be in present-day England" (186). Lowe makes a similar argument: "The novel takes its title from this scene, and reminds us that this generation, insiders though some might have become, still has to fight racism" (170). By contrast, Ball connects "teeth" to "roots" via (root) canals: "[Smith's] obsession with 'roots' is...familiar, though her controlling metaphor of teeth is original; moreover, by naming her flashback chapters 'Root Canals,' she hints at the roots/routes duality of migrancy, since outside of dentistry a canal is a route. It is, notably, an inland waterway, a local route; Smith also links roots to oceanic, global routes when she extends Samad's belief that 'tradition was culture, and culture led to roots, and these were good' with the following metaphor: 'Roots were what saved, the ropes one throws out to rescue drowning men, to Save Their Souls. And the further Samad himself floated out to sea,...the more determined he became to create for his boys roots on shore, deep roots that no storm or gale could displace.'... Strong local roots, in other words, are a defence against the dangers of ocean-crossing routes" (242).

[15] This campus chronotope, which initially suggests an academic novel of the kind discussed by Robbins in his "What the Porter Saw," then becomes a foil against which the competing aesthetic universes of the outside world get recast to fit within the narrow discursive parameters of the American "culture wars." *On Beauty* thus transvalues the campus novel in a similar way as it does the postcolonial and the modernist novels.

[16] P. 175.

[17] *On Beauty* begins with "One may as well begin with Jerome's e-mails to his father" (3); *Howards End* with "One may as well begin with Helen's letters to her sister" (*HE* 1). Quotations from *On Beauty* will hereafter be referenced as *OB* and from *Howards End* as *HE*.

[18] Mandakini Dubey draws a relation between *On Beauty* and *Wide Sargasso Sea*, arguing that Smith's novel differs from Rhys's only because "Smith does not mount a radical critique of the original text so much as use it, lovingly, as a guide" (5). The question of whether *On Beauty* is

a critique or an homage to Forster's novel misses, I think, its key points of engagement with *Howards End*, which cannot be described as either all-out acceptance or all-out rejection.

[19] This is not to say that all similarity between the plots and themes of the two novels ends here; for instance, Margaret and Kiki have a similar experience when Mrs. Wilcox and Carlene Kipps, respectively, invite them on a spontaneous trip to see their houses. There is also the question of the interference with the two women's rightful inheritance, which will be mentioned below.

[20] Forster's narrator describes Leonard Bast in the following way: "He was inferior to most rich people, there is not the least doubt of it. He was not as courteous as the average rich man, nor as intelligent, nor as healthy, nor as lovable. His mind and his body had been alike underfed, because he was poor, and because he was modern they were always craving better food" (*HE* 35). Also compare the description of Carl's teeth to those of Jacky Bast, Leonard's wife, who is significantly less genteel than Leonard: "[The photograph] represented a young lady called Jacky, and had been taken at the time when young ladies called Jacky were often photographed with their mouths open. Teeth of dazzling whiteness extended along either of Jacky's jaws, and positively weighed her head sideways, so large were they and so numerous" (*HE* 37).

[21] Zora, too caught up at the concert with the perceived affront she perceives in Carl's accusation that she has accidentally mistaken his CD player for hers, only notices Carl's beauty later, when she runs into him at the swimming pool to engage in a parodic repeat of the CD player incident—this time with goggles: "For the time it takes to swim one length she stood by the side of the lifeguard's chair and…watched the initial seal-pup flip-flop of the boy's torso, the ploughing and lifting of two dark arms in turbine motion, the grinding muscles of the shoulders, the streamlined legs doing what all human legs could do if only they tried a little harder. For a whole twenty-three seconds the last thing on Zora's mind was herself" (*OB* 133).

[22] Carl is accused of stealing a piece of art from Monty Kipps's office; Levi is constantly suspected by his suburban neighbors because of his clothing and his race.

[23] P. 155.

[24] "Harold's face creased into the picture of distressed aesthetic sensitivity, as if Howard had just put his foot through *The Mona Lisa*. *The Mona Lisa*. A painting Harold loves. When Howard was having his first pieces of criticism printed in the sorts of papers Harold never buys, a customer of Harold's had shown the butcher a cutting of his son writing enthusiastically about Piero Manzoni's *Merda d'Artista*. Harold closed the shop and went down the road with a handful of twopence to use the phone. 'Shit in a jar? Why can't you write about somefing lovely, like *The Mona Lisa*? Your mum would be so proud of that. *Shit in a jar?*'" (*OB* 299).

[25] Race is not an aesthetic problem for any of the primary characters in the text (that is, none of the main characters is *racist*, in the narrow sense of the word), but Howard's father, Harold Belsey, has in the past shown significant hostility to his marrying a black woman, suggesting,

for instance, that "you couldn't expect black people to develop mentally like white people do" (*OB* 296). Again, Howard's own anti-aesthetic theory is an attempt—however misguided—to refute such aesthetic valuations, which are a part of his background.

[26] A similar point is made by Amardeep Singh, who writes: "Belsey, [Smith's] main purveyor of deconstructive thinking, appears deeply delusional about his own relationship to beauty and art. While he rigorously 'interrogates' the myth of Rembrandt's 'genius,' his susceptibility to female beauty in particular leads him into a series of disastrous affairs, which bring down his marriage."

[27] The narrative description of Victoria when Howard first sees her in his class is focalized through Howard's awed perspective—one which, ironically, is full of the kinds of traditional aesthetic valuations that he claims to despise: "The first thing to note were two spots of radiant highlights on her face—maybe the result of the same cocoa butter Kiki used in the winter. A pool of moonlight on her smooth forehead, and another on the tip of her nose; the kind of highlights, it occurred to Howard, that would be impossible to paint without distorting, without misrepresenting, the solid darkness of her true complexion. And her hair had changed again: now it was wormy dreadlocks going every which way, although none was longer than two inches. The tips of each were coloured a sensational orange, as if she had dipped her head into a bucket of sunshine. Because he was not drunk this time he knew now for certain that her breasts were indeed a phenomenon of nature and not of his imagination, for here were the spirited nipples again, working their way through a thick green ribbed woollen jumper" (*OB* 156).

[28] Smith explicitly cites Elaine Scarry's *On Beauty and Being Just* as an influence for this novel, and titles her final section in the novel, "On Beauty and Being Wrong," after Scarry (and a poem entitled "On Beauty" written by Smith's husband, Nick Laird). Howard has clearly "been wrong" in his aesthetic judgments throughout the novel, but it does not occur to him until this particular moment, at the very end.

## Works Cited

Armstrong, Isobel. *The Radical Aesthetic*. Oxford: Blackwell, 2000.

Ashcroft, Bill. "Excess: Post-Colonialism and the Verandahs of Meaning." In *De-Scribing Empire: Post-Colonialism and Textuality*, edited by Chris Tiffin and Alan Lawson, 33–44. London and New York: Routledge, 1994.

Bahri, Deepika. *Native Intelligence: Aesthetics, Politics, and Postcolonial Literature*. Minneapolis: University of Minnesota Press, 2003.

Ball, John Clement. *Imagining London: Postcolonial Fiction and the Transnational Metropolis*. Toronto: University of Toronto Press, 2004.

Björkén-Nyberg, Cecilia. "'Listening, Listening': Music and Gender in *Howards End, Sinister Street* and *Pilgrimage*." *Rodopi Perspectives on Modern Literature* 25 (2002): 89–116.

Born, Daniel. "Private Gardens, Public Swamps: *Howards End* and the Revaluation of Liberal Guilt." *Novel: A Forum on Fiction* 25, no. 2 (1992): 141–59.

Brennan, Timothy. "The National Longing for Form." In *Nation and Narration*, edited by Homi K. Bhabha, 44–70. London and New York: Routledge, 1990.

Cuder-Domínguez, Pilar. "Ethnic Cartographies of London in Bernardine Evaristo and Zadie Smith." *European Journal of English Studies* 8, no. 2 (2004): 173–88.

Dubey, Mandakini. "Only Conflict." *Biblio* 10, nos. 11–12 (2005): 5.

Eagleton, Terry. *The Ideology of the Aesthetic*. Oxford: Basil Blackwell, 1990.

Forster, E.M. *Howards End*. New York: Bantam Books, 1985.

Hall, Stuart. "New Ethnicities." In *Stuart Hall: Critical Dialogues in Cultural Studies*, edited by David Morley and Kuan-Hsing Chen, 441–49. London and New York: Routledge, 1996.

Head, Dominic. "Zadie Smith's *White Teeth*." In *Contemporary British Fiction*, edited by Richard J. Lane, Rod Mengham, and Philip Tew, 106–19. Cambridge, UK: Polity Press, 2003.

Howard, Catherine E. "'Only Connect': Logical Aesthetic of Fragmentation in *A Word Child*." *Twentieth Century Literature* 38, no. 1 (1992): 54–65.

Israel, Nico. "Tropicalizing London: British Fiction and the Discipline of Postmodernism." In *A Concise Companion to Contemporary British Fiction*, edited by James F. English, 83–100. Malden, MA: Blackwell, 2006.

Levine, George. "Introduction: Reclaiming the Aesthetic." In *Aesthetics and Ideology*, edited by George Levine. New Brunswick, NJ: Rutgers University Press, 1994.

Lloyd, David. "Arnold, Ferguson, Schiller: Aesthetic Culture and the Politics of Aesthetics." *Cultural Critique* 2 (1985–86): 137–69.

Loesberg, Jonathan. *A Return to Aesthetics: Autonomy, Indifference, and Postmodernism*. Stanford, CA: Stanford University Press, 2005.

Lowe, Jan. "No More Lonely Londoners." *Small Axe* 9 (2001): 166–80.

McCarthy, Cameron, and Greg Dimitriadis. "The Work of Art in the Postcolonial Imagination." *Discourse: Studies in the Cultural Politics of Education* 21, no. 1 (2000): 59–74.

Procter, James. "New Ethnicities, the Novel, and the Burdens of Representation." In *A Concise Companion to Contemporary British Fiction*, edited by James F. English, 101–20. Malden, MA: Blackwell, 2006.

Robbins, Bruce. "What the Porter Saw: On the Academic Novel." In *A Concise Companion to Contemporary British Fiction*, edited by James F. English, 248–66. Malden, MA: Blackwell, 2006.

Rushdie, Salman. *The Moor's Last Sigh*. London: Vintage, 1995.

Scarry, Elaine. *On Beauty and Being Just*. Princeton, NJ: Princeton University Press, 1999.

Schmidt, Benjamin Marius. "From 'Self vs. Other' to 'System/Environment': Joseph Conrad and Salman Rushdie Mark Steps on the Way Towards an Ecology of the Mind." *European Journal of English Studies* 5, no. 3 (2001): 367–83.

Schülting, Sabine. "Peeling Off History in Salman Rushdie's *The Moor's Last Sigh*." In *Hybridity and Postcolonialism: Twentieth-Century Indian Literature*, edited by Monika Fludernik, 239–60. Tübingen, Germany: Stauffenburg Verlag, 1998.

Schultheis, Alexandra W. "Postcolonial Lack and Aesthetic Promise in *The Moor's Last Sigh*." *Twentieth Century Literature* 47, no. 4 (2001): 569–95.

Schwarz, Henry. "Aesthetic Imperialism: Literature and the Conquest of India." *Modern Language Quarterly* 61, no. 4 (2000): 563–86.

Siebers, Tobin. "Kant and the Politics of Beauty." *Philosophy and Literature* 22, no. 1 (1998): 31–50.

Singh, Amardeep. "Zadie Smith's Academic Tomato-Meter." August 31, 2006.http://www.lehigh.edu/~amsp/2006/03/zadie-smiths-academic-tomato-meter.html.

Smith, Zadie. *On Beauty*. London: Hamish Hamilton, 2005.

———. *White Teeth*. New York: Vintage, 2000.

Spivak, Gayatri Chakravorty. "Can the Subaltern Speak?" In *Marxism and the Interpretation of Culture*, edited by Cary Nelson and Lawrence Grossberg, 271–313. Urbana and Chicago: University of Illinois Press, 1988.

Stein, Mark. *Black British Literature: Novels of Transformation*. Columbus: Ohio State University Press, 2004.

Stokes, Eric. *The English Utilitarians and India*. Delhi: Oxford University Press, 1959.

Viswanathan, Gauri. "The Beginnings of English Literary Study in British India." In *The Post-Colonial Studies Reader*, edited by Bill Ashcroft, Helen Tiffin, and Gareth Griffiths, 431–37. London and New York: Routledge, 1995.

———. *Masks of Conquest: Literary Study and British Rule in India*. New Delhi: Oxford University Press, 1989.

Weiss, Timothy. "At the End of East/West: Myth in Rushdie's *The Moor's Last Sigh*." *Jouvert: A Journal of Postcolonial Studies* 4, no. 2 (2000).

Young, Robert J.C. "Ideologies of the Postcolonial." *Interventions* 1, no. 1 (1998): 4–8.

# CHAPTER III

## The Impossible Self and the Poetics of the Urban Hyperreal in Zadie Smith's *The Autograph Man*

Urszula Terentowicz-Fotyga, Maria Curie Skłodowska University,
Lublin, Poland

The publication of *White Teeth* almost instantly canonized Zadie Smith as a new voice of multicultural Britain. The novel, contrasted with the writings of Naipaul, Selvon, or Caryl Phillips, was said to open a new chapter in the history of the postcolonial novel. Even though some criticized it for depoliticizing race, it was generally praised for representing "a third generation of postwar Black-British experience, a generation for which the concepts of 'migrancy' and 'exile' have become too distant to carry their former freight of disabling rootlessness" (Head 107–8). *The Autograph Man* came in for a more mixed reception. While some praised its treatment of the contemporary celebrity culture, many felt it had fulfilled the curse of the second novel and not lived up to the expectations raised by the assured debut. Somewhat unexpectedly, however, *The Autograph Man* was said to be wanting in what in *White Teeth* was Smith's greatest strength—a convincing picture of multicultural London and high-spirited characterization. The portrait of the city in *The Autograph Man* many found wan and lifeless; the characters were deemed paper thin and unconvincing.[1]

Smith's second novel sits uncomfortably with the label of postcolonial fiction. Despite superficial similarities in setting and characterisation, its main concerns are very different from those explored in *White Teeth*. Although both novels represent London as a multicultural city, they differ significantly in their representation of multiculturalism, especially in the way the second generation of migrants is portrayed. In *White Teeth*, the acceptance of multiculturalism is the destination of the protagonists' youthful quest for identity; in *The Autograph Man*, it is a point of departure. While in *White Teeth* the theme of migration is filtered through the lenses of history, the second novel is organized around the theme of culture industry and the hyperreal experience of space. A fluid sense of identity in *The Autograph Man* is not so much an effect of migration and displacement as of problematic experience of reality.

The purpose of this essay is to explore the themes of postmodern, urban identity in view of Baudrillard's idea of simulacrum and Benjamin's concept of the aura. The structure of *The Autograph Man* is based on the complex dialectic of the real and the imaginary, the authentic and the fake, the fictional and metafictional, written into the novel's bipartite composition. In book one, both the author and her protagonists seem immersed in the reality of self-referential signs. The main characters use media reality as the principal frame of reference, and Smith appears to follow suit, filling the novel with clichés of popular culture and scraps of contemporary literary and cultural theory. Book two, I argue, can be read as a tentative attempt to recuperate the notion of "the Real" in the textual reality defined by "the precession of simulacra" (Baudrillard 166). As her characters set off on a quest for "the Real," the parodic character of metafictional strategies becomes more apparent. The way Smith uses literary and cultural theory to contextualize fictional reality illustrates the transition from the multicultural concerns of the debut novel to the intertextual themes explored in *On Beauty*.

*The Autograph Man*, like *White Teeth*, is set in the northern suburbs of London. In both books, Smith focuses on a specific religious community—the Muslim one in the debut novel and the Jewish diaspora in *The Autograph Man*. However, different experiences of the first and second generations, central to the meaning of the first novel, remain in the background in *The Autograph Man*, and the plot focuses firmly on the immigrants' children. Alex's father, who sees difference as a burden and wants his son to melt in, "to be part of...everybody,"[2] figures only briefly in the prologue. For Alex and his friends, *alterity* is a backdrop to identity rather than its defining characteristic; it is "this weird but cool thing you just got landed with, like an extra shoe" (AM 31). Once the center has been redefined by migration and globalisation, "difference [is] both acknowledged and irrelevant" (Weeks 92). The fluid, slippery, hybrid identity is the norm, as is the migratory character of the city. Alex's family roots are dispersed among various places in Eastern Europe, Russia, and China. Family history is limited to several photographs; a "tram ticket for a defunct line through a defunct city," probably somewhere in Poland; "[t]he qualification certificates of an émigré Russian teacher, distant cousin. One bowler hat, crushed" (AM 92). The Jewish diaspora in *The Autograph Man* is depicted as a cultural melting pot rather than integrated community. The main protagonist is the son of a Jewish Buddhist mother and Chinese father, preaching "*imperceptible* Judaism" (AM 7). His best friends are Rubinfine—the Jewish rabbi fascinated by Harrison Ford and "goyish in the extreme" (AM 74) and Adam—"the only black kid for miles" (AM 8), who came from Harlem with his grandparents, "claiming the tribe of Judah. Dressed like Ethiopian kings!" (AM 11). Even though all the main characters are Jewish, religious beliefs are a matter of contention. They range from Alex's arbitrary reading of reality in terms of Jewishness and Goyishness, to Adam's fascination with Jewish mysticism and Kabbalah, to the different Talmudic schools represented by the three rabbis. Thus, while Judaism is used to structure the novel, it is, as Gilman rightly contended, "the pop Jewish mysticism of the 1990s, watered down to become a universal experience separate from its Jewish religious context" (140). The characters' experiences are deliberately depicted as universal. Jews, Elizabeth Grosz observed, traditionally serve as "a trope of *alterity*," "a metaphor for a more universal (even ontological) alienation" (60, 61).

In *The Autograph Man* there are no Chalfens to claim the purity of the centre, and the fluid character of identity is taken for granted. In this sense, Alex's change of name (from Chinese "Tan" to the ineffectively neutral "Tandem") may be read as a symbolic transition from the reality of fixed identity (with a name as an indicator of background and origin) to the space of shifting meanings and multiplied signifieds. The furthest Alex gets in asserting his identity is when he feebly protests being mistaken for Japanese. The "endlessly performative self" (Hall 1) is defined through the multiplicity of subject positions it adopts. As Alex comments about Adam:

> Handsome, bright, enlightened, thin—what happened to that fat weird freak Black Jew kid? Who lurched from one ill-fitting "identity" to another every summer; going through hippiedom, grunge, gangsta-lite, various *roots*isms (Ebonics, Repatriation, Rastafarianism), Anglo-philia, Americanization, afros, straightened, corn-rowed, shaved, baggy jeans, tight jeans, white girls, black girls, Jew girls, conservatism, Conservatism, socialism, anarchism, partying, drugging, hermiting, schizing, rehabbing—how did he get from there to *this*? (AM 129)

If *The Autograph Man* offers a vision of reality in which place is not a clear support of identity, it is not because of migration and displacement but because of a problematic sense of "the Real." The "philosophy" behind Smith's second novel seems less inspired by postcolonial critics and more by such theoreticians as Jean Baudrillard and Walter Benjamin.

Baudrillardian inspiration can be seen in Smith's subversive mapping of urban space. Although, as in *White Teeth*, the action is set in the northern part of London, it is no longer a unique, bustling, multicultural community, but standardized urban suburbia, deprived of its own identity: "This is not the Promised Land. This is an affordable, fifties built, central heating/locking as standard, schools included, commuter village on the northernmost tip of the city of London" (AM 8). The unattractive suburbia is sufficiently standardized to prevent any potential identification. The people of Mountjoy, we are told, "based their lives on the principle of compromise," "looking for a way out" (AM 8). Smith deliberately questions the identity of the place by emphasizing its mediocrity and lack of originality but also by avoiding detailed descriptions or using proper names. Instead of Leicester Square, we have "a popular square, framed on every side by giant cinemas" (AM 184). Rambling through the city, Alex goes "down a famous road to a monument, and then...up a forgotten lane...finding the next place I am meant to be" (AM 179–81). This denial of mapping leaves readers with a very schematic picture of the city, with bold outlines rather than details or landmarks. London is meant to stand for any metropolis, Mountjoy for all the suburbia of big cities, "sitting directly in the flight path of an international airport" and "promising that fantastic—perfectly fictional...—thirty-minute" journey to the center (AM 8). The indistinct, universal character of space is foregrounded by the parallels between London and New York. As soon as Alex finds himself in New York, he feels the familiarity of "the suburbs between an airport and a city" (AM 227). Roebling, where Kitty Alexander lives, like Mountjoy, is a space of "will-do"; it "has seen better days. It has also seen so-so days and worse days. Now it is settling for just 'days'" (AM 230). Calling England "a little country that seems a shrunken parody of [America]" (AM 104), Smith underscores structural reproducibility of urban relations and effaces the individual character of the cities.

But the (meta)fictional reconstruction of Baudrillard's conceptualizations is even more ostentatious. Smith undermines the sense of reality by presenting the city as fake, simulated space. "[T]he great suburb of Mountjoy," we find out, actually takes its name from the artificial mount. Its streets, sneers Rabbi Green, were made from scratch, indoors. The town's center point is the War Memorial—"a proud commemoration of Mountjoy's wartime sacrifices, although [as Smith ironizes] Mountjoy itself had not been built until 1952" (AM 67–68). The memorial serves as a theatrical stage where the three rabbis, like the chorus in Greek drama, preach the Word, about which they disagree substantially. Mountjoy is thus denied not only true identity but also history. The city no longer functions as a site of cultural memory; the past proves but a fake spectacle, representation deprived of a referent. The memory Smith's flâneur refers to is not of historical past, but of culture industry, the global language of the mass media. Social, cultural, and political practices become subsumed by media simulations, and the city turns into the matrix of postmodern mediaspace.

The simulated character of space becomes more apparent when the action moves to America. Featured in numerous films, ads, and documentaries, the space of New York seems "[f]amiliar, like from another life." "Everyone's been here before," says Alex (AM 226). In New York, reality and reproduction become indistinguishable. The urban reality shaped by the language of cinema, television, and advertising blurs the boundaries between fiction and reality, otherness and sameness, repetition and difference. The Technicolor city, as Alex calls it, compartmentalized in convenient chunks, is infinitely reproduced on the multitude of television channels: "Here goes the city. Here it goes. There it is. On television. In a magazine. Written on a towel. In a photograph that hangs above the bed in moody black and white, as you sit indoors in this Technicolor city. There it is again. On channel nine, on twenty three, briefly on seven, in cartoon form on fourteen and always on number one, which is the channel of the city" (AM 301).

Coming to New York, Alex takes a full blow of simulated space, of endless reproductions and simulated activities. In the hotel, he notes, a corporate virus has spread everywhere—from the odorless flowers, through the fake marble water feature, the repeating monogram pattern in the carpet, to the professional smile of the staff. As soon as he digs in his bag for the camera to capture the view from the window, he finds it replicated on the cover of the hotel magazine. In the Rothendale Hotel, where Autographicana is held, plastic palms and murals of tropical scenes reconstruct "the Miami Dream" in the center of New York. Simulated spaces project simulated existence. Alex observes how in a gym "people were busy going exactly nowhere, running at great speeds towards impassive glass" (AM 260).

The passage from the city of *White Teeth* to the city of *The Autograph Man* can be interpreted as the passage from Cosmopolis to what Iain Chamber calls "a cinematic city" (54). In the city of simulation, the differences between the real and the imaginary, true and false, the original and the copy, become effaced. What we experience and what we know from films, television, and commercials cannot be told apart. Distinguishing between what is real and what is imagined has become practically impossible. We are no longer involved in the mapping of urban space but in the refabrication of urban imaginary; we are, to borrow Soja's term, in the urban hyperreal with its "confusion and fusion of the realandimagined" (324).

The novel explores the existential consequences of the implosion of the boundary between mass consciousness and media phantasmagoria and the consequent obliteration of the social. Social life becomes part of the infinite process of reproduction. No phrase, gesture, or emotion is truly authentic. A smile is a "Panavision smile" (AM 186), a disturbed man is "a bad King Lear" (AM 118), having an opaque conversation is "like reaching the twenty-seventh minute of a French film, the point at which he usually began to have some hazy idea of what was going on" (AM 239). As Smith aptly comments: "It is impossible these days to follow a man or quit a job without an encyclopaedia of cinematic gestures crowding you out" (AM 268). The images, signs, and codes of film are the matrix of the characters' experience of reality. "Men, who don't want to go home, go to a bar. Alex knew this because he'd seen it in the films" (AM 375), ironizes Smith when her protagonist refuses to see Esther and face the consequences of his actions. Popular culture and film are not only the source of meaning but also a model which outer reality aspires to recreate: "He pressed his thumbnails into the soft of his palm, as she prattled on, shaping her body into a deliberate echo of the famous silhouette, the Marilyn hourglass. Back arched, abdomen retracted, turning out the lips like blushing petals, tilting the head low but looking to the ceiling— what an incredibly powerful gift! The ultimate in International Sexual Gestures: the metamorphosis from woman to vase" (AM 193).

Clichés from films, ads, and popular entertainment mediate the characters' thoughts, provide ready-made responses, evoke scripted stories with happy endings. Sentimental contexts pre-empt and mock words, gestures, and emotions. For the novel's protagonists, the experience of reality has been ousted and taken over by "illusion-promoting spectacles" (Benjamin, "Work" 226). As the faked world becomes the template for reality, simulation replaces the sense of "the Real." The characters become immersed in the hyperreal world of self-referential signs—whatever happens has already happened in cinema, every creation is a recreation, every phrase a quotation. In the world that Umberto Eco called the "already said" (530–31), camp recycling becomes the only possible means of communication.

Smith's diagnosis of the problematic sense of "the Real" in the contemporary, media society was indicted for remaining immersed in the reality it meant to expose.[3] Her use of clichés of popular culture and ostentatious literalization of the arguments of Situationists Baudrillard and Eco in the first part of the novel indeed seem to belong to the reality of endless reproductions. At first glance, the novel appears to join in uncritically in an ever-growing trend in postmodern literature, which, in Steven Connor's words,

> obediently falls into step with the motifs and preoccupations of institutionalised post-structuralist theory...resonating in sympathy with all its hermeneutic requirements...serv[ing] to concentrate radical or skeptical theory into an institutionally usable form, allowing the business of the literary academy—the interpretation of texts, the production and accreditation of readings and methodologies—to go on as usual. (133)

But the way theory and popular culture are used alongside each other may suggest a more ironic and self-conscious perspective.[4] In the climactic scene of book one, being also the most obvious metafictional intrusion into the narrative, the main character says: "Forgive the twin lies of entertainment and enlightenment" (AM 181), drawing attention to the commodification of writing and reading practices. If *The Autograph Man* conflates fictional equivalents of theoretical arguments with clichés of popular culture, it does so with a blessing of the academy. After all, Smith's instant canonization on the publication of *White Teeth* was an effect of the novel's clever mixing of high and low, the literary and the cultural, the popular and the theoretical.[5]

Smith's underlying critique of publishing and university industry, if such it is, is further foregrounded by the evocation of Walter Benjamin. Smith quotes Benjamin's definition of the aura from "The Work of Art in the Age of Mechanical Reproduction"—"the unique phenomenon of distance, however close an object may be" (AM 43)—and uses it to introduce the main themes of the text: the relationship between aura and authenticity, the impact of film on human perception of reality, and the negative influence of film industry.[6] The quotation from Benjamin is juxtaposed with that of Madonna, both figures introduced by a parallel phrase—"the popular singer Madonna Ciccone" and "the popular wise guy Walter Benjamin" (AM 43). Even if references to "The Work of Art" are addressed to more erudite readers, Benjamin's function in the novel is equivalent to that of Madonna. They bring together the novel's two main themes—Jewish mysticism and culture industry. As popular culture and Kabbalah normally do not belong to the same semiotic field, Benjamin and Madonna, in different ways, provide a convenient link, Madonna as an icon of the society of spectacle, propagating a pop version of Kabbalah, and Benjamin, as a German Jew, influenced by Scholem's version of Judaic mysticism, offering an important early insight into culture industry.

Contextualizing the aura in terms of the cult of celebrity, Smith takes on Benjamin's ambivalent attitude to culture industry. Benjamin, on the one hand, argues for the potential of photography to transform the nature of human perception, to change the way we experience reality. In a vocabulary that evokes the formalist concept of defamiliarization and Brechtian theory of theatre, he points to the film's ability to make us see what ordinarily is not detected. Such cinematic techniques as enlargement, close-up, and slow motion, he writes, "made analyzable things which had heretofore floated along unnoticed in the broad stream of perception" ("Work" 229). Yet, arguing for the film's potential for authenticity, Benjamin also acknowledges the artificiality of Hollywood spectacles: "In Western Europe the capitalistic exploitation of the film denies consideration to modern man's legitimate claim to being reproduced. Under these circumstances the film industry is trying hard to spur the interest of the masses through illusion-promoting spectacles and dubious speculations" ("Work" 226).

> The film responds to the shrivelling of the aura with an artificial build-up of the "personality" outside the studio. The cult of the movie star, fostered by the money of the film industry, preserves not the unique aura of the person but the "spell of the personality," the phony spell of a commodity. ("Work" 224)

Smith revisits and revises Benjamin's argument from the perspective of Baudrillard's "precession of simulacra" (166). Alex's fascination with older productions is based on the conviction that in early films actors "play themselves, they just play essences of themselves" (AM 136). But Smith takes a more ironic view and uses Book mottos to point out multilayered recodings of reality involved in filmmaking and acting: "You see, this is my life. It always will be. There's nothing else. Just us, and the cameras—and those wonderful people out there in the dark" (AM 223).

Although in Benjamin the aura is a very complex and elusive term, in "The Work of Art" it is associated with spatial distance.[7] An interesting reference can be found in *The Arcades Project*, where Benjamin clarifies the meaning of "the aura" by juxtaposing it with "trace": "The trace is appearance of a nearness, however far removed the thing that left it behind may be. The aura is appearance of a distance; however close the thing that calls it forth. In the trace, we gain possession of the thing; in the aura, it takes possession of us" (447). It is the obsessive/possessive aspect of the aura that Smith brings into focus and satirizes. Exploring the theme of authenticity through the motifs of autograph collecting and celebrity obsession, she gives Benjamin's concept an inordinately literal meaning—spatial distance becomes synonymous with physical unavailability. For Alex, Kitty is more desirable than his girlfriend Esther precisely because she is unattainable. When he meets another celebrity in person, he "feel[s] oddly offended that she made herself so accessible to him" (AM 300). It is only when celebrities are surrounded by bodyguards "the size of a water-buffalo and about fifteen people of the kind the magazines call 'handlers'" does Alex have a sense that "[t]he aura was being effectively handled" (AM 300).

In *The Autograph Man*, the air of unreality is not just a prerogative of celebrity but the essence of modern experience. Throughout the first part of the novel, Smith makes it clear that in contemporary media culture the concept of "the Real" cannot be safely used. The novel's main motif—autograph collecting—is a perfect illustration of how the notion of authenticity is both essential and impossible. Autograph collecting, as the main protagonist explains, is all about "what is real and what is forged"; like art and religion it is "[n]ot much, without your belief" (AM 59). Yet, an autograph is designed for reproducibility; it is also, inevitably, entangled in the whole series of faked representations—an autograph evokes not a real person but a film star, itself a conglomeration of the real and the faked, the actor and the character he/she portrays, the person and the image, the private persona and the celebrity.

The quest for "the Real," the true person behind Kitty Alexander's media image, is the theme of the second part of the novel. With a characteristically subversive take on one of the most familiar cultural *topoi*, Smith takes her Wandering Jew on a pilgrimage following the ten steps of the Zen path to self-realization—the ten bulls. Alex's experiences in the second part of the novel gradually take him beyond the comfort zone of "telematic hyper-space" (Chambers 54). Meeting Kitty, seeing the scars on Esther's body after the heart operation, witnessing Duchamp dying, and reliving the death of the father in preparation for the Kaddish become a way of making him see "the Real" beyond the spectacle, taking him out of the hyperreal space of films and film stars. His pilgrimage to New York leads through spaces of urban simulation (the plane, chain hotel, the auction room of Autographicana) to the suburban house of Kitty Alexander. Meeting the actress in person and bringing her to his flat in London become a very tangible way of transferring her from the distant auratic existence into the center of the everyday.

The scenes in Kitty's home are constructed on a complex dialectic of the real and the fictional. Alex comes to discover that his knowledge of cinematic conventions fails him. The script either does not fit—"All the opening lines he can think of call for a younger woman in the role" (AM 304)—or simply goes wrong. Before he has a chance to put into action a familiar script of a romantic breakfast in bed, "with a tray of fresh OJ and eggs-over-easy, and a flute glass with a single rose and the rest of the movie props" (AM 315), the object of his veneration quickly jumps out of bed and disappears in the kitchen. More important, however, Kitty refuses to be delegated into the realm of the fictional. Films and fame, she says, belong to the past; the reality of the present is that of the aging body and cancer. What is more, she remains sensitive to the perils involved in the implosion of the boundary between life and fiction:

> "We talk at breakfast, hmm?" she says as neutrally as she can, turning to find him kneeling by her side in an artificial panic, and with a cast to his face that she has played opposite, many times. "We sleep now. It's terribly late—too late to play a B-movie."
>
> She rolls away from him and grips the coverlet. Her fingers have gone cold. Even making those films, even as a know-nothing girl, she had slept badly on the suspicion of just how many of these people, these movie-goers, take a line, take a look, and use it on a loved one. (AM 310)

Although Kitty's transition from the auratic existence on the television screen onto the center of Alex's everyday is a turning point in his quest for reality, his relations with Esther remain just as crucial. While Kitty moves from one realm to the other, Alex's girlfriend consistently remains on the side of "the Real." Like Kitty, Esther refuses to become part of the mediascape: "Don't tell me you'd *never do anything to hurt me*. Please. Please try not to say anything you've heard on television" (AM 350), she urges Alex. Alex himself contrasts "real people (Esther, only her, always)" with "fantasy people (Kitty, Anita, Boot, porn girls, shop girls, girl girls)" (AM 161). As his friend Adam puts it, in contrast with other women, mere discourses in the palimpsest of endless substitution, Esther is "the thing itself":

> "But all these women," he said, cutting Alex off, "they're all the same woman, really. Don't you *see* that? Kitty, Boot, Anita—they just overlap each other. Think of an art restorer peeling the paint off a portrait to find other portraits underneath. You ruin a perfectly good painting out of some misplaced curiosity—the possibility of other portraits. It's a kind of endless substitution—and all because you don't know how to deal with things as they are...."

> "...And Esther—the first face? The last?"

> "Well, that's obvious mate," said Adam coldly. "She's the paint." (AM 177)

The quest for "the Real" and the impossibility of "the Real" is one of Smith's primary concerns in *The Autograph Man*. In the first part of the novel, the hyperreality of the everyday is the main source of comedy, harmonizing with Alex's binge moods. In book two, the tone gradually changes to become wryly ironic and occasionally rather sentimental. References to popular culture become drier and less entertaining. With the plot focusing on Alex's meeting with Kitty, his preparations for the Kaddish in memory of his father, Esther's heart operation and Duchamp's death, the second part of the novel offers a surprising accumulation of momentous events, of life-and-death situations. As the tone changes, there is a sense that behind the "illusion-promoting spectacles" Smith tries to uncover the sense of reality. The shift in tone and characterization in book two is accompanied by the change in the novel's construction.

The first part of *The Autograph Man* offers a whole array of metafictional elements: pictures, diagrams, elongated lists, boxed jokes, informational interpolations, and intertextual references to texts of both high and popular culture. Smith plays with the language, exposing the process of the novel's construction: "All of a sudden they run at each other once more and if you have a better phrase than *like thundering elephants* insert it here [    ]" (AM 38). Through a number of strategies, she lays bare the novel's condition of artifice, playing with fictional framing and the status of the author. The climax of book one is the scene in which Alex addresses the reader directly, rebelling against his fictional status:

> Please remember this.... Things cannot in reality fit together the way the evidence does when I write it down—please remember this, please. The lunch wasn't just so,

so tidy; I didn't walk down a street to divert you; the scenes didn't follow one to the other, flawless and meaningful—please remember this is my *life* [YOU ARE NOT WATCHING TV]. This is a description of a struggle. Judge it accordingly. (AM 181)

Alex's passionate address to the reader clearly is meant to be taken with a pinch of salt—after all, like most of his experiences in book one, it is an effect of binging. But it is also a herald of the more serious tone of book two and the criticism of culture industry.

In book one, each chapter is accompanied by headings, some of which relate to the theme and events of the chapter; others seem to suggest deeper and more abstract references and contexts. The titles of the chapters are taken from the names of ten Sefirots of the Kabbalistic Tree of Life, reproduced in the form of a diagram at the end of the novel. The diagram, entitled The Kabbalah of Alex Li Tandem, is contrasted with two other diagrams in the body of the text, one representing Alex's recreation of The Ten Sefirot of Elvis and one painted by Alex's friend Adam on the wall of his room (completed with photographs of nine celebrities). Yet, even though the reader is faced with three separate, complementary texts—the narrative, the titles of the chapters, and the Kabbalistic diagrams, the complex cross-referencing among the three textual elements does not seem to underlie the dialogic aspect of the text. Neither the chapter headings nor the diagrams enrich the interpretation of the main narrative. In fact, instead of foregrounding the conflict of interpretation, the three diagrams seem to erase it. For example, the differences between Alex's and Adam's interpretations of the Kabbalah, as dramatized in chapter four, are cancelled by the diagram in chapter six, when it turns out that the names of the celebrities appearing in their respective trees are exactly the same. Thus, rather than illustrating the characters' different interpretations of the sacred, the diagrams suppress their dialogue.

A similar strategy is apparent in Smith's play with the status of the author. At the beginning of the novel, Alex says: "He believed utterly that there are days in which it is revealed that someone has written a cruel story about you for their own entertainment. He believed, further, that on such days all you can do is follow, dumbly, with your knuckles grazing the ground" (AM 55). In book one, there are numerous hints pointing to a correlation between *The Autograph Man* and the book written by Alex, suggesting that he is both a character aware of his own fictionality and a writer constructing a version of reality. While Alex's book aims at dividing the whole world into two categories—things Jewish and things Goyish—Smith herself often describes people, objects, and aspects of reality as either Jewish or Goyish. Both in Alex's book and in the novel's prologue, sections are marked with the Tetragrammaton—God's four-letter name. "Occasionally, when the section [is] particularly contentious...its more potent Hebrew incarnation" (AM 89) is used.[8] But the parallel between *The Autograph Man* and Alex's book is not developed, and in the second part of the novel it disappears completely.

As the novel progresses, there is a strong sense of faked metafictionality—metafictional devices and strategies only purport to create a multitudinous space of discursivity, flaunting the dialogism of the text only to suppress it. Critics tend to follow in Frederic Jameson's footsteps and read *The Autograph Man* as a symptom of postmodern exhaustion, an instance of shallow mimicry, empty pastiche. But the changes introduced in the second part of the novel suggest that in *The Autograph Man* metafictionality itself is the target of parody. Smith openly mocks fictional framing and circular self-referentiality of novel-writing: "You should ask that the writer lady makes you this bloke in the book who organizes an auction and then buys his place in, er...wait—no, yeah, in a book as a character who organizes an auction and then buys his place in a book and asks..." (AM 114). In book two, Smith gradually withdraws from metafictional strategies, scrapping the chapter headings and references to the diagram. The painful literalness with which the pictures reflect the titles of the chapters plays with the arbitrariness of the relationship between the signifier and the signified. As her protagonists embark on the journey in search of "the Real," Smith resorts to a more traditional narrative.

The metafictional aspect of the novel is neither fully developed nor naturalised or recontextualized. If we agree with most critics that metafictional play in the first part of *The Autograph Man* is to be read as sign of exhaustion, book two might be interpreted as an attempt on the part of the author to redress it. One might argue that Smith shares Benjamin's belief in the redemptive quality of the Word and uses literary narrative to rescue her character from the blankness of self-referential discourse; that Benjamin's philosophy is employed to redeem Madonna's spectacle. In fact, in chapter six Benjamin is referred to in the context of the metaphysics of language. His photograph ("The wise guy Walter Benjamin in need of a comb, a better tailor, a way out of France") is put up on the wall of Adam's living room next to a "pin-board of notes and reminders, aphorisms ('All names and attributes are metaphoric with *us* but not with *Him*') and scraps of prayers" (AM 126) and, as we learned earlier, Twenty-two Foundation Letters, which in Kabbalistic doctrine of language are the divine substance of reality. For Benjamin, the belief in the sacred word and "language as an ultimate reality" ("On Language" 67) is the foundation of the idea of redemptive criticism. As Richard Wolin recapitulates:

> For the Kabbalists the texts which revealed the most immediate contact with the word of God were those of Scripture. In Benjamin's quasi-secularized reinterpretation of this doctrine, not scripture alone, but also *literary works of art*, are legitimate objects of the exegetical quest for the key to redemption. The preeminent status he accords literary works of art follows, above all, from their *linguistic* nature. (43)

Adam's beliefs resonate with those of Benjamin; his name evokes the time before the Fall, when the word turned into empty prattle (Benjamin, "On Language" 72). Yet, his teaching is lost on Alex; his words remain meaningless. The only thing Alex understands out of Adam's lengthy and elaborate parable on the truth hidden "under the garment" (AM 211) of sacred narratives is the word Torah. Consequently, his Kaddish in memory of the father balances between the lofty and the low, between the word and prattle, between entertainment and enlightenment.

The novel's epilogue shuns resolution; the fictional and metafictional quests for "the Real" end in a liminal zone. Alex's transformation is neither complete nor truly believable. At the end of the novel, he seems suspended between the real and the hyperreal in the same way that the text hovers between the slapstick and the sentimental. Returning from America, Alex comes to read space literally. He takes an overground train, because he "[c]ouldn't face the Underground, *being under ground*" (AM 372). Yet, despite his refusal to metaphorize reality, his destiny is to remain a character in a work of fiction, immersed forever in the reality of self-referential signs. By the same token, the text of the novel remains trapped in an endless reproduction of literary conventions. Discarding the postmodern play, Smith takes recourse in the hackneyed motifs of a dying friend and gravely ill lover.

The novel balances two contrasting impulses. Smith denounces the emptiness of the hyperreal but also gives readers a wink by remaining, like Alex, fully immersed in it; she writes an experimental novel that fits in with the contemporary theoretical fads but at the same time makes the best of a traditional story with a moral. The poetics of "either and" (Bernard 169) aims neither at resolution nor at antithesis. After all, in the hyperreal, parody is impossible. Cancelling out "the difference upon which the law is based," it leaves us with an "indefinite recurrence of simulation" (Baudrillard 178, 179).

## Notes

[1] Deborah Moggach, in *The Independent*, argues that in contrast to the characters in *White Teeth*, who are "rooted in a real world," the protagonists of *The Autograph Man* "exist in limbo and remain strangely unconvincing, hijacked by their own larky prose" (23). James Wood, likewise, considers the novel to be constructed around "an empty centre" (17). For a positive account of the novel, see, for example, Childs 201–16.

[2] Zadie Smith, *The Autograph Man*, p. 6. Hereafter referred to in the main text as AM.

[3] John Wood, for example, found it full of pop culture trivia and meaningless metafictional riffs.

[4] In an interview given at the Book Festival in Edinburgh, Smith spoke about her mixed feelings about academia and the university "theory machine": "I thought Cambridge was going to be about loving books and walking around in a floppy hat. But it was about hardcore French theory. It was scary for me. And it was very good and I'm glad and I don't resent it any more. But for a while I was really angry at what they did to my affection for fiction, and to my academic life. I became a real psycho, I think. And when I got to Harvard I felt like a lot of kids in my class were having a similar experience" ("Skindeep" 11).

[5] In a paper read at the 2005 Lancaster Conference ("The Twenty-First-Century Novel") entitled "Forgive the Twin Lies of Entertainment and Enlightenment: Conflation of Theory and Fiction in Zadie Smith's *The Autograph Man*," I discussed the strategies used by Smith to appeal to a variety of readers and fit in with contemporary academic fads and theoretical trends.

[6] There are also other allusions to Benjamin—to his writing on fetishism and art collecting, the idea of flâneur and the city as space of cultural memory. One might argue, as I do at the end of this essay, that Benjamin's philosophy of language and his idea of redemptive criticism are also relevant for the reading of the novel.

[7] On an insightful analysis of the changing definitions of the aura, see Rochlitz 149–66.

[8] The link is also suggested by the lack of distance between the narrator and the character, which some critics see as the novel's weakness. See, e.g., Wood.

## Works Cited

Baudrillard, Jean. "Simulacra and Simulations." *Selected Writings*. Edited by Mark Poster, 166–84. Cambridge, UK: Polity, 1988.

Benjamin, Walter. *The Arcades Project*. Translated by Howard Eiland and Kevin McLaughlin. Cambridge, MA: Belknap, 1999.

———. "On Language as Such and on the Language of Man." *Selected Writings*. Vol. 1, 62–74. Cambridge, MA: Belknap, 1996.

———. "The Work of Art in the Age of Mechanical Reproduction." In *Illuminations*, translated by Harry Zohn, 211–44. London: Fontana, 1973.

Bernard, Catherine. "The Cultural Agenda of Parody in Some Contemporary English Novels." *European Journal of English Studies* 3, no. 2 (1999): 167–89.

Chambers, Iain. *Border Dialogues. Journeys in Postmodernity*. London: Routledge, 1990.

Childs, Peter. *Contemporary Novelists. British Fiction Since 1970*. Houndsmills, UK: Palgrave Macmillan, 2005.

Connor, Steven. *Postmodernist Culture: An Introduction to Theories of the Contemporary*. Oxford: Blackwell, 1989.

Eco, Umberto. *The Name of the Rose*. San Diego, CA: Harcourt Brace, 1980.

Gilman, Sander L. "'We're Not Jews': Imagining Jewish History and Jewish Bodies in Contemporary Multicultural Literature." *Modern Judaism* 23, no. 2 (2003): 126–55.

Grosz, Elizabeth. "Judaism and Exile: The Ethics of Otherness." In *Space and Place: Theories of Identity and Location*, edited by Erica Carter, James Donald, and Judith Squires, 57–72. London: Lawrence & Wishart, 1993.

Hall, Stuart. "Introduction: Who Needs Identity?" In *Questions of Cultural Identity*, edited by Stuart Hall and Paul du Gay, 1–17. London: Sage, 1996.

Head, Dominic. "Zadie Smith's *White Teeth*: Multiculturalism for the Millennium." In *Contemporary British Literature*, edited by Richard Lane, et al., 106–19. Cambridge, UK: Polity, 2003.

Moggach, Deborah. "*The Autograph Man* by Zadie Smith." *The Independent*, September 21, 2002, 23.

Roberts, Julian. *Walter Benjamin*. London: Macmillan, 1982.

Rochlitz, Rainer. *The Disenchantment of Art: The Philosophy of Walter Benjamin*. Translated by Jane Marie Todd. New York: Guilford, 1996.

Smith, Zadie. *The Autograph Man*. London: Penguin, 2003.

———. "Skindeep. Interview with Craig McLean." *The List: Glasgow and Edinburgh Events Guide*, August 25–September 8, 2005, 10–11.

Soja, Edward W. *Postmetropolis: Critical Studies of Cities and Regions*. Malden, MA: Blackwell, 2001.

Weeks, Jeffrey. "The Value of Difference." In *Identity, Community, Culture, Difference*, edited by Jonathan Rutheford, 88–100. London: Lawrence & Wishart, 1990.

Wolin, Richard. *Walter Benjamin: An Aesthetic of Redemption*. New York: Columbia University Press, 1982.

Wood, James. "Fundamentally Goyish." *London Review of Books*, October 3, 2002, 17–18.

# CHAPTER IV
## "Only Connect":
## Intertextuality and Identity in Zadie Smith's *On Beauty*

*Maeve Tynan, Mary Immaculate College, University of Limerick, Ireland*

## Postcolonial Elements

Zadie Smith's writing concerns itself with themes such as ethnic (dis)orientation, identity politics, and the latter-day consequences of colonialism, thus firmly locating her within a postcolonial paradigm.[1] Dealing with the already diasporized identities of characters whose only known home is the metropolis, Smith's writing marks a point of departure from the traditional portrayal of an immigrant population that is seen as despondently stranded between two cultures. Though hybrid, her characters inhabit a comfortable zone of cultural self-fashioning. A comic novelist, her multicultural vision traverses the mores of ethnic and cultural existence in an upbeat celebration of fusion and hybridity. Her current novel, *On Beauty*, implements a popular postcolonial strategy of rewriting, taking E.M. Forster's *Howards End* as a point of departure. However, as this essay will argue, Smith's work veers from the typical path of adversarial "writing back," seeking instead the more diffident aim of establishing links. The now-infamous epigraph of Forster's novel that instructs the reader to "only connect..." would appear to be a *modus operandi* in a novel that blends literary texts, contending ideologies, and diverse races and ethnicities within its covers.

Though racially heterogeneous, the characters she creates are for the most part integrated into the metropolis, which provides a space on which to draft the blueprints for their various identities. In Smith's first novel *White Teeth*, for example, we find a cast of characters gathered together in the city of London as a consequence of imperialism, in a development that has come to be known as reverse colonization.[2] Hortense Bowden, an aggressive Jehovah's Witness impatiently awaiting the end of the world, is the product of a union between a West Indian mother and a British officer. Muslim waiter Samad Iqbal proudly (and repeatedly) traces a genealogy back to a rebellious ancestor in the Indian Mutiny of 1857. Characters like Samad cling to their national culture in an effort to maintain a coherent sense of self. If the first generation of immigrants holds on defiantly to the fading emblems of a cultural past in an effort to maintain a clear sense of identity, then its offspring

are more adventurous in their adaptations. Growing up in a multiethnic suburb, they confidently negotiate the various strands of cultural inheritance and
adolescent trauma.

*On Beauty* is also actively concerned with the process of navigating and
constructing identities from sources that are often regarded as incompatible
or contradictory. In Smith's novels identity is as much about forging links in
the present as it is about staking a claim on the past. Identity, in this light, is
a matter of identification with reference points in the outside world. Rejecting notions of stable, coherent claims of identity based on exclusion and difference, *On Beauty* highlights the idea that identity is as much a matter of
conscious positioning as of simply being. As Stuart Hall contends:
"Cultural identities are the points of identification, the unstable points of
identification or suture, which are made, within the discourses of history and
culture. Not an essence but a *positioning*" (Hall, Cultural Identity and Diaspora 53).

The fluid and malleable identities created by Smith are a little hard to
swallow for some. In a response to *White Teeth*, Ziad Haider Rahman, the
inspiration for one of the book's central Muslim characters, has urged Britain
to "abandon the dogma of multiculturalism" (quoted in Chittenden), which
ignores the ghettoization of the East End of London. The novel that made
"Britain feel good about its race relations" has been charged with "white-
washing the truth" (Chittenden). If Smith's cheerful multiculturalism opens
her writing to charges of playing to the masses, her explicit literariness leaves
her vulnerable to accusations of elitism.

In her latest novel, *On Beauty*, a contemporary re-working of E.M.
Forster's *Howards End*, Smith manages both to pander to her stated preoccupation with her literary predecessors and to explore several key concerns of
postcolonial literature. Like *Howards End*, *On Beauty* focuses on the pain and
joy inherent in human relationships and the role of art in a changing world.
Smith's stated relation to the source-text indicates the multifarious webs of
meaning and relations that pattern the plot, relationships, and identities of
characters from both. *Howards End* introduces the reader to two families, the
Schlegels and the Wilcoxes. Where the Schlegels are intellectual and idealistic, the Wilcoxes are materialistic and sensible. Their interrelations docu-
ment the clashing and commingling of their contrasting worldviews with
comedic and tragic results. Likewise, Smith's novel *On Beauty* turns on the
relationship between two equally ill-matched families, the Kippses and the

Belseys. Their respective patriarchs, Sir Monty Kipps and Howard Belsey, stand at ideological loggerheads. Monty is Trinidadian, right wing, anti-gay, anti-affirmative action, and strongly Christian. Howard, by contrast, is trenchantly liberal. His mixed-race family is an odd assortment of personalities, whose vaguely defined laissez-faire attitudes and beliefs—anti-state religion and anti-war—only highlight their difference from the more hard-line Kippses.

It is clear, then, that both novels are structured around a series of oppositions. Yet the movement of these novels is to consistently undermine these seeming contradictions, dwelling on their various points of intersection, rejecting the hollowness of a dualistic view of the universe, and embracing complexity and hybridity – connecting. Through a series of encounters, these discrete worlds internalized within the various family members collide and break through, altering subjectivities in the process.

## Rewriting: Intertextuality and the Ethics of Indebtedness

Rewriting is a common strategy employed by postcolonial narratives. The process involves entering into a dynamic critical dialogue with a source text, or *hypotext*,[3] in the creation of an entirely new narrative, or hypertext. The hypotext, or intertext,[4] serves as inspiration or a point of departure for the hypertext. For some writers the relationship between the two is openly adversarial, the hypertext functioning to resist or challenge representations within the hypotext that are deemed objectionable. Marilyn Butler's suggestion that many postcolonial academics are "provisionally willing enough to tolerate the canon, because they are so accomplished at turning it into cannon-fodder: apt material for a brutal, totalizing, highly political form of deconstruction" (Butler 11), highlights this confrontational element to treatments of the classics. Postcolonial hypertexts, therefore, challenge colonialist representations of colonized peoples and cultures in the same way that feminist hypertexts tend to dispute patriarchal systems and depictions. Many hypertexts have intersecting agendas. Jean Rhys's *Wide Sargasso Sea*, for instance, is a highly celebrated rewriting of Charlotte Brontë's novel *Jane Eyre* that simultaneously embodies a postcolonial *and* feminist counter-discourse. In the novel, Rhys resuscitates the figure of the Creole woman Bertha, "the mad woman in the attic," transporting this marginal character from the periphery to center stage, giving her a voice. Other well-known postcolonial hypertexts include J.M. Coetzee's *Foe*, a postcolonial re-working of Daniel

Defoe's *Robinson Crusoe,* and Peter Carey's appropriation of *Great Expectations* in his novel *Jack Maggs.* These texts activate the reader to call into question that which had previously been regarded as a given. Consequently, when Jean Rhys's novel provides an independent subjectivity for Antoinette "Bertha" Mason, we are forced to ask why the same character in Brontë's *Jane Eyre* was capable of only bestial shrieks and moans. This process points to a general mode operating within postcolonial rewritings—that of providing a voice for marginalized characters. To recast Spivak's expression, these narratives enable the subaltern to speak.[5] Postcolonial rewritings, therefore, tend to bestow agency. As Charles Pollard remarks:

> Even though these fictional and dramatic reconfigurations are varied in their subject matter, they are fairly standard in their strategy. The postcolonial novelist focuses on the oppressed character maligned in the canonical work—Caliban, Bertha, Friday, or Magwitch—and retells the story from, or at least with sympathy with, that character's perspective. (62)

Pointing to and elaborating on gaps and elisions in their narrative predecessors, these hypertexts place the source text under the microscope, inviting the reader to arbitrate. The method at work here is defamiliarization, a process which invites us as readers to review a canonical text from an alternative slant in order to reveal what is repressed or occluded in an original. The creation of the hypertext is cathartic for the hypotext, transforming it from a "readerly" text to a "writerly" text in Barthes's formulation. Barthes delineated the "readerly" text as engaging "a passive reader who tends to accept the text's meanings as predetermined and already made," whereas a "writerl'" text "constantly challenges the reader to rewrite and revise it, and, in this rewriting and revision, to make sense of it" (Scaggs 74). Thus the hypertext contains within itself the power to irreversibly transform our conception of the hypotext.

This brief sketch already highlights a significant difference with the reformulation embarked upon by Smith to those of Rhys, Coetzee, or Carey. *On Beauty* is not an attempt to interrogate *Howards End* for any perceived patriarchal or imperial investment. Though E.M. Forster has had his work examined in the light of colonialist representations on previous occasions,[6] Zadie Smith is not in the business of putting Forster on trial. Therefore, though we are informed that the Wilcoxes had the "colonial spirit, and were always making for some spot where the white man might carry his burden unobserved" (Forster 190), this fact is not central to Smith's project. Despite the rich ground for investigation provided by the Wilcoxes' activities in the Imperial and West African Rubber Company,[7] the relationship between the hypertext and hypotext is nonconfrontational. As Smith openly declares in her acknowledgments, *On Beauty* is an "homage" (1) to *Howards End*. The mode is not so much counter-discursive as dialogic. We are dealing with a peaceful negotiation of the source text rather than a hostile takeover. A pleasure principle is clearly in operation here, drawing attention to the play of similarity and difference, both the familiar and the new alerting the reader to additional levels of significance buried within the text. Forster fans will instantly be able to recognize key scene parallels between the two books, such as the concert scene, the shopping trip, the destruction of the "will," and so on. These scenes emerge intact though amended for a more contemporary audience: Leonard Bast's pilfered umbrella is substituted for Carl's Discman, Leonard the ill-fated London clerk is himself updated in the form of Carl, an African American rapper. Other allusions are more subtle: the briefly-referred-to New England Art Club, which the Schlegel ladies belong to in *Howards End*, could perhaps explain the choice of an art lecturer living *in* New England as protagonist. Clearly Smith does not feel the need to overly reconfigure or contradict the faint skeleton framework provided by the antecedent; rather she elaborates on and supplements it to suit her own purposes. Thus we see Forster's highly stratified Edwardian England relocated to an equally tiered East Coast American university. The fictional campus of Wellington provides an appropriate contemporary equivalent. The privileged, insulated world of the Wellington campus, congratulates itself on its liberal principles, whilst remaining largely removed form the actual social conditions outside its walls.

Forster and Smith both draw attention to the fact that the ideological battleground of their warring tribes still represents a privileged high ground of restricted access. In the same way that Leonard Bast can feel that "to trust people is a luxury in which only the wealthy can indulge" (Forster 35), Carl reaches a realization that "People like me are just toys to people like you.... I'm just some experiment for you to play with" (*On Beauty* 418). Likewise, the middle-class affluence of many of the African American characters rejects a simplistic black-white dualism that would seek to associate blackness with victimhood. The presence of the Haitian underclass, as cleaners in the university, as servants in the houses of the rich, as political malcontents in the Bus Stop bar, underscores the extent to which issues of class are decided by power as well as race relations. Supplementing Forster's analysis on class relations with an investigation of racial dynamics in contemporary society, Smith updates rather than challenges the concerns of the previous novel. Thus, while being a novel dealing with hallmark postcolonial concerns, and a rewriting of a canonical Western novel, Smith's *On Beauty* veers from the traditional format of a typical postcolonial rewriting.

While broadly applauded for their contribution to the literary canon, postcolonial rewritings also come in for a fair share of criticism. One charge laid against literature that openly wears its literariness is that it addresses an educated elite, an audience who must be familiar with the source text(s) in order to fully appreciate its significance. In postcolonial writings this relationship is potentially problematic, requiring a readership versed in the literary output of the colonizing culture, and denying the possibility of independent status for the newly created text. However, novelists such as Zadie Smith, who are frequently housed under the banner of black British writers, *are* British. The term "black Britain" is itself contested since although its existence was voiced as part of a vital attempt to make visible and install black peoples into the narrative of the British nationhood from which they had been expelled...the phrase always risked a potential contradiction between "Black" and "Britain," suggesting that black peoples were fated to exist in a semi-detached relationship with Britain, not fully within but not entirely beyond its imagined borders (McLeod 69). The term thus implies exclusion as well as inclusion. However, it is, I feel, conceptually worthwhile to the extent that the very Britishness it espouses underlines the entitlement of its writers to claim the culture of the colonizer as part of *their own* literary tradition. Though the terminology hints at discrepancy, or a somehow anomalous affiliation due to diverse traditions or ethnicities, it also highlights continuity and prerogative—the passing on of traditions.

*On Beauty* is a literary text abounding in references and allusions. The acknowledgments alone cite Simon Schama's *Rembrandt's Eyes*, Forster's *Howards End*, and Harvard professor Elaine Scarry's essay on aesthetics entitled "On Beauty and Being Just": "from which I borrowed a title, a chapter heading and a good deal of inspiration" (*On Beauty* 1). The mention of Scarry's essay on aesthetics is particularly apt as it concerns the generative, self-perpetuating nature of beauty and art. Scarry maintains:

> Beauty brings copies of itself into being. It makes us draw it, take photographs of it, or describe it to other people. Sometimes it gives rise to exact replication and other times to resemblances and still other times to things whose connection to the original site of inspiration is unrecognizable. (Scarry 3)

Thus Scarry's essay implicitly *authorizes* the act of reformulation with which *On Beauty* incorporates it and other sources within itself. Beauty inspires us to create and encourages reproduction. It may inspire a work of art or piece of music, or even the desire to procreate in an effort to bring duplicates into being. Beauty thus enacts a continuing cycle of replication and reformulation. Though Scarry's essay reiterates the natural tendency to reproduce, not all acts of appropriation are so kindly regarded within the novel. In an incident where Kiki mistakes Shakespeare for Sylvia Plath, she is informed: "It's Shakespeare," said Christian, wincing slightly. "*The Tempest. Nothing of him doth fade, But doth suffer a sea-change, Into something rich and strange.* Plath stripped it for parts" (*On Beauty* 102). This reference may be seen as a coy, self-deprecating gesture on behalf of the author regarding her own indebtedness, outlining her own method of replication. Modesty aside, Smith's own project clearly goes far beyond the realms of "stripping it [*Howards End*] for parts."

Literary allusions persist throughout Smith's novel. On occasion these references are clumsy or forced. Attributing her husband Nick Laird's already-published poetry to the character of flaky poetess Claire, is a decision that is questionable at best. Again, when we are told that Carol (a barely mentioned character who takes care of Howard's father Harry) is reading *A Room with a View*, the information feels unnecessary in the extreme. We feel here the heavy hand of authorial intrusion; Smith's predilection for scholarly reference taking precedence over believable representations of her characters. The move is an artificial insertion whose sole function is to introduce a note of dramatic irony: Howard, it seems, "Can't stand Forster" (*On Beauty* 298). Like Joyce's Bloom, who has no inkling of his Homeric embodiment, Howard is unwittingly attached to the author he professes to despise. Characters throughout the book are implicated in this compulsion of retelling the same old stories. So when Victoria jumps into Howard's lap, it is art as much as life that inspires her:

> She did it. She jumped off the bed and into his lap. His erection was blatant, but first she coolly drank the rest of his wine, pressing down on him as Lolita did on Humbert, as if he were just a chair she happened to sit on. No doubt she had read

*Lolita*. And then her arm went round the back of his neck and Lolita turned into a temptress (maybe she had learned from Mrs. Robinson too). (*On Beauty* 315)

Victoria, in her performative approach to sexuality, is interpellated by cultural ideologies present in books and films that instruct her in the art of seduction. *On Beauty* presents a world in which the characters, as well as their author, exist intertextually. To approach their significance is to plunge headfirst into a tangled web of textual relationships. Although this constant referencing to literary sources is to some extent justifiable within the academic diagesis created by Smith, the effect is often heavy handed. Unfortunately, in an otherwise engaging novel, the end result of this glib knowingness is some very sketchy writing. Though clearly the lapse of a mind perhaps a little too enamored with literature, Smith would do well to recall Helen Schlegel's appraisal of books, that they "mean us to use them for sign-posts, and are not to blame, if, in our weakness, we mistake the sign-posts for the destination" (Forster 114).

An allegation facing literary appropriations is that they serve to reinforce the canonical status of their literary progenitors. Existing in a constant state of referral, these works consistently perpetuate their literary progenitors. In fact, as the works we have so far considered would seem to suggest, canonicity is practically a prerequisite for appropriation. Chantal Zabus offers the opinion that certain "interpellative dream-texts" hail the would-be appropriator, inciting him/her to the act of appropriation:

Each century has its own interpellative dream-text: *The Tempest* for the seventeeth century; *Robinson Crusoe* for the eighteenth century; *Jane Eyre* for the nineteenth century; *Heart of Darkness* for the turn of the twentieth century. Such texts serve as pre-texts to others and underwrite them (quoted in Sanders 120).

Without the guaranteed reputation and knowledge of the source-text, the force of the pleasure principle at work in the recognition of references and allusions is greatly diminished. For this reason it is advisable, if not necessary, for appropriation to work within the parameters of an established canon. Accordingly to rewrite a text is also to confer canonicity on that text. The postcolonial rewrite therefore occupies an interstitial site, vacillating continuously between positions of subservience and resistance. Smith's choice of *Howards End* thus reflects the already-established canonicity of Forster's hypotext as well as perpetuating this status through reference and allusion. The relationship that links the two texts forms a bond that cannot be severed. Although arguably a novel that can exist in its own right, *On Beauty* will remain forever tethered to its literary precursor and will thus be read relationally to its antecedent. This eventuality is anticipated by Scarry, who writes:

> I began here with the way beautiful things have a forward momentum, the way they incite the desire to bring new things into the world: infants, epics, sonnets, drawings, dances, laws, philosophic dialogues, theological tracts. But we soon found ourselves turning backward, for the beautiful faces and songs that lift us forward onto new ground kept calling out to us as well, inciting us to rediscover and recover them in whatever new things get made. (Scarry 31)

The intertextual drive, therefore, is Janus-faced, incorporating a dual gaze into past and future. As a theoretical term intertextuality is highly useful in that it "foregrounds notions of relationality, interconnectedness and interdependence in modern cultural life" (Allen 5). In undermining the boundaries of the textual artifact, it offers a means for the book to escape from its cover, meaning moving between texts.

However, the connection between books also highlights the delicate question of literary debt. The "complex ethics of indebtedness" (Sanders 40) raises the contentious dilemma in ascertaining when does homage end and plagiarism begin? Julie Sanders[8] has examined the accusations thrown at Graham Swift's novel *Last Orders* that challenged the book's originality on the basis of prominent structural overlaps with William Faulkner's *As I Lay Dying*. The main thrust of these charges implied that "Swift had somehow been intellectually dishonest by reworking Faulkner's remarkable novel into a late twentieth-century and vernacular English idiom without paying due acknowledgement" (Sanders 35). While Smith avoids the charge of obfuscating her influences by making broad references to them in her acknowledgments and also in sly allusions throughout the book, the act of rewriting is itself enough to boil the blood of many critics. In a review for *The Sunday Times* dated September 4, 2005, Peter Kemp unleashed a merciless attack on Smith's novel. Commenting that her reworkings of *Howards End* are "all but daubed with highlighter pen," Kemp questioned Smith's classification of *On Beauty* as an "homage" (*On Beauty* 1) to Forster. Instead he charges her with "cannibalizing one of his novels, giving its components a gaudy respray and recycling them into what turns out to be a ramshackle vehicle for an ill-sorted heap of concerns" (Kemp).

Yet this tendency to construe the process of literary appropriation in solely negative terms raises some serious problems of its own. It fails to acknowledge the extent to which appropriation and cross-referencing have been central to literary productions throughout the ages. Many of the harshest critics of Shakespearean adaptations and appropriations, for example, fail to acknowledge the extent to which the bard himself was "an active adaptor and imitator, an appropriator of myth, fairy tale, and folklore, as well as the works of specific writers as varied as Ovid, Plutarch, and Holinshed" (Sanders 46).

Though rewriting is currently enjoying a self-conscious vogue in the wake of late-twentieth-century postmodernist and postcolonial cultural productions, it is important to remember that this process is far from new. Similarly, a focus on "debt" would prove problematic across the arts. Jazz music, for example, is based on the process of improvisation or "signifying": that is, taking well-known, recognizable riffs and altering or supplementing them to create new sounds. "Sampling" in modern rap and hip-hop denotes a process of incorporating fragments of other songs in a celebratory exploration of sound possibilities. Cover versions of songs underline the transformative aspect of performance and re-interpretation where the same piece of music can generate an entirely new effect. Distinct art forms revel in the process of referencing as well, marking a further blurring of boundaries across the arts. Books refer to works of art—for example, Tracey Chevalier's *Girl with a Pearl Earring* creates a history for the eponymously titled painting by Johannes Vermeer; and conversely works of art refer to books—for example John Everett Millais's painting of the drowned Ophelia.[9] Television programs such as *The Simpsons* are liberally endowed with popular cultural quotations from the stories and poems of Edgar Allan Poe to well-known musical hits.[10] Referencing across the arts allows Forster and Smith to confidently inform us that Helen Schlegel can hear goblins and elephants in Beethoven's *Fifth Symphony* and that Kiki Belsey is able to imagine apes and mermaids in Mozart's *Requiem*. In our contemporary cultural climate, audiences and readers exhibit a sophisticated appreciation of intertextual effects such as pastiche, parody, and mimicry. Rather then focusing on what is owned or owed, as our current age of copyright laws and property rights would seem to encourage, Sanders suggests: "We need to view literary adaptation and appropriation from this more positive vantage point, seeing it as creating new cultural and aesthetic possibilities that stand alongside the texts which inspired them, enriching rather than 'robbing' them" (Sanders 41).

## Constructing Identities

Central to most politically or ethically minded acts of appropriation is a process of retrieval. Gaps, silences, and omissions are sounded out, and priorities are weighted in toward the disadvantaged. A sketchily drawn figure from the margins is moved to centre stage. The previously maligned character is shown in a sympathetic light. Thus a typical rewriting of *Howards End* might be expected to focus on the novel's underdogs. A postcolonial rewriting of *Howards End* might be expected to focus on the impact of Paul Wilcox's work in Nigeria for the Imperial and West African Rubber Company, on the country or the local people, typically from the point of view of an indigenous protagonist. A feminist rewriting might involve a detailed examination of characters such as Jacky Bast, who falls foul to the patriarchal systems of Edwardian London.[11] For some critics these processes of recuperation tend to operate on overly simplistic lines. As Charles Pollard argues, prevailing realist expectations about characters in postcolonial narratives leads to a crisis of representation: "The novelist or dramatist rightly recuperates the oppressed character, but this recuperable character is expected to have a single, coherent identity" (Pollard 62).

Although this claim is itself questionable—Susan Barton, in Coetzee's *Foe*,[12] for example, providing a stark contrast—it highlights again a disparity between Smith's novel and other more politically inspired rewritings. Rather than trying to rescue an oppressed "Bertha" or "Friday" from an unsympathetic source text, Forster's characters inhabit Smith's more as echoes or types than fully imagined identities. They provide partial presences in otherwise unpopulated characters. Thus while Carlene Kipps might adequately provide us with a contemporary Ruth Wilcox, her husband Henry is not so easily assimilated. Aspects of Henry reside in both Howard Belsey *and* in Monty Kipps, who acts as a foil to Howard. In fact, the central appeal of Forster's writing for Smith would appear to be his characters' *lack* of a single, coherent identity. In an essay for *The Guardian* on November 1, 2003, Smith wrote of the appeal of Forster's "chaotic, irrational human beings" who 'wouldn't stand a chance against Austen's protagonists' (Smith, "Love, Actually"). Whereas Austen created characters who were "good readers" who could successfully "read situations, refine them, strip the irrelevant information" and use their sense to navigate the realms of pride and prejudice, "Forster wanted his people to be in a muddle: his was a study of the emotional, erratic and unreasonable in human life" (Smith, "Love, Actually"). Likewise, Smith's protagonists have a tendency not just toward error, but toward repeated error. The extent to which Howard Belsey is lacking in both sense and sensibility to those in the world around him underscores this observation. So while Meg can diagnose Henry's failures as his "inability to connect," Jerome identifies Howard's "*no* to the world" as a "denial of *joy*" (*On Beauty* 236).

Another reason that Smith does not feel the need to rehabilitate characters maligned by the metropolitan power is that her characters themselves belong to the metropolis. They can no more oppose an external colonial power than they can oppose that identity that resides within themselves. As previously mentioned, her characters are frequently racially mixed or culturally hybrid. Their bodies alone would contest the black-white dualism on which many debates regarding racial and ethnic relations are based. Much of the ongoing debate concerning the theme of identity in Smith's *On Beauty* can be read as a confrontation between different epistemologies that inform conflicting ways of understanding the self in relation to concepts such as "blackness." The fact that almost every character in the novel at one point questions what it means to be black emphasizes the confusion and contesting claims surrounding the term. For Michael Kipps "being black was not an identity but an accidental matter of pigment" (*On Beauty* 44), this view reducing the concept of blackness to a simple biological variant. In an argument with Zora, Carl shouts, "You people aren't even black no more...you don't live right" (*On Beauty* 418), making blackness a matter of behavior, a scale against which worth is measured.

The blackness of Kiki's body adds extra layers of meaning to a reading of identity as inscribed on the body. Kiki's enormous bosom acts as a signifier of broad discursive capabilities:

> The size was sexual and at the same time more than sexual: sex was only one small element of its symbolic range. If she were white, maybe it would refer only to sex, but she was not. And so her chest gave off a mass of signals beyond her direct control: sassy, sisterly, predatory, motherly, threatening, comforting—it was a mirror-world she had stepped into in her mid-forties, a strange fabulation of the person she believed she was. (*On Beauty* 47)

In a process of reverse interpellation, Kiki's chest always precedes her, as it were. It directs her personality, denying her the possibility of shyness or meekness. The competing ideologies it signifies, interpellates[13] those who encounter it, thus setting in motion a chain of discursive associations. Their response to her bosom's interpellative hail in turn hails Kiki, calling for her recognition of this new self, forged in the eyes of others. Responding to the hail, she finds she is transformed. This implicit association throughout the novel of Kiki with the body/nature in contrast to Howard's as mind/culture might seem a galling affiliation both to feminist and racial theorists. Yet it is an interesting observation on the manner in which the living body becomes a text that can be read and interpreted. Notable is the mode in which such readings intersect with gender and ethnicity relations. If Kiki were white, her large breasts would probably interpellate others toward a recognition of her as a female who is an object of desire. Her black skin, however, unleashes a chaotic realm of possibility beyond the merely sexual in the eyes that behold her.

Kiki's middle-class existence arouses feelings of guilt in her regarding her Haitian maid Monique. However, her middle-class status is also a source of pride and achievement for her. A series of photographs half way up the stairs provides a description of the Simmonds's maternal line:

> These are placed in triumphant, deliberate sequence: Kiki's great-great-grandmother, a house-slave; great-grandmother, a maid; and then her grandmother, a nurse. It was nurse Lily who inherited this whole house from a benevolent white doctor.... An inheritance on this scale changes everything for a poor black family in America: it makes them middle class. (On Beauty 17)

Kiki thus has no clear core or center from which to produce a single, fixed identity. She must negotiate a plurality of centers, weaving a self from intersecting discourses of race, gender, and class, among others. These conflicting identity determinants induce a heightened sense of awareness in her. For example, Kiki is highly conscious of the way in which her body is perceived: "I'm the Aunt Jemima on the cookie boxes of their childhood, the pair of thick ankles Tom and Jerry played around" (*On Beauty* 51). Her encounters with people are peppered with introspective musings as to the range of signals her body gives off, and of which she is unable to control: "Sometimes you get a flash of what you look like to other people. This one was unpleasant: a black woman in a headwrap, approaching with a bottle in one hand and a plate of food in the other, like a maid in an old movie" (*On Beauty* 98). Kiki, in turn, is interpellated by the reactions of others around her and constructs a personality out of their refracted expectations. In general this manifests itself as an exaggerated version of the self: "Her body had directed her to a new personality" (*On Beauty* 47).

For Levi, the youngest Belsey, being black is a matter of being "street." As Zora explains for her bemused father, "It's like, 'being street,' knowing the street—in Levi's sad little world if you're a Negro you have some kind of mysterious holy communion with sidewalks and corners" (*On Beauty* 63). Levi cannot reconcile his notion of "authentic" blackness with his family's comfortable middle-class existence. The existence of a white father who lectures at Wellington University is just another detail to be kept under wraps in his conversations with others. Throughout the novel Levi seeks ways to achieve authenticity by continuously re-inventing himself. This process includes adopting a *faux* Brooklyn accent, feigning residence in the poorer area of Roxbury, and taking up the cause of the Haitian underclass in Wellington. Levi fashions his "authentic" blackness by identifying with "blackness" as a concept and through fashioning representations of himself as a part of this concept. He thus occupies a contradictory position: while assuming "blackness" to be a fixed, stable category, his desire to *become* authentically black highlights a view of the concept as contingent and available through identity construction. Though this "desire to emerge as 'authentic' through mimicry" might be seen as "ironic" (Bhabha 88), the importance of the process of identification that it highlights should not be underestimated. Stuart Hall reminds us that "questions of identity are always questions about representation. They are always questions about the invention, not simply the discovery of tradition" (Hall, "Negotiating Caribbean Identities" 282).

Identity, then, is a matter of *positioning* as well as simply being. This understanding of identity as journey to be navigated rather than a destination is central not only to Smith's own writing but also to her appreciation of Forster's work. Existence is not the successful resolution of conflicting thoughts, histories, cultures, and ideologies; existence resides *in* the chaos of a constant becoming.

## Notes

[1] The term "postcolonial" literature is itself a much-disputed one, and the borders of its literatures are hotly contested. Within this essay I will be employing it "to cover all the culture af-

fected by the imperial process from the moment of colonization to the present day" (Ashcroft et al., 1989, 2), be it written in either center or periphery. For a broader view of the debates surrounding the postcolonial, see Ann McClintock, "The Angel of Progress: Pitfalls of the Term Post-Colonialism," in *Colonial Discourse and Post-Colonial Theory: A Reader*, ed. Patrick Williams and Laura Chrisman (Hemel Hampstead, UK: Harvester Wheatsheaf, 1993); and Bill Ashcroft, Gareth Griffiths, and Helen Tiffin, eds., *The Empire Writes Back: Theory and Practice in Post-Colonial Literatures* (London: Routledge, 1989).

[2] In a poem entitled "Colonization in Reverse," Louise Bennett humorously muses on the phenomenon by which Jamaicans undertook mass migration to Britain from the 1950s onward. See Louise Bennett, "Colonization in Reverse," in *An Anthology of African and Caribbean Writing in English*, ed. John J. Figueroa (London: Heinemann Educational Books, 1982).

[3] The term "hypertextuality" as employed by French theorist Gérard Gennette describes "any relationship uniting a text B (which I shall call the *hypertext*) to an earlier text A (I shall, of course, call it the *hypotext*), upon which it is grafted in a manner that is not that of commentary" (quoted in Allen 107–8).

[4] "What Gennette terms the *hypotext* is termed by most other critics the *inter-text*, that is a text which can be definitely located as a major source of signification for a text" (Allen 108).

[5] For further reading see Gayatri Chakravorty Spivak, "Can the Subaltern Speak," in *The Postcolonial Studies Reader*, ed. Bill Ashcroft, Gareth Griffiths, and Helen Tiffin, 24–28 (London: Routledge, 1995).

[6] Forster's study of latter-day colonial India in *A Passage to India* has been analyzed in terms of ambivalent colonialist representations. For further reading see Elleke Boehmer, *Colonial and Postcolonial Literature* (Oxford: Oxford University Press, 1995), and Abdul R. JanMohamed, "The Economy of Manichean Allegory," in *The Postcolonial Studies Reader*, ed. Bill Ashcroft, Gareth Griffiths, and Helen Tiffin (London: Routledge, 1995).

[7] For example, Edward Said's essay "Jane Austen and Empire," in *Literary Theory: An Anthology*, ed. Julie Rivkin and Michael Ryan (Oxford: Blackwell, 1998), centers around the Antiguan sugar plantation that is the source of wealth for the inhabitants of Mansfield Park.

[8] See Julie Sanders, "Sustained Appropriation: Homage or Plagiarism?," in *Adaptation and Appropriation*, 32–41 (London: Routledge, 2006).

[9] The examples provided have been taken from Julie Sanders, "Appropriating the Arts and Sciences," in *Adaptation and Appropriation*, 147–55 (London: Routledge, 2006).

[10] Popular episodes include a Halloween version of "The Raven" and a rewriting of the song "It Was a Very Good Year."

¹¹ Chantelle Williams does replace Jacky as the victim of patriarchal attitudes to the world. Similarly, Howard and Monty both provide negative exemplars of masculinity in a world of females "more sinned against than sinning," highlighting a feminist slant to Smith's writing.

¹² Susan Barton's very existence in the novel questions stereotypical representations of marginalised characters and revolts against notions of essentializing identities.

¹³ Louis Althusser uses the term "interpellation" to explain the way in which subjects are recruited into subject-positions through recognizing themselves.

## Works Cited

Allen, Graham. *Intertextuality*. London: Routledge, 2000.

Ashcroft, Bill, Griffiths, Gareth, and Tiffin, Helen, eds. *The Empire Writes Back: Theory and Practice in Post-Colonial Literatures*. London: Routledge, 1989.

Bennett, Louise. "Colonization in Reverse." In *An Anthology of African and Caribbean Writing in English*, edited by John J. Figueroa. London: Heinemann Educational Books, 1982.

Bhabha, Homi K. *The Location of Culture*. London: Routledge, 1994.

Castle, Gregory. *Postcolonial Discourses: An Anthology*. Oxford: Blackwell, 2001.

Butler, Marilyn. "Repossessing the Past: The Case for an Open Literary History." *Literature in the Modern World*, edited by Dennis Walder, 9-17. Oxford: Oxford University Press, 1990.

Castle, Gregory. *Postcolonial Discourses: An Anthology*. Oxford: Blackwell Publishers, 2001.

Chittenden, Maurice. "Zadie Didn't Tell the Real Race Story." *The Sunday Times*, February 19, 2006. http://www.timesonline.co.uk/article/0,,2087-2047388,00.html (accessed April 1, 2006).

Forster, E.M. *Howards End*. London: Edward Arnold, 1910.

Hall, Stuart. "Cultural Identity and Diaspora." In *Concepts of Identity and Difference*, edited by Kathryn Woodward, 51–59. London: Sage Publications, 1997.

———. "Negotiating Caribbean Identities." In *Postcolonial Discourses: An Anthology*, edited by Gregory Castle, 280–93. Oxford: Blackwell, 2001.

Kemp, Peter. "On Beauty by Zadie Smith." *The Sunday Times*, September 4, 2005. http://www.timesonline.co.uk/article/0,,2102-1758074,00.html (accessed April 1, 2006).

Loomba, Ania. *Colonialism/Postcolonialism*. London: Routledge, 1998.

McLeod, John. "Black Britain." In *A Historical Companion to Postcolonial Literatures in English*, edited by Prem Podder and David Johnson. Edinburgh: Edinburgh University Press, 2005.

Pollard, Charles W. *New World Modernisms: T.S. Eliot, Derek Walcott, and Kamau Brathwaite*. Charlottesville: University of Virginia Press, 2004.

Said, Edward. "Jane Austen and Empire." In *Literary Theory: An Anthology*, edited by Julie Rivkin and Michael Ryan. Oxford: Blackwell, 1998.

Sanders, Julie. *Adaptation and Appropriation*. London: Routledge, 2006.

Scaggs, John. *Crime Fiction*. London: Routledge, 2005.

Smith, Zadie. "Love, Actually." *The Guardian*, November 1, 2003. http://books.guardian.co.uk/review/story/0,12084,1074217,00.html (accessed April 1, 2006).

———. *On Beauty*. London: Hamish Hamilton, 2005.

———. *White Teeth*. London: Hamish Hamilton, 2002.

Scarry, Elaine. "On Beauty and Being Just." *The Tanner Lectures on Human Values*. New Haven, CT: Yale University, 1998. http://www.tannerlectures.utah.edu/lectures/scarry00.pdf (accessed April 1, 2006).

# CHAPTER V
## Colonization in Reverse:
### *White Teeth* as Caribbean Novel

Raphael Dalleo, Florida Atlantic University

Separating Caribbean literature from British literature has never been simple or straightforward.[1] From its nineteenth-century origins, Anglophone Caribbean literature has been deeply embedded in a British literary field, with the tradition's major practitioners frequently located in England both in terms of geography and sensibility.[2] The fields of Commonwealth and postcolonial studies emphasize the common British ancestry of a variety of world literatures, bringing writers like V.S. Naipaul, Sam Selvon, Derek Walcott, Beryl Gilroy, and Fred D'Aguiar to an international reading public. While this (post)colonization of Caribbean literature has continued to perpetuate the reading of the Caribbean as a broadly defined British space, recent British fiction—in particular, Zadie Smith's *White Teeth*—reverses this process, writing British literature—British in material, characters, and locale—with a distinctively Caribbean sensibility.

The dominant conversation surrounding *White Teeth* has positioned the novel as thoroughly, if not definitively, British. Jan Lowe describes *White Teeth* as "a deeply English novel" (167); Tracey Walters notes how "the literary establishment has elected to define *White Teeth* as British" (314); and Dominic Head argues that "*White Teeth...*is artfully constructed as the definitive representation of twentieth-century British multiculturalism" (106). These readings place *White Teeth* alongside writings by Salman Rushdie, Hanif Kureshi, Paul Gilroy, Stuart Hall, and other foundational black British texts to show how the novel engages with the same problematic of British multiculturalism and self-definition. In this essay, I would like to supplement this reading of *White Teeth* as exemplar of contemporary British literature to argue for the novel as *Caribbean*.[3] An examination of the "Caribbeanness" of the characters and setting, as well as the novel's concerns with syncretism and hybridity, demonstrate that *White Teeth* deploys tropes and participates in the debates characteristic of Caribbean literature, and is itself a Caribbean novel.

The Caribbean has long been considered a prime site to examine the process of cultural mixing. As site of "the first cycle of globalization" (*Global-*

*ization* 41) in the sixteenth and seventeenth centuries, the production of the Caribbean *through* contact has meant that whether under the name of transculturation (Fernando Ortiz), creolization (Kamau Brathwaite), relation (Edouard Glissant), or the cross-cultural imagination (Wilson Harris), a variety of thinkers have identified the Caribbean as a crucible within which a new conception of identity is being fashioned. *White Teeth* extends the borders of the Caribbean to include London, acknowledging the global Caribbean George Lamming identifies when he describes "London, Paris, New York Amsterdam" as "the Caribbean external frontiers" (vii). Smith shows how Caribbean people have moved into London and made it their own, and how Caribbean culture has become a central part of the culture of the city. Even more than that, the novel depicts London as a womb-space, a site of creolization, a far-flung island of Caribbeanness adrift in the sea of the English countryside. *White Teeth* shows how London has become a contact zone for cultures from around the world.

Mary Louise Pratt describes contact zones as "social spaces where disparate cultures meet, clash, and grapple with each other, often in highly asymmetrical relations of domination and subordination—like colonialism, slavery, or their aftermaths as they are lived out across the globe today" (4). The contact zones that Pratt examines are primarily non-European sites, particularly Africa, Latin America, and the Caribbean. *White Teeth* unearths the historical processes that have made London such a contact zone. In addition, the novel explores the nature of that contact. Contemporary cultural theorists attuned to Caribbean realities agree that cultural transformation takes place not only as acculturation; immigrants and "arrivants" do not simply take on the culture of the new country. Cuban anthropologist Fernando Ortiz offers transculturation as an alternative model: "the result of every union of cultures is similar to that of the reproductive process between individuals: the offspring always has something of both parents but is always different from each of them" (103). The cultural syncretism Ortíz describes in this passage goes by many names; Néstor García Canclini is one of many to suggest calling this hybridization: "Hybridization transcends the simple fusion of discrete social structures or practices that existed separately; by combining, they generate new structures and new practices" (43). *White Teeth* portrays the world created by this complex cultural interaction, at the same time interrogating the biological language (Ortiz's "offspring") used by so many commentators to describe cultural transformation.[4] The discourse of hybridity in particular, framed by García Canclini in terms of "biodiversity" (38) and cultural/genetic engineering, becomes the target of parody and critique throughout the second half of *White Teeth*.

The novel highlights how the contact that sets these processes in motion comes from the revenge of the empire: as acclaimed Jamaican poet Louise Bennett puts it, the rest of the world check title "colonizin Englan in reverse" (106). *White Teeth* traces the varied routes this contact creates: what happens when Caribbean people go to London; what happens when Caribbean culture goes to London; and what happens when London becomes, in one way or another, Caribbean. That London turns out to be Caribbean is typical of Smith's ironic sense of humor, but also of her more serious anti-essentialist agenda. The novel undermines bordered constructions of Englishness, but also of Caribbeanness. Caribbeanness is never an essence but rather a process, the borders of the archipelago infinitely fluid. At the same time, *White Teeth* is never a blind celebration of cultural syncretism, but rather a reminder of the roots of what too often becomes a dehistoricized hybridity discourse.[5] The novel explores the ramifications and outcomes of cultural mixing, aware of the dangers and possibilities of a globalized world in which purity is impossible. The future for London immigrant subcultures cannot be reduced to either assimilation or marginalization; instead, Smith shows us the emergence of something else entirely, a London that is British and Caribbean and South Asian and American all at the same time.

The novel moves throughout London at ground level, depicting a cityscape in the process of being Caribbeanized. Most obviously, the landscape of the metropolis has been literally darkened by successive waves of immigrants.

> The 52 bus goes two ways. From the Willesden kaleidoscope, one can catch it west like the children; through Kensal Rise, to Portobello, to Knightsbridge, and watch the many colours shade off into the bright white lights of town; or you can get it east, as Samad did; Willesden, Dollis Hill, Harlesden, and watch with dread (if you are fearful like Samad, if all you have learnt from the city is to cross the road at the sight of dark-skinned men) as white fades to yellow fades to brown, and then Harlesden clock comes into view, standing like Queen Victoria's statue in Kingston—a tall stone surrounded by black. (164)

This passage transports Harlesden Square to Jamaica, and Kingston to the heart of London. The narrator draws a direct equivalence between the darkening pigmentation of London's residents and the changing face of its cultural landscape. The Caribbeanization of the cityscape is not limited to its darkening, however. Its streets have become a cultural hodge-podge where one can buy mangos and coconuts from street vendors (166), where "you can get fourteen types of dal, but you can't get a bloody cigar in the Euston Street for love nor money" (67), where O'Connell's Pool House "is neither Irish nor a pool house" (183). What is so Caribbean about this London is not only the presence of Caribbean culture grafted onto its British host: it is the prominence of "complex linkages and mixed traditions" (35), which Wilson Harris and others consider constitutive of Caribbean, black Atlantic identity.

These mixed traditions are most readily apparent in the youth culture. Much of the energy of the novel comes from its focus on this youth culture, primarily through the eyes and mouths of Millat and Irie, in contrast with the more rigidly hermetic view of culture embodied by the older characters. As Jan Lowe realizes in her review of *White Teeth*, the novel's real cultural revolution occurs at the level of language, specifically the language spoken by the novel's younger generation.[6] The kids' speech jumps across registers and incorporates a variety of influences. Two passages in particular highlight this polyglot language. In the first case, as the kids head west on the bus to deliver God's' harvest on Harvest Day, Millat exclaims, "*Cha*, man! Believe, I don't *want* to tax dat crap," at which point the narrator describes Millat's speech as "the Jamaican accent that all kids, whatever their nationality, use to express scorn" (167). It is in this language that the novel makes one of its most explicit nods to London as Caribbean space; while Irie's language exhibits a recognizable Jamaican vocabulary and cadence, these ways of speaking have an influence that goes beyond ethnicity. Later, Millat shows off another level of his personal language spectrum. Arguing with a ticket-man in the underground, Millat calls upon his Jamaican once again, but also sprinkles his speech with words like "barii" (230), "somokami" (230), and "bidayo" (232). The narrator again enters to describe this speech as "a strange mix of Jamaican patois, Bengali, Gujarati, and English" (231). These observations serve to highlight the impurity of this language and its historical roots in empire.

Millat's language in this scene is only one way in which he and his friends mark off their cultural territory. Their gang, known by the neologistic moniker "the Raggastanis," becomes *White Teeth*'s epitome of the cultural mixing typical of postcolonial London. In addition to their polyglot language, the narrator describes "their ethos, their manifesto, if it could be called that" as "equally a hybrid thing" (232). This hybridity draws from a variety of sources:

> Allah *featured*, but more as a collective big brother than a supreme being, a hard-as-fuck *geezer* who would fight in their corner if necessary; Kung Fu and Bruce Lee were also central to the philosophy; added to this was a smattering of Black Power (as embodied by the album *Fear of a Black Planet*, Public Enemy).... Naturally, there was a uniform. They each dripped gold and wore bandanas, either wrapped around their foreheads or tied at the joint of an arm or leg. The trousers were enormous, swamping things, the left leg always inexplicably rolled up to the knee; the trainers were equally spectacular, with tongues so tall they obscured the entire ankle; baseball caps were compulsory, low slung and irremovable, and everything, everything, everything was *Nike*™; wherever the five of them went the impression they left behind was of one gigantic swoosh, one huge mark of corporate approval. (232)

This indiscriminate borrowing suggests the kinds of syncretic fusion seen in contact zones like the global Caribbean. One of the great ironies of this very ironic novel is that, on the one hand, Millat and his friends are poster children for corporate globalization, mimicking African American, Italian American, Latino, Afro-Caribbean, and Far Eastern cultures, all apparently via Hollywood; yet these boys wear their Hollywood uniforms while they fight the forces of secularization and Western imperialism, in the name of a traditional Islamic way of life.

In addition to the Caribbeanization of London space and culture, then, the novel also engages with the hybridity discourse that Shalini Puri identifies in *The Caribbean Postcolonial* as foundational to a Caribbean national imaginary.[7] In this way, *White Teeth* argues that contemporary London imagines itself not through the government-sanctioned management strategy of multiculturalism—despite Molly Thompson's reading of the novel as primarily invested in "problematizing the notion of 'multiculturalism'" (123)—but through the complex and self-conflicted lens of hybridity. Each time one of these scenes of the unrepentant cultural syncretism of youth culture appears in *White Teeth*, it occurs in contrast to the attitudes, liberal or conservative, of the older generation toward this impure youth culture. For example, Millat, Magid, and Irie's bus trip takes them to the door of Mr. J.P. Hamilton, a man "from a different class, a different era" (169) who immediately suspects them of coming to rob him, and then tells the children gruesome stories of wiping out "niggers" in the Congo during his days in the army in World War I (171). He betrays his attitude toward black Britain when Magid and Millat try to convince him that their father fought for the British in World War II: "I'm afraid you must be mistaken.... There were certainly no wogs as I remember—though you're probably not allowed to say that these days are you? But no...no Pakistanis...what would we have fed them.... The Pakistanis would have been in the Pakistani army" (172). In this short passage, Hamilton represents a generation even older than Archie's, who, though showing a vague awareness of political correctness, conveniently forgets (despite qualifying all of his observations with "as I remember") the presence of colonial subjects in British history. His memory produces a hermetic, albeit fictional, past world in which the English fought in the British army, and the Pakistanis in the Pakistani army, and never the twain did meet. One of the novel's purposes appears to be to combat this decontextualization with the historical realities of contact.

At the other end of the political spectrum is Poppy Burt-Jones. Unlike Mr. J.P. Hamilton, she acknowledges diversity, in fact celebrates it. Yet her ignorant celebration of difference leads to some of *White Teeth*'s most humorous scenes, such as her shocking discovery that Millat listens to Bruce Springstein and Michael Jackson. This moment illustrates the impossibility of identifying what in the culture is British and what is black British in a Caribbeanized cultural space. She regards music as a vehicle for teaching her students about other cultures, because "we can learn about each other through each other's culture, can't we?" (156). But her efforts are derailed by the fact that the other's culture turns out to have a great deal of overlap with her own. Asking Millat what music he listens to, she is appalled to hear that his favorite songs are "Born to Run" and "Thriller" (156), rather than some more "traditional" Bengali music. Even after this incident, though, Poppy cannot accept cultural mélange, still preferring to see everything through the lens of difference. Seeing Magid dressed in black and refusing to speak, she asks Samad, "I meant what *day* is it; I mean, for Muslims" (159), to which question Samad is forced to make up an outrageous story about the day of "closed-mouth worship of the Creator" (159). Like the waiters in the Indian restaurant who make up stories about the origin and history of the food (203), Samad realizes that the truth of the matter is not what Poppy wants to hear.

Again, what's the relevance? Joyce Chalfen shares the same worldview as Poppy. Her initial encounter with Millat shows her inability to cope with the reality of a no-longer-English London:

Joyce: "Where are you from, if you don't mind me asking?"

Millat: "Willesden."

Joyce: "Yes, yes, of course, but where *originally*."

Millat: "*Oh*, you are meaning where from am I *originally*."

Joyce: "Yes, *originally*."

Millat: "Whitechapel, via the Royal London Hospital and the 207 bus." (319)

These liberal Englishwomen want their *Others* othered. When confronted with the reality of the hybrid Millat, dark-skinned but born and raised in London (one of England's so-called "immigrants" who never really immigrated, who were born and raised in London and "whose furthest expedition East was the one they made daily, back home to Whitechapel, Smithfield's, the Isle of Dogs" [203]), neither is sure how to proceed. Despite all of Joyce's consultations with Millat's analyst, Marjorie, and her reading up on "brown strangers" (326), and finding out that "60 per cent of Asian men did *this*...and 90 per cent of Muslims felt *that*..." (375), she never gets close to understanding Millat's situation, which Millat realizes full well: "[T]he problem with Millat's subconscious (and he didn't need Marjorie to tell him this) was that it was basically split-level" (444). Looking at Millat as strange and foreign blinds Joyce to the fact that his psychological dislocation comes not only from his difference, but from the sameness of his hybrid doubleness that Frantz Fanon describes as "third person consciousness" (110).

Clara and Alsana occupy an in-between position, not of the same generation as the much older J.P. Hamilton, Archie, Samad, and Joyce, but not as young as their children. So while Alsana defends arranged marriages, she also enrages her husband's sense of tradition when he sees her in "running shoes and a sari" (198). At first glance, this outfit appears to be precisely the type of mixing we would expect of the immigrant: East and West, traditional and modern, homeland and present residence. But Alsana adds another touch: "It was one of Clara's African headscarves, a long, beautiful piece of orange Kenti cloth in which Alsana had taken to wrapping her substantial mane" (199). This eclectic syncretism, not reducible to a synthesis of ancestral and metropolitan culture, is typical of the Caribbeanized culture depicted in *White Teeth*: Alsana's ethnicity is part British, part South Asian, but—as this African headscarf borrowed from a West Indian neighbor indicates—always in contact with other immigrant cultures as well. She relishes attacking her husband's faith in the purity of tradition: it is she who, after being told by Samad that "You're a Bengali. Act like one" (236), consults the dictionary to find that "The vast majority of Bangladesh's inhabitants are Bengalis, who are largely descended from Indo-Aryans who began to migrate into the country from the west thousands of years ago" (236). Alsana triumphantly reads this as proof that there is no pure culture: to be Bengali is already to be mixed, to be "Indo-Aryan." The novel never explicitly identifies whether Alsana's and Clara's openness for accommodating different cultures is due to their age or gender. *White Teeth* only hints at the different attitudes of men and women when confronted with difference. In this light, Joyce and Poppy become examples of this openness gone too far, in which women without real contact with difference try to show themselves to be accommodating of it.

In the second half of the novel, as the story of FutureMouse© moves to center stage, hybridity and the presence of the Caribbean becomes much more ambivalently valued as its historical and biological roots come to the surface. The novel focuses on the colonial origins of migration and the ominous side of hybridity as social project, taking Irie and company back to the turn of the century to the great experiments of Sir Edmund Glenard and Captain Charlie Durham. The novel depicts British gentlemen cut from Victorian cloth; whether from an early form of liberal guilt, from economic, spiritual, or sexual self-interest, or from genuine goodwill (for as the narrator of *White Teeth* puts it, Captain Durham truly loved Ambrosia Bowden, "just as England loved India and Africa and Ireland; it is the love that is the problem, people treat their lovers badly" [361]), these men take it upon themselves to uplift less fortunate Jamaicans. Of course, their notions of uplift are at best misguided: Sir Edmund, for example, uproots hundreds of Jamaicans and sends them off to North London in the hopes that proximity with hardworking Brits will instill in the Jamaicans a good English work ethic, while the Jamaicans might teach Englishmen the proper way to worship and express their faith in the Lord. This grand experiment in cultural hybridity has the added pecuniary bonus that the Jamaicans will provide a cheap labor source for Glenard's cigarette-packaging factory, which the novel assures us is nothing more than a fortuitous side benefit. The experiment goes badly:

the immigrants do not take to England, the business goes under, and the whole affair ends with the Jamaicans hungry and unemployed.

This tale of the best-laid plans gone awry appears as a digression during the kids' meeting with their principal, in which he sends Irie and Millat to the Chalfens so that they might benefit from a more stable home environment: "And you know, the exciting thing is, this could be a kind of guinea-pig project for a whole range of programmes.... Bringing children of disadvantaged or minority backgrounds into contact with kids who might have something to offer them" (308). The narrative juxtaposes these moments to play up their historical irony; the multicultural present is both product and repetition of the nearly erased Caribbean-based past. The principal, inheritor of the legacy of Sir Edmund Glenard, after whom the school is named, is embarking on a social experiment no less radical than Glenard's, and no less fraught with the complications inherent in dealing with human beings, not guinea pigs.

This allusion to the similarities between the cultural and scientific experimentation in hybridity that have defined Caribbean history once again returns us to the discourse surrounding this mixing as target of Smith's critique. The academic version of hybridity discourse is particularly critical of the participation of biology in constructing intolerant versions of race and nation: García Canclini, one of the most prominent theoreticians on the subject, writes about the advantage of hybridity as a concept because of how it goes "beyond biologistic and essentialist discourses of identity authenticity and cultural purity" (43). Yet it takes little digging to uncover how García Canclini relies on the same biological language that he seeks to disrupt: he writes that "we know that examples of productive, enriching hybridizations exist in biology which generate expansion and diversification" (42). As *White Teeth* reminds us, just as hybridity discourse cannot escape its biological roots, in offering hybridization as social project it may be only another repetition in the Enlightenment history of social experiments.

In support of his celebration of hybridity, García Canclini uses the example that "the majority of corn developed commercially in the United States is the result of processes of hybridization undertaken by geneticists to improve its strength" (43). This slippage between the metaphor of cultural syncretism and the literal idea of genetic crossbreeding haunts Caribbean hybridity discourses from creolization to mestizaje. The uncomfortable residue that these concepts still contain, of biological racism's attention to bloodlines and genes, takes center stage during the second half of the novel through the Chalfen family and the FutureMouse© project. This shift in emphasis brings to the foreground *White Teeth*'s critique of hybridity discourse. The Chalfens are the perfect English family, despite or because of the fact that they are "after a fashion immigrants too (third generation, by way of Germany and Poland, née Chalfenovsky)" (328). Marcus and Joyce seem to be constantly striving both to secure their Englishness through emphasizing Irie and Millat's Otherness, and looking to inject new blood into the family to keep from "falling victim to Darwinism" (318). As much as Joyce wants to save Millat from himself and his family, Irie, Millat, and especially Magid become the Chalfens' saviors, just as "diversity" becomes that which can save Englishness from stagnation. Joyce's belief in "cross-pollination" expresses hybridity in positively scientific terms: "A species cloning such uniform offspring runs the risk of having its entire population wiped out by a single evolutionary event…the fact is, cross-pollination produces more varied offspring that are better able to cope with a changed environment" (308). If this language sounds vaguely like that of eugenics, the novel plays up the resemblance.

While Joyce uses García Canclini's language of genetics, pollination, and hybridity as vaguely metaphoric, Marcus, in discussing FutureMouse, speaks in nakedly biological terms. For example:

> But if you *re-engineer* the actual genome, so that *specific* cancers are expressed in *specific* tissues at *predetermined* times in the mouse's development, then you're no longer dealing with the *random*. You're eliminating the *random* actions of a mutagen. Now you're talking the *genetic program* of the mouse, a force activating oncogenes *within* cells…and its only with transgenic mice, by adding experimentally to the genome, that you can understand those kind of differences. (340)

Marcus's language echoes that of Joyce, and even that of Ortiz, Benítez-Rojo, and other theorists of hybridity. Admittedly, this discourse stands at a remove from eugenics: "Nowhere in the book did Marcus even touch upon human eugenics—it wasn't his field, and he had no particular interest in it" (419). Nonetheless, the underlying logic remains the same, whether of programming a mouse in order to remove the random chance of disease from its future, of cross-pollinating plants to create new and more resilient species, of taking the strengths from different cultural groups to form a stronger culture, or of "choosing who shall be born and who shall not—breeding persons as if they were so many chickens, destroying them if the specifications are not correct" (119).

*White Teeth* offers a position learned from the lived reality of Caribbean history: while cultural mixing is something unavoidable and potentially productive, it is painful, and attempts to prescribe, mandate, or control it often prove disastrous.

By pairing Marcus and Dr. Marc-Pierre Perret, the brilliant French scientist who worked loyally for the Nazis during World War II, *White Teeth* underlines all of these connections and resemblances. The future lies with the next generation, but it will not be genetically minded racial couplings that produce a mestizo super-race. The future is Irie's daughter, who at first appears to be such a hybrid offspring. The daughter will be born to a half-Jamaican, half-English mother; she will have an Anglicized Bengali father; and it seems entirely likely that she will be raised in England by an assimilated Jewish stepfather. Even this description disguises how her bloodlines can be both uncertain and definitely known: the genes she inherits may be either the "good" genes of Magid or the "bad" genes of Millat, but ironically, both turn out to have the same genes anyway. Once again, Joyce, with her proclamation that "it *is* the genes" (355), appears to be proven wrong. In the case of the twins, genes make no difference at all. Any laboratory-formulated social experiments that make blood and biology the determining factor are destined to go the way of FutureMouse, disappearing "through the hands of those who wished to pin it down" (542).

*White Teeth* contrasts the Chalfens' biological attitudes toward hybridity with a more Caribbean way of understanding diaspora, associated in the novel with the youth cultures of immigrant London. Despite their willingness to celebrate difference, the Chalfens have chosen to allow themselves to be incorporated by Englishness rather than continue to identify themselves as hyphenated and conflicted.[8] Most of the novel's older generation join the Chalfens in continuing to see identity as either-or, whether Samad, who clings to tradition as something pure on which he can build identity, or Poppy Burt-Jones, who thinks of herself as promoting respect for other cultures. And even those who pursue hybridity, like Joyce, rely on being able to distinguish between two unlike elements that can come together to create a new mixture. As in the Caribbean, where centuries of mixing have obliterated hope of finding any originary roots, in the world of *White Teeth*, the legislating or planning of hybridity is impossible, if only because there are not two different strands to cross-pollinate: the mixture to which hybridity discourse aspires has always already occurred. The appeal of *White Teeth* comes from this Caribbean-inflected approach to the cultures and subcultures of London. This cultural cauldron demonstrates that the confluence of cultures that the Caribbean has claimed as its unique contribution to the world is moving into metropoles, and turning them into Caribbean space.

## Notes

[1] Thanks to María Cristina Rodríguez and Loretta Collins for reading early versions of this essay.

[2] For two early and still-influential explorations of this phenomenon, see Kamau Brathwaite's "Sir Galahad and the Islands" and George Lamming's *The Pleasures of Exile*. In *Making Men*, Belinda Edmondson talks especially about the presence of this "British sensibility" in the writers of the 1950s and 1960s by identifying the "discourse of Victorian manhood" (19) deployed by V.S. Naipaul, Lamming, C.L.R. James, and Derek Walcott.

[3] This argument, for the Caribbeanness of *White Teeth*, can be seen to parallel Andrew Furman's claim of *The Autograph Man* as an "arguably Jewish text" (8).

[4] In an extreme example of such biological language, Antonio Benítez-Rojo describes Caribbean culture as "engendered by the copulation of Europe—that insatiable solar bull—with the Caribbean archipelago," continuing with the particularly graphic metaphor of "Europe conceiv[ing] the project of inseminating the Caribbean womb with the blood of Africa" (*Repeating Island* 5).

[5] For this reason I find Laura Moss's article on *White Teeth* especially suggestive. Moss initially argues for the novel as "a portrait of hybridity" and seems to suggest that Smith celebrates the "'normalisation' of hybridity in contemporary postcolonial communities" (12). Toward the end of the article, Moss modifies her position somewhat, noting that in addition to this celebration, "the mouse, however, seems to be a warning to a reading of the comfortable nature of the multiplicity. It is the result of a scientific experiment in creating a self-destructive hybridity" (15). While Moss essentially ends there, without drawing out what makes the mouse's hybridity so dangerous, I believe that her idea of a positive "everyday hybridity" and the mouse's "self-destructive hybridity" resonates with the distinctions that I am drawing here.

[6] Lowe's review starts by describing how "Zadie Smith's inventiveness with language pops open like a bottle of champagne and the fizz lasts to the end" (166) and ends by arguing that "the key to explaining the importance of the novel and why it has made such a huge impact in Britain is found in decoding its semiotics" (179).

[7] Puri begins her chapter titled "Theorizing Hybridity: Caribbean Nationalisms" with "a bold claim: the very vision of the Caribbean as a place of historical possibility turns on the question of hybridity" (43).

[8] This focus on the Chalfens as one iteration of Jewish diaspora is one of the many ways in which *White Teeth* evokes Paul Gilroy's *The Black Atlantic*. The last chapter of *The Black Atlantic* discusses links between the Jewish and African diasporas. Gilroy puts forward his relationary project in contrast to the narrative of an authentic African essence predating slavery and independent of the West, which he identifies as the equivalent of the most exclusionary, chauvinist forms of imagining Israel.

## Works Cited

Benítez-Rojo, Antonio. *The Repeating Island.* Translated by James Maraniss. Durham, NC: Duke University Press, 1996.

Bennett, Louise. *Selected Poems.* Kingston: Sangster's, 1982.

Brathwaite, Kamau. "Sir Galahad and the Islands." 1957. In *Roots*, 1–27. Ann Arbor: University of Michigan Press, 1993.

Coatsworth, John. "Globalization, Growth and Welfare in History." In *Globalization: Culture and Education in the New Millennium*, edited by Marcelo Suárez-Orozco and Desirée Baolian Qin-Hilliard, 38–55. Berkeley: University of California Press, 2004.

Edmondson, Belinda. *Making Men: Gender, Literary Authority, and Women's Writing in Caribbean Narrative.* Durham, NC: Duke University Press, 1999.

Fanon, Frantz. *Black Skin, White Masks.* Translated by Charles Lam Markmann. New York: Grove Press, 1967.

Furman, Andrew. "The Jewishness of the Contemporary Gentile Writer: Zadie Smith's *The Autograph Man.*" *MELUS* 30, no. 1 (Spring 2005): 3–18.

García Canclini, Néstor. "The State of War and the State of Hybridization." Translated by Kristin Pesola. In *Without Guarantees: In Honor of Stuart Hall*, edited by Paul Gilroy et al. London: Verso, 2000.

Gilroy, Paul. *The Black Atlantic: Modernity and Double Consciousness.* Cambridge, MA: Harvard University Press, 1993.

Harris, Wilson. "Creoleness: The Crossroads of a Civilization?" In *Caribbean Creolization: Reflections on the Cultural Dynamics of Language, Literature, and Identity*, edited by Kathleen Baluntansky and Marie-Agnès Sourieau, 23-35. Miami: University Press of Florida, 1998.

Head, Dominic. "Zadie Smith's *White Teeth*: Multiculturalism for the Millennium." In *Contemporary British Fiction*, edited by Richard Lane, Rod Mengham, and Philip Tew, 106–19. Malden, MA: Polity, 2003.

Lamming, George. *The Pleasures of Exile.* Ann Arbor: University of Michigan Press, 1960.

———, ed. *Enterprise of the Indies.* Port of Spain: Trinidad and Tobago Institute of the West Indies, 1999.

Lowe, Jan. "No More Lonely Londoners: Review of *White Teeth*, Zadie Smith." *Small Axe* 9
    (March 2001): 166–80.
Moss, Laura. "The Politics of Everyday Hybridity: Zadie Smith's *White Teeth*." *Wasafiri* 39
    (Summer 2003): 11–17.
Ortiz, Fernando. *Cuban Counterpoint: Tobacco and Sugar*. Translated by Harriet de Onís. Dur-
    ham, NC: Duke University Press, 1995.
Pratt, Mary Louise. *Imperial Eyes: Travel Writing and Transculturation*. London: Routledge,
    1992.
Smith, Zadie. *White Teeth*. London: Penguin Books, 2000.
Thompson, Molly. "'Happy Multicultural Land'? The Implications of an 'Excess of Belong-
    ing' in Zadie Smith's *White Teeth*." In *Write British, Write Black: From Post Colonial to
    Black British Literature*, edited by Kadija Sesay, 122–40. London: Hansib, 2005.
Walters, Tracey. "'We're All English Now Mate Like It or Lump It: The Black/Britishness of
    Zadie Smith's *White Teeth*." In *Write British, Write Black: From Post Colonial to Black Brit-
    ish Literature*, edited by Kadija Sesay, 314–21. London: Hansib, 2005.

# SECTION II.
## Race Mixing: Britishness, Blackness, and the Construction of Racial Identities

# CHAPTER VI
## "Gimme Shelter": Zadie Smith's *On Beauty*
### Susan Alice Fischer, Medgar Evers College (CUNY)

Zadie Smith's most recent novel, *On Beauty* (2005), updates E.M. Forster's
*Howards End* (1910), which famously exhorts: "only connect." Citing a line
by her husband, the poet Nick Laird, Smith rephrases this sentiment as
"there is such a shelter in each other" (93). While Smith's Belseys and Kippses—her stand-ins for Forster's Schlegels and Wilcoxes—appear to be at opposite ends of the ideological spectrum, their actions ultimately reveal them
to be much more alike than first supposed. The short-lived engagement between Jerome Belsey and Victoria Kipps at the beginning of Smith's novel
propels the two families into each other's orbit. As in Forster's original, it is
the women in the families—Kiki and Carlene—who develop a deep connection that breaks the "binary" paradigm of their husbands' ideological differences (175).[1] Yet Smith's allusions go well beyond *Howards End*. The most
obvious is Elaine Scarry's *On Beauty and Being Just*, which gives Smith her
title. Equally significant is Smith's debt to an author she claims as a favorite,
Zora Neale Hurston (see PBS interview). Indeed, for her vision in *On
Beauty*, Smith draws upon both Hurston's novel *Their Eyes Were Watching
God* and her study of voodoo in Haiti and Jamaica, *Tell My Horse*. From
these various starting points, Smith sets her characters upon the mined landscape of human relations, as she urges us to reject binary paradigms and to
connect across socially constructed differences so that we can see the full
beauty of humanity.

The main male character of *On Beauty*, Howard, is a middle-aged white
British professor of aesthetics who, despite his profession and his surname—
Belsey—refuses to *see beauty*. Married for thirty years to his African American wife, Kiki Simmonds, he is the father of three children, Jerome, Zora,
and Levi, whom he does not understand. As the novel opens, he is making
half-hearted amends to his wife for what he claims was an anonymous one-
night stand, though it was actually a long-standing affair with a colleague.
Howard's career is also in crisis. He is somehow still untenured after ten
years at Wellington College, and the pages of the book he has been writing
on—or against—Rembrandt lay scattered on the floor of his study, rather
than bound between covers (21). He has been humiliated by his academic

archrival, Sir Montague Kipps, who has not only had the effrontery to have
published a book of his own on Rembrandt—and a successful one to boot—
but to have gleefully and quite publicly exposed Howard's poorly aimed critique of Kipps's work.

As in Forster's original, a house stands at the center of Smith's novel.
The Belseys live in Wellington, Massachusetts, a mostly white, middle-class
college town, in a house which been passed down through Kiki's maternal
line. While "a little shabby," the house has a certain "grandeur" (17); the
house thus takes on larger proportions, symbolic of race relations in the
United States and emblematic of who "belongs." For instance, when the
younger son, Levi, approaches their house on the day of his parents' anniversary party, his sister Zora, who is also outside, yells sarcastically at a white
woman who is staring at her brother from the street: "Thank you! Yes, move
along now—he *lives* here—yes, that's right—no crime is taking place—thank
you for your interest!" (83). Howard, however, is reluctant see Levi's experience as a young black man in America. Despite being married to a black
woman for almost thirty years and having three children with her, Howard
"disliked and feared conversations with his children that concerned race"
(85). Smith's point seems to be that, although the United States, and the
West generally, is built on the legacy of slavery, many white people still fear
this conversation. Such avoidance is symbolically represented in the Belsey
house by the multicolored spot created by the skylight with its "harlequin
pane that casts a disc of varicoloured light upon different spots on the upper
landing as the sun passes over America" (16). Indeed, it is the "family super-
stition never to step through it" (16). Although the Belseys are a multiracial
family, the avoidance and discord in the house stops them from embracing
this reality.

The rest of the house seems oddly devoid of color, suggesting an inability
to see beyond the binary of black and white. As one descends the spiral stair-
case, one views black and white photographs of the children, followed by
"four generations of the Simmondses' maternal line" beginning with Kiki's
great-great-grandmother, a house slave (17), and culminating in the photograph of Kiki, with Howard's eerily "rogue white arm clinch[ing her] waist"
(18), in a synecdochic gesture of ownership. Hung high is "a charcoal portrait
of Howard's own father," described as looking upon his mixed-race descen-
dents in dismay (18). Pictures of Howard through the decades follow, ending
with a photograph of Howard and Kiki in Eatonville, Florida, in which Kiki

is "shielding her eyes from either Howard or the sun or the camera" (19). This suggests that, like Howard, Kiki has her own difficulties seeing the truth. Although Kiki's, the house feels much more like Howard's, thus bolstering its symbolic value. During her own anniversary party, Kiki gets "a flash of what [she] look[s] like to other people. This one was unpleasant: a black woman in a headwrap, approaching with a bottle in one hand and a plate of food in the other, like a maid in an old movie" (98). In a similar vein, Levi, the son most committed to connecting with his black identity, dwells in the basement.

The Belsey house was built in 1856, when the tension over slavery was at fever pitch. The Dred Scott case went to the United States Supreme Court in that year, when it was still an open case, with the possibility of a positive outcome. The devastating verdict came the following spring.[2] Whether Smith was thinking specifically of the events of 1856 or more generally of the ideological split in the country in the years leading up to the Civil War when she selected the year for the construction of the Belsey house remains open to question. Yet, she clearly selects the other dates that appear in her novel carefully: 1910, the year of the publication of *Howards End* (15), and September 11, obviously, though not explicitly, the date of Kiki and Howard's wedding anniversary and when their marriage collapses (68). The Belsey household is indeed a "house divided." In this way, Smith shows the divisions that do not allow the inhabitants of this "house"—whether the Belseys or wider society—to find "a shelter in each other." Moreover, by bracketing much of the novel between the historical events suggested by the year 1856 and September 11, Smith signals the dangers of binary and dehumanizing ideological divides.

As the novel moves out into the wider world of Wellington, both town and college, Howard Belsey and Monty Kipps represent the destructive divisions in the American academy and society. While the novel focuses on the mostly self-inflicted unraveling of Howard's personal and professional lives, the events are larger than Howard himself. Academic "culture wars" fuel the plot: the anti-affirmative action, old-school, pull-yourself-up-by-your-bootstraps, Trinidadian-turned-hyper-English Sir Montague Kipps versus the liberal, don't-believe-in-anything, beauty-is-just-antiquated-false-consciousness Howard (see Rich). Kipps expects people to will themselves into a better life and hence opposes affirmative action. Apparently more "liberal," Howard refuses to see the beauty in the art he studies and thus devitalizes the academy. As it turns out, they are both wrong and hypocritical; neither behaves in a just manner, their corruption culminating in exploitative affairs with their female students.

Smith draws upon Elaine Scarry's *On Beauty and Being Just* to set the ideological conflict between Howard Belsey and Monty Kipps in motion. Monty's conservative worldview is patently retrograde. In her send-up of the American academy, Smith presents Howard as ideologically opposed to the notion of the sublime in art. While at times affected to the point of tears by the music he hears, Howard tries to escape its beauty. Smith illustrates Scarry's assertions that the absence of beauty imperils the university: "To misstate, or even merely understate, the relations to beauty is one kind of error that can be made. A university is among the most precious things that can be destroyed" (Scarry 8). Instead, Scarry argues, beauty is "sacred," "unprecedented," and "life-saving" (23–24). Similarly, Scarry's definition of beauty's effect on the beholder and beauty's relation to justice provides an important theme for Smith's novel. Scarry postulates that the "presence of what is beautiful" invites "ethical fairness" (95) and thus "assists us in getting to justice" (94). The symmetry in the beautiful object enables the beholder to imagine the equality that leads to just actions (101). Therefore, "beauty is a call" (109).[3]

It is a call, however, that Howard fails to heed. In his personal life, he is blind to the beauty of his wife, Kiki, who now inhabits a much larger, middle-aged body. Instead, he is bowled over by Kipps's daughter, Victoria, who, though she knows that men see only "her face, her breasts, her hips" (390), rather than the full beauty of her being, apparently participates in her own objectification. It is one of the great ironies of the novel that Howard, an art historian and the only member of his family who is not myopic, is so incapable of seeing. Indeed, sight—and to a lesser extent hearing—are used symbolically throughout the novel, and Howard's blindness is a trait he has passed on to others in his family.

It is primarily the women in the novel who provide an alternate vision that moves beyond the ideological stalemate that the men present. Yet while Kiki generally *sees* much more clearly than her husband, she struggles to be seen. In the current state of her marriage, it is clear that Howard no longer sees her; he is surprised, for instance, when Victoria tells him that his wife is a beautiful "African queen" (313). Even so, one wonders how much of her he saw earlier in their relationship: when Howard had "thrown her over his shoulder like a light roll of carpet, to be laid down, and laid upon, in their first house for the first time" (14). Relegating her to the position of object—even chattel—rather than subject hints not only at the legacy of slavery in current interracial relations, but also his objectification of her as a woman. After all, people walk on carpets.

Thus freighted with an excess of symbolic value, at times Kiki reads like a stereotype (see Anjaria and Walters); at others she appears to see herself performing for the white inhabitants of Wellington. She muses about how young white boys see her: "I'm the Aunt Jemima on the cookie boxes of their childhoods, the pair of thick ankles Tom and Jerry played around. Of course they find me funny" (51).[4] When she meets a colleague of Howard's and her husband, she performs blackness: "'Honey,' said Kiki, moving her head from side to side *in a manner she understood white people enjoyed*, I done set already'" (52; emphasis added), referring to her interlocutor's insistence that she looks like a sunset because of all the colors she is wearing. Thus, in the context of Howard's world, and even their house, she has moments when she sees herself the way white America constructs blackness.

It is, perhaps, Smith's propensities for both literary allusion and for making her characters do double-duty as vehicles for the ideas in her books that make her characters read rather like stereotypes. While suggesting Kiki's need to be seen for who she is, Smith also loads her with so many allusions that her individuality is swamped. As James Lasdun points out, "Kiki Belsey...seems intended to embody a kind of feelingful alternative to Howard's hyper-intellectuality but never quite comes out from behind the enormous bosom with which her creator has a little too symbolically endowed her." This leaves the reader asking the same question that Kiki asks at the beginning of the novel, and Howard at the end: "What am I looking at, exactly?" (Lasdun 7, 434).

Yet with her insistent descriptions of Kiki, Smith is up to something more. In addition to the details cited above, Smith portrays Kiki as wearing her hair in "two thick ropes of plait that reached to her backside" under a "flame-coloured headwrap" (14)—a style that can, as Kiki notes in her double-consciousness, make her see herself as a maid in her own house. This description not only shows Kiki's awareness of how white America sees her, but also links her to other texts by African American women writers and, through these connections, allows Smith to undercut the stereotypes she sets up and to re-envision beauty—particularly that of black women.

In *The Bluest Eye*, Toni Morrison details the devastation caused by a standard of beauty that excludes blackness. While Pecola Breedlove is taught to see her dark skin as ugly and to revere white images of beauty—such as those she consumes by drinking milk with her Shirley Temple mug and by eating her Mary Jane candies—another young girl, Maureen Peal, is seen to be "beautiful" because she is lighter. That Maureen's two waist-length plaits are described as "lynch ropes" underlines how exalting this form of beauty destroys Pecola (Morrison 62).[5] In Smith's *On Beauty*, however, the darker Kiki wears her long hair in a similar style and is repeatedly described as beautiful, which allows Smith to reclaim beauty for all black women through allusion to Morrison's novel.

Yet Zora Neale Hurston's *Their Eyes Were Watching God* and *Tell My Horse*, her study on voodoo culture in Jamaica and Haiti, are even more significant texts for *On Beauty*. Smith drops several broad hints at Hurston's importance: Kiki is from Florida; the photo of Kiki and Howard was taken in Eatonville, Florida, Zora Neale Hurston's birthplace; and Kiki's daughter is named Zora. Like Kiki, Hurston's protagonist, Janie, wears her hair in a thick braid "swinging well below her waist." During her marriage to the oppressive and jealous Joe Starks—and Howard is also described as intensely jealous—Janie's hair is hidden under a headwrap. Upon his death, Janie uncovers her long plaited hair and destroys "every one of her head rags" (Hurston 137). Kiki's association with Hurston's Janie suggests something less simplistic than the "majestically overweight earth mother with a feminist's spine" that Frank Rich describes. Instead, she is a strong woman who will come to a more powerful sense of herself following disillusionment in her marriage. However, unlike Janie, whose transformation is enacted through her marriage to Teacake, Kiki's is sparked by her connection with another woman, Carlene Kipps.

As in Forster's *Howards End*, two women in *On Beauty* step across the boundaries established by family and societal biases and provide the greatest hope for human connection. When she moves from London to Wellington, Carlene Kipps spots Levi walking down the street and instantly sees his relation to Jerome, whom she has met in London. Recognition is an unusual experience for Levi; as a young black man, he is accustomed to being perceived only as a negative stereotype. Having met Kiki's sons, Carlene expresses an interest in Kiki, and when they meet, Kiki begins to apologize for the misunderstanding between their families. Carlene interjects, "whatever problems our husbands may have, it's no quarrel of ours" (91). It is during this first encounter that Carlene quotes the line from Nick Laird's poem, "There is such a shelter in each other" (93). Carlene's vision for human connection will flourish in their friendship and become part of Kiki's legacy.

At another meeting between the two women, Carlene clearly sees Kiki's beauty (172), and she shows her the painting of Maîtresse Erzulie, the Voodoo Goddess or Black Virgin. Rachel Stein defines voodoo as a

> syncretic religion, constantly evolving in response to changing cultural and social conditions. [It] encourages a view of human transformative possibilities, rather than of externally fixed, eternally static identities. Crucially, Voodoo spiritually contests the binaristic hierarchies within colonial structures that prove so damaging to black women. (Stein 469)

These "transformative possibilities" that go beyond "binaristic hierarchies" enable Smith—and Hurston before her—to use the figure of Erzulie and the ideas of voodoo to envisage a world where the beauty of human connection valued by Carlene and Kiki can displace the destructive "binary" paradigms that their husbands foment with their culture wars (Smith 175).

Carlene tells Kiki that Erzulie "represents love, Beauty, purity, the ideal female"—and that she "avenge[s] herself on men" (175). Like Kiki, the Erzulie in the painting wears a "red bandanna" (174). As the two women talk about love and life, Kiki mentions that she had once thought of living with women, rather than men (177). These details establish Kiki's identification with Erzulie: Erzulie, though heterosexual, is associated with lesbians, and her muted cry of "ke-ke-ke-ke-ke" suggests Kiki's name (see Voodoomama). As Joan Dayan states, "Erzulie vacillates between her attraction for the two sexes...and thus goes beyond false dichotomizing" (Dayan 6). This also explains Howard's frequent references to Kiki's lesbian friends at the end of the book. According to Rachel Stein, Zora Neale Hurston's study of voodoo, *Tell My Horse*, suggests that the syncretic voodoo religion counters

> the denigration of Caribbean black women, in particular by revising the terms of their negative Western association with nature. Voodoo undermines the ground of racist and sexist colonial hierarchies and provides black women a means of redefining themselves in positive and defiantly fluid terms. The revisionary potential of Voodoo spirituality becomes even clearer in Hurston's classic novel of a black woman's struggle for self-creation, *Their Eyes Were Watching God*. (Stein 474)

Thus, by extension, and through Smith's use of literary allusion, Kiki, who is associated with both Hurston's Janie and with the voodoo goddess Erzulie, can be read less as a stereotypical black earth mother, as white Wellington sees her, and more as a powerful woman who is defining her own reality away from the paradigms of racist and sexist America.[6]

That the loa Erzulie has varied and fluid manifestations allows her to be associated with another character in *On Beauty*, to redefine female sexuality and, like "Voodoo belief and ritual [to] subvert the Western belief that sexuality is merely animalistic and that black women's sexuality epitomizes bestial bodily desire" (Stein 472). As Joan Dayan writes, most ethnographers focus on only "three emanations [of Erzulie]—as Erzulie-Fréda, the lady of luxury and love; as Erzulie-Dantor, the black woman of passion...; as Erzulie-gé-rouge, the red-eyed militant of fury and vengeance—Erzulie bears witness to far more complicated lineage" (6). Hurston's description of Erzulie in *Tell My Horse* is of Erzulie Frieda, "said to be a beautiful young woman of lush appearance.... She is represented as having firm, full breasts and other perfect female attributes.... To men she is gorgeous, gracious and beneficent" (122). In the context of *On Beauty*, this description of Erzulie clearly summons up Victoria Kipps.

Indeed, Victoria—or Vee as she insists on being called—initially seems yet another iteration of the stereotype of the hyper-sexualized black woman. Yet Vee—for voodoo, perhaps—is an Erzulie spirit who embodies the possibility of transformation. In *Tell My Horse*, Hurston describes Erzulie Frieda as having followers who are either "reclamé," i.e., chosen by her, or who are "voluntary" (123). Victoria sets much of Smith's narrative in motion through her sexual encounters with her devotees Jerome, Howard, and, at the end of the novel, with Carl, the Spoken Word poet. Read within the context of Hurston's description of Erzulie Frieda, Victoria's sexuality is recuperated and redefined because of its transformational power.[7] As Stein argues, "Voodoo ceremonially worships black women's sexuality as the female aspect of the deity" (472).

Writing about the connection between Hurston's study of voodoo and *Their Eyes Were Watching God*, Rachel Stein reminds us that Hurston spoke of the "tree-shrine" at which "women had an opportunity for affirming their bodies" (471). Counter to prevailing Christian attitudes, women's sexuality and sexual pleasure are celebrated in Hurston's work on voodoo and in her fiction: "the ritual of the tree embraces female sexuality as a natural manifestation of spirit. [It is ] a central Voodoo symbol and often signifies the sexual and spiritual union of the primary male and female deities" (Stein 471–72). One need only recall Janie's sexual awakening "beneath the pear tree soaking in the alto chant of the visiting bees" to see how Hurston uses this symbol in *Their Eyes Were Watching God* (24). Similarly, at the beginning of *On Beauty*, the encounters between Jerome and Victoria take place "under the tree in the Kippses' back garden" (45). Like Janie, who sees her beloved Tea Cake as "a glance from God" (216), Jerome sees Victoria "as beautiful as the idea of God" (45). Victoria's transformative role in the novel recalls that of a transformative voodoo loa who presents an alternate vision. As in Hurston's work, "the tree vision affirms black women's erotic energy as [a] vital source of life" (Stein 476).

In *Tell My Horse*, Hurston states, "Voodoo is a religion of creation and life" (113). In response to ritual questions, the priestess, Hurston tells us, "replies by throwing back her veil and revealing her sexual organs. The ceremony means that this is the infinite, the ultimate truth. There is no mystery beyond the mysterious source of life" (113). This display of the vulva recalls Vee, who spreads her buttocks for Howard to view all at the beginning of their sexual encounter and who later in the novel sends him pictures of her orifices. Joan Dayan describes Erzulie as the "loa of 'love,' but she demands that we re-invent the word. As desire for what has been stunted by the minds of men, she forces us to enter a world where the word is undone, where certain tenets of affection or attachment undergo some strange, instructive metamorphoses" (10). After her first sexual encounter with Howard, Victoria meets him at a sleazy hotel where she is dressed up as a cheesy seductress. Realizing that he does not want her, Howard flees. One senses that her work with Howard is done.

Associating Victoria with Erzulie and with Hurston's use of the voodoo loa adds a much-needed dimension to understanding Victoria's sexuality and its transformative power in the novel. At the end, Howard belatedly recognizes "that he actually liked her. There was something courageous there, flinty and proud" (390). However, the problem remains that she can still be read—perhaps more easily—as exploited, confused, or indeed as the usual stereotype of aberrant black female sexuality. While Smith is known for requiring a lot of her reader—particularly in terms of intertextuality—her transformative vision might have been better served by rather broader hints.

Shortly after the friendship between Victoria's mother, Carlene, and Kiki begins, the ailing Carlene Kipps dies, leaving Kiki the painting of Erzulie. As this is not mentioned in the will, Kiki will only discover this legacy accidentally later in the novel. Even before, however, Kiki recognizes the significance of their friendship: Carlene has not only seen and befriended her, but offered her the central message of the novel, Smith's equivalent to Forster's "only connect": "there is such a shelter in each other," adding that "eyes and the heart are directly connected" (268). With these two thoughts, Carlene and Kiki step outside their husbands' limiting ideologies. They are able to see beauty and recognize the centrality of human relations. Implicitly, Scarry's ideas about the connection between beauty and justice are made through the women's connection and conversations. Kiki's ability to see the beauty in the painting of Erzulie endears her to Carlene and will ultimately enable her to use beauty, as represented by the painting, to act in a just manner.

The Belsey children also undergo varying degrees of transformation. Like their parents, the Belsey offspring search for meaning in different spheres of life: through religion, the academy, and politics. Jerome, the eldest, is a Christian and initially believes he has found the right direction when he stays with the Kipps family in London during an internship at the beginning of the novel. Attracted by the apparent cohesiveness of the family, as well as their belief in god and the divine beauty of great art, Jerome falls in love not only with their daughter, Victoria, but with the family itself. Howard is horrified by his son's attraction to religion as well as to the Kippses, while Kiki accuses Howard of being "terrified of anyone who believes anything" (393).

Of all Howard's children, Zora is most like her father. A sophomore at Wellington College, Zora throws herself into academic life. An academic in the making, she has her eye on the future and a lust for campus politics that surpasses her passion for interesting ideas. Like her father, she ignores the beauty that is before her and experiences it second-hand. Observing Zora listening to lecture-notes about Mozart's *Requiem*, instead of the music itself, Kiki recognizes that her daughter "lived through footnotes. It was the same in Paris: so intent was she upon reading the guide book to Sacré-Coeur that she walked directly into an altar, cutting her forehead open" (70). Even so, beauty does not seep into her brain. Placing theory between herself and art, she buys into Howard's sterile ideas. She is appalled, for instance, that her creative writing instructor, Claire, fails to discuss theorists such as Foucault.

Zora thus assumes Claire must be "barely intellectual. With her, it was always 'in Plato' or 'in Baudelaire' or 'in Rimbaud,' as if we all had time to sit around reading whatever we fancied" (219).

Significantly, we learn early that Zora is myopic. Her inability to see manifests itself most obviously in her interactions with Carl, the young, black Spoken Word poet from Roxbury—and Smith's version of Forster's Leonard Bast, the aspiring but financially constrained writer. Zora wavers between seeing his physical beauty and a stereotype of him leading her to worry that he may rob her. Several times she believes he has stolen from her: her CD player (when she actually took his), her goggles (he borrowed them, symbolically trying to see the world through her eyes), and her wallet (which remains safely tucked in the bottom of her bag). On the other hand, she believes she is championing his cause—to stay in the creative writing class as a member of the community, rather than as a matriculated student—but as one of Howard's colleagues will say of her, "She loves to make a fuss, but she is rarely very attached to the fuss she makes" (370). Like her father, she believes in nothing.

The child that seems farthest from Howard—and closest to Kiki—is their son Levi. Indeed, his connection to his mother is also evoked by his name: Zora Neale Hurston opens *Tell My Horse* by introducing "Brother Levi," who is one of the "two greatest leaders of the cult in Jamaica" (3). As we see later in the novel, Levi emerges as a leader as well. However, Howard frankly does not understand his son. When we first see Levi, Howard is "surprised by" him (21) and is trying to figure out what he is wearing. Distanced from his family by the location of his room in the basement and his after-school job in nearby Boston, Levi invents a black identity for himself by dissociating himself from white Wellington and his family through the "black Brooklyn" speech he has adopted and his dress. In this youthful exuberance, Levi identifies with the "street," which he romanticizes. As the novel progresses, he quits his job at the megastore and connects with a group of young black men from Haiti and other parts of the diaspora who sell goods on the street. From them he learns about the struggles of the Haitian people who populate the edges, yet gird the lifestyle, of white Wellington, working for poor pay by doing the more menial jobs in the town and in the homes, including the Belseys'. Indeed, Monique, their Haitian cleaner, makes Kiki "nervous of what this black woman thought of another black woman paying her to clean" (11).

Touched by the beauty of Haitian music, which expresses the pain of the people, Levi is moved to act in a way that will bring greater justice to the world. Upon hearing "the lovely sadness of that Haitian music...the plangent, irregular rhythm, like a human heartbeat, the way the many harmonized voices had sounded, to Levi, like a whole nation weeping in tune," Levi returns home red-eyed from crying and says the single word "Beautiful" to no one in particular (408). Yet, while his actions are well intentioned, they are not necessarily well judged. With a friend, he steals the painting of Erzulie that now hangs in Monty Kipps's office. Levi erroneously believes that Kipps stole the painting from Haiti and he wants the money it raises to be redistributed to the Haitian people. Ironically, it is through this "theft" that Kiki will learn of her legacy, which the Kippses have stolen from her. It is during the tussle over the painting that Kiki finds the note designating her as the owner of the painting: *"To Kiki—please enjoy this painting. It needs to be loved by someone like you. Your friend, Carlene."* Under that, the line of poetry appears once more: *"There is such a shelter in each other"* (430–31).

Just as Levi's intervention brings about Kiki's legacy, Zora uncovers her father's affair with Victoria when she finds Victoria and the equally beautiful Carl embracing: "He on top of she" (412). The encounter recalls the voodoo ceremony that Hurston describes in *Tell My Horse* in which "the mysterious source of life" is "the infinite, the ultimate truth" (113). Zora's eyes are indeed watching god in this hurricane, which clears the detritus from the eyes of the Belsey family. Victoria and Carl—whose name echoes Victoria's mother's, and whose "face was doing *silent voodoo* on [Zora], just as it seemed to work on everybody" (137; italics mine)—force Zora to "undergo some strange, instructive metamorphoses" (Dayan 10). Zora sees more clearly at the end of the novel: "She could not remember ever feeling as focused as she did this morning. The first day she wore glasses had been a little like this: lines sharper, colours clearer. The whole world like an old painting restored. Finally, she understood" (420). (Having achieved clarity of vision, Zora will also attempt to make amends to Carl, but he has vanished.)

These two events—Kiki's delayed legacy from Carlene, which strengthens her understanding of what a relationship should be, and Howard's exposure—make it clear that the Belsey family house fails to provide the "shelter in each other" they may have assumed. Early in the novel, Kiki recalls thinking "that if her family could only speak the truth, together they would emerge, weeping but clear-eyed, into the light" (60). By the end of the novel, her family has cried, though the clarity of vision still eludes them to some degree. Music has moved Howard to tears before, and he listens to the *Lacrimosa* in the last chapter (440). Jerome and Zora have cried over Victoria and Carl, and Levi has wept over the beauty of Haiti's music and the plight of its people. As the novel ends, the extent to which all this weeping has removed the distorting film from their eyes and allowed the Belseys to see truth and beauty remains an open question. The last chapter ends with Howard asking the same question that Kiki asked at the beginning: "What am I looking at exactly?" (434). What he is looking at is a letter separating his bank account from his wife's, but he still refuses to see the point. As Zora says: "You're separated…. That's the point," to which Howard replies, "Temporarily" (434). Howard is now alone in the house with his children where he is forced to recognize "the life cycles of his house" (435) and to "deal with this family" (436).

From Levi, we learn that with her legacy from Carlene, Kiki will demonstrate that beauty—and the ability to perceive it—leads to social justice, as Elaine Scarry claims. Significantly, Smith departs from Forster's original, in which the legacy one friend leaves the other is a house. The Belsey house, representing something larger than itself, has a legacy of its own with mismanaged relations that Howard is now left to sort out. Instead, Smith chooses a work of art—the sole purpose of which is to be beautiful—as Kiki's inheritance. Kiki will sell the portrait of Erzulie and give the proceeds to the Haitian Support Group (437). Here, Levi's and Kiki's recognition of both beauty and human connection leads quite literally to greater justice.

Kiki's departure from the family home reads like a goddess decamping, her work done. She reappears only at the very end of the novel during Howard's tenure lecture. In the audience, he sees Kiki, who wears "a scarlet ribbon threaded through her plait,…her shoulders…bare and gleaming" (442). Like Janie in Hurston's *Their Eyes Were Watching God*, Kiki's hair and her considerable attractions are no longer under wraps, and she emerges as a woman who has, like Janie, journeyed to herself. As she catches Howard's glance, smiles, and looks away, she is also reminiscent of Janie's mythical lover, Tea Cake, who, though gone, is yet with her at the end of the novel: "He could never be dead until she herself had finished feeling and thinking. The kiss of his memory made *pictures of love and light against the wall*…She called in her soul to come and *see*" (286; emphasis added). Howard also projects a picture of "love and light against the wall"—the slide of "Rembrandt's love, Hendrickje" (443). Incapable of finding the words he needs to deliver for his lecture, Howard sees "only Kiki" (443) and in the "intimation of what is to come," his own mortality—Howard's end. We are left to wonder whether he can at last see beauty and if his eyes are watching god.

This essay was reprinted with permission of the author who retains all copyright.

## Notes

[1] Many plot details of *On Beauty* draw directly from *Howards End*. For a discussion of some of the many similarities between the novels, see Susan Alice Fis[c]her, "The Shelter of Each Other," review of *On Beauty*, *The Women's Review of Books* 25, no. 2 (2006): 30–31. Some of the ideas first presented there are elaborated upon in this essay.

[2] If Zadie Smith had the Dred Scott case in mind, it is interesting that she chose the year the case went to the United States Supreme Court—when the possibility of a positive outcome existed—rather than the year of defeat. Dred Scott argued that, although a former slave, he was free because he resided in a free state; the United States Supreme Court did not agree (see Christyn Elley). In Smith's novel, Howard Belsey and Montague Kipps argue about the value of affirmative action in the current culture wars, which derive from a legacy of slavery. Smith seems to be leaving the verdict open for today's ideological conflicts.1856 was also the year that saw the tussle over Kansas entering the union as free or slave state. Senator Charles Sumner, an antislavery Republican from Massachusetts, denounced absent proslavery Senator Andrew Butler of South Carolina as having a "mistress...ugly to others...lovely to him...the harlot, Slavery" (U.S. Senate). Three days later, the Southern Senator's relative, Representative Preston Brooks, waylaid Sumner and beat him on the head with a metal-tipped cane. That each man was celebrated as a hero in his own part of the country shows the state of the country: "The nation, suffering from the breakdown of reasoned discourse that this event symbolizes, tumbled onward toward the catastrophe of civil war" (ibid.).

[3] I am grateful to Michael Manson for allowing me to read his unpublished paper entitled "'On Beauty and Being Wrong': Zadie Smith Meets Elaine Scarry," which goes into much greater detail about Scarry's work than I do here. Some of my points in this paragraph in relation to Scarry parallel his work.

[4] These two images seem to be the mirror images of the Shirley Temple cup and the Mary Jane candies that represent the sort of "beauty" that Pecola Breedlove wishes for herself in Toni Morrison's *The Bluest Eye*. The images in both Morrison and Smith underline how U.S. race relations have created a flawed notion of what constitutes beauty and humanity. In Zora Neale Hurston's *Their Eyes Were Watching God*, to which Smith also alludes, Janie's "Cauca-

sian characteristics" make her acceptable to Mrs. Turner, who has similarly internalized notions of beauty (216).

[5] I am grateful to Tracey L. Walters for reminding me of Maureen Peal's plaits.

[6] The problem remains, of course, that without access to these allusions, Kiki and Victoria can still both be read as stereotypes.

[7] Hurston describes Erzulie Frieda as "a mulatto," like her character Janie in *Their Eyes Were Watching God* (122). However, in the context of Smith's redefinition of beauty, Victoria, like Kiki, is darker.

### Works Cited

Dayan, Joan. "Erzulie: A Women's History of Haiti." *Research in African Literature* 25, no. 2 (Summer 1994): 1–31.

Elley, Christyn. "Missouri's Dred Scott Case, 1846–1857." *Missouri State Archives*, February 2002. http://www.sos.mo.gov/archives/resources/africanamerican/scott/scott.asp (accessed March 6, 2007).

Fischer, Susan Alice. "The Shelter of Each Other." Review of *On Beauty*, by Zadie Smith. *The Women's Review of Books* 25, no. 2 (2006): 30–31.

Forster, E.M. *Howards End*. London: Edward Arnold, 1910.

Hurston, Zora Neale. *Tell My Horse: Voodoo and Life in Haiti and Jamaica*. New York: Perennial Library. 1990.

———. *Their Eyes Were Watching God*. London: Virago Modern Classics, 1987.

Lasdun, James. "Howard's Folly." Review of *On Beauty*, by Zadie Smith. *The Guardian*, September 10, 2006. http://books.guardian.co.uk/review/story/0,,1565470,00.html (accessed December 21, 2006).

Morrison. Toni. *The Bluest Eye*. New York: Plume, 1994.

Rich, Frank. "Zadie Smith's Culture Warriors." Review of *On Beauty*, by Zadie Smith. *The New York Times*, September 18, 2005. http://www.nytimes.com/2005/09/18/books/review/18rich.html?ex=1284696000&en=36254da61bf8821c&ei=5088&partner=rssnyt&emc=rss (accessed December 21, 2006).

Scarry, Elaine. *On Beauty and Being Just*. Princeton, NJ: Princeton University Press, 1999.

Smith, Zadie. "An Interview with Zadie Smith." Public Broadcasting Service (PBS). N.d. http://www.pbs.org/wgbh/masterpiece/teeth/ei_smith_int.html (accessed March 11, 2007).

———. *On Beauty*. London and New York: Penguin, 2005.

Stein, Rachel. "Remembering the Sacred Tree: Black Women, Nature and Voodoo in Zora Neale Hurston's *Tell My Horse* and *Their Eyes Were Watching God*." *Women's Studies* 25, no. 5 (July 1996): 465–82.

Voodoomama. "Erzulie Dantor, Fierce Defender of Women." N.d. http://www.squidoo.com/erzuliedantor/, 2006 (accessed December 21, 2006).

# Chapter VII
## Still Mammies and Hos: Stereotypical Images of Black Women in Zadie Smith's Novels

*Tracey L. Walters, Stony Brook University*

Black women writers have been diligent in their attempt to combat three "controlling images" of black womanhood: the mammy, the jezebel, and the matriarch.[1] Countless novels, poems, and essays, Michelle Wallace's *Black Macho and the Myth of the Superwoman* or Maya Angelou's "Phenomenal Woman," for example, serve to debunk the unflattering characterization of black women: "Black women who understand the origin and purpose of the stereotype champion a massive revolutionary effort to redeem and reclaim slave women and their daughters from discursive dishonor. These writers invest their creative energy into (re)membering ancient, spoken texts and alternative mythologies where the African woman's presence is respected" (Tucker 163). While some black female writers are clear about their endeavor to alter false representations of black women, transforming them from stereotypes into positive images of black womanhood, writer Zadie Smith does not always leave readers with the sense that she wishes to move her black female characters beyond stereotypical archetypes. In all three of her novels, Smith features black female characters that exemplify the mammy, jezebel, and matriarch figures. Kiki Belsey of *On Beauty* is the consummate maternal mammy, Hortense Bowden of *White Teeth* is a ball-breaking matriarch, and Honey Brown of *The Autograph Man* serves as the sexually deviant jezebel. The question for consideration then, is what is Smith's motivation for presenting these kinds of black female characters? Does Smith intend to endorse the negative portrayal of black women or is there another agenda at play?

Before delving into an examination of Smith's novels it is first important to consider a major event that occurred in the Spring of 2007. On April 4, 2007, radio shock jock Don Imus referred to members of the Rutgers University basketball team as "nappy headed hos." Imus' referral to the black female players' hair as "nappy" (an offensive term used to describe the texture of black people's tightly coiled hair) and his use of the word "ho" (short for whore) sparked a national debate concerning the portrayal of black women in media. For the first time on a national scale the relevance of black women's race, gender, and beauty politics was pushed to the forefront of American public discourse. Imus' comment was met with outrage from members of the black community, women's groups, and other sympathizers who demanded an apology and called for Imus' termination from CBS radio. Following the incident Imus expressed his regret to members of the basketball team and others who were insulted by the comment. Interestingly though, in addition to apologizing, Imus defended his use of the term "nappy headed hos" arguing that he was appropriating the same vernacular employed by rap musicians and some members of the black community; and therefore felt justified in his use of the same terminology to refer to black women. In an instant, Imus' rebuttal shifted attention away from his own racist and sexist comments and redirected the focus toward the black community and its acceptance of the misogynist language and degrading portrayal of black women in black vernacular, rap songs, and rap videos. However bigoted Imus might have been, he had a strong point: derogatory language used to describe black women (and women in general) *is* pervasive in black music and culture. But it is also important to note that while the black community should indeed be held accountable for the manner in which black women are represented, mainstream America also plays a role in perpetuating false images of black women. In her short piece "Confessions of a Hip-Hop Critic" Dream Hampton underscores this point:

> Because I love rap music, its cadences, intonations, and mood swings, I've recognized and struggled to reconcile the genius and passion of my brothers—even when it meant betraying my most fundamental politics. I'm in the same position I imagine I would have assumed had my peers been eloquently sexist Ishmael Reed or genius/woman beater Miles Davis. Hip hop may be guilty of pimping and parading the worst of black America, but rap music cannot be made responsible for this government's institutional racism and sexism...". (107)

As with any sensational news item, within a few days interest in the Imus story waned and black women were no longer relevant. Imus' comment offended many, but his statement was significant because it forced mainstream America to engage in a discussion concerning the misrepresentation of black women both in rap music and the entertainment industry in general. Most rap and R & B songs that receive radio play depict black women as sex objects, willing participants in the sexual escapades of the male studs the musicians bring to life. In rap videos video vixens, as they are called, parade around scantily dressed, wildly gyrating their hips or standing in provocative poses alongside the male subject of the video. Mainstream media is also guilty of contributing to the denigration of black women. Although there have been more opportunities for black female actresses in television and film, black women are still largely invisible or are often reduced to the demeaning role of mammy, prostitute, or "sassy" black sapphire. These images of Black women's sexuality and dominance adds to their inability to be respected by black males and the society at large—thus reinforcing Imus' point: if others did not revere black women why should he? The debate concerning images of black women in music, radio, film, and television highlights the fact that despite all of their achievements (think Condeleeza Rice or Wangari Mathaii)[2] black women in the West continue to remain imprisoned by the three stereotypical images often portrayed in Smith's fiction.

In *Black Feminist Thought: Knowledge, Consciousness, and the Politics of Empowerment*, Patricia Hill Collins examines the development and impact of the mammy, jezebel, and matriarch stereotypes. Hill defines the mammy as "the faithful, obedient domestic servant. Created to justify the economic exploitation of house slaves and sustained to explain Black women's longstanding restriction to domestic service, the mammy image represents the normative yardstick used to evaluate all Black women's behavior" (72). The second stereotypical image of black womanhood, the matriarch, symbolizes the 'bad' Black mother" (Collins 75) an "overly aggressive, unfeminine" woman who "emasculated [her] lovers and husbands" (75). Finally, the jezebel "is constructed as a woman whose sexual appetites are at best inappropriate and, at worst, insatiable; it becomes a short step to imagining her as a "freak" (Collins 83). The mammy, matriarch, and jezebel images denigrate black women and maintain their marginalized position as *other* to white women. These controlling images continue to exist because they are perpetuated in our media, pop culture, and literature.

An examination of *White Teeth*, *The Autograph Man*, and *On Beauty* reveals that Zadie Smith has a problem with black women—that is, Smith has difficulty creating female characters (both black and white) that are more than one-dimensional character types. Smith's female characters lack development because they are overshadowed by white male protagonists. In *White Teeth*, for example, the experiences of the female characters (Clara Jones and Alsana Iqbal) are dependent upon the male characters (Archie Jones and Samad Iqbal) whose stories drive the narrative. In the short story "Martha,

Martha" Smith creates a black female protagonist, but this character is as flat as the female characters in her novels. In an interview with British *Vogue,* Smith reveals why women occupy a marginalized role in her writing. She admits, "Women are a very complex sex [to write about]. Men are much simpler" (356). If Smith is honest about her difficulty writing from the female perspective she helps explain why her black female characters often fail to move beyond their portrayed stereotypes. At times though, as is indicated with the character Kiki, Smith manages to create female characters that transcend their stereotypical image.

A stereotype, according to Craig McGarty, "is a set of associated beliefs. That is, the stereotype can be thought of as a relatively enduring system of interrelated concepts that inform perceptions of members of certain groups" (7). The problem with stereotypes, both negative and positive, is that they create preconceptions about groups of individuals that lead to generalizations and the failure to recognize individuality. One of the most damaging impacts of stereotypes is that they can be used to create a power dynamic that legitimizes racist and sexist beliefs. During slavery racist stereotypes about black people's inferiority gave whites license to enforce a system of racial hierarchy resulting in the creation of binaries centered upon intellectuality, civility, and morality. In an effort to remind themselves of their superiority whites dehumanized blacks and treated them like cattle. Racist language was used to classify the Africans they had captured and enslaved. Slaves were not men and women; rather, they were strong bucks or fertile fillies. Plantation owners also defined their slaves according to character types; older slave women were classified as mammies and mature slaves were referred to as "uncle." These character types were satirized in minstrel shows featuring whites in blackface portraying blacks as indolent, sexually deviant, childlike, and unintelligent.[3] While over time blacks were able to counter the aforementioned stereotypes, before long new stereotypes such as the welfare queen and the negligent Black father replaced the old images. In the infamous 1965 Moynihan report *The Negro Family: The Case for National Action,* Daniel Patrick Moynihan stereotyped black men as irresponsible absentee husbands and fathers who failed to provide for their families and support their women. Black women were stereotyped as dominant matriarchs who governed their households with a strict hand. The matriarch's independence supposedly emasculated black males, who either abandoned their women or refused to marry them (Collins 75). Many in the black community were angered by

Moynihan's generalizations about black men and women, especially his suggestion that the discord between black men and women accounted for the dysfunction of the black family and the "social problems in Black civil society" (Collins 75). Essentially, Moynihan's report contributed to the racist discourse involving black inferiority and immorality that was established during slavery.

In literature stereotypes are often used "not to reflect or represent a reality but to function as a disguise or mystification, of objective social relations" (Carby 22). In *White Teeth*, *The Autograph Man*, and *On Beauty* Smith shows how stereotypes in literature can also be used as a satirical device to expose racism, sexism, and other biases. It should be noted that black women are not the only figures stereotyped in Smith's writing. Smith has a fondness for writing satirical narratives featuring a full cast of stereotypical characters, oftentimes, as a reviewer for *The Economist* observes, "turn[ing] racial stereotypes on their head." (81). Smith's pervasive use of stereotypes has drawn criticism from literary critics who find her characters unrealistic. In her intensive study of *White Teeth*, Claire Squires observes that a number of critics have complained about the stereotypical portrayal of the main characters in the novel. "The Chalfen family were a particular source of contention, with several reviewers thinking them drawn too much for comic effect to have an existence beyond stereotype" (Squires 73). Similarly, Susan Horsburgh maintained that in *White Teeth* Smith "sketches characters that hover on the human edge of caricature." In *White Teeth* racial stereotypes appear in every section of the narrative. The novel features familiar contemporary British character types such as the South Asian anglophile who is more "English than the English" (Samad's son Magid), the racist white Briton who remains locked in the past and unaware of political correctness (Mr. J. P. Hamilton), and well-meaning white liberals who are infatuated with the exoticism of the oppressed groups for whom they rally to support (Poppy Burt-Jones and the Chalfens). At various points in the narrative these characters consciously and unconsciously betray their bigotry and prejudice. A humorous exchange between Marcus Chalfen and the Iqbal's lesbian niece and her partner serves as a prime example of the hidden prejudices and offensive views possessed by even the most liberal minded. When Marcus meets the Iqbal couple he treats the women like sexual objects and uses homophobic language to refer to their same sex relationship.

"You two are terrible temptations for a man."

"Are we[?]."

"Oh, dykes always are. And I'm sure [a] certain gentleman would have half a chance—though you'd probably take beauty over intellect, I suspect, so there go my chances." (289)

Following this statement Marcus offends the women again: "I can't help thinking," said Marcus, unheeding, "that a Chalfen man and an Iqbal woman would be a hell of a mix. Like Fred and Ginger. You'd give us sex and we'd give you sensibility or something. Hey? You'd keep a Chalfen on his toes— you're as fiery as an Iqbal. Indian passion" (290). In this instance Smith features Marcus as the stereotypical sexist male who is oblivious to the fact that his misogynist language is inappropriate and demeaning. Marcus' comments are also sexist and racist. Not only does he reduce the women to the status of sex slaves, but he suggests that as Indian women, full of what he calls "Indian passion," their contribution to an interracial relationship would rely upon their primal nature (sexual favors) while his own (white) contribution to the relationship would be intellectual. Ultimately, by underscoring the binaries of male/female, White/Indian, and primal/civilized, Marcus—whether consciously or unconsciously—reveals his feelings of racial and gender superiority. In addition to using stereotypes to reveal people's biases, on other occasions Smith's incorporation of stereotypes into her narratives allows for social commentary concerning the detrimental nature of stereotypes. In *On Beauty* Smith drives home the point that stereotypes can have a damaging impact upon the psyche of those who identify with the stereotypical image applied to them. In the narrative, Kiki Belsey, an overweight, black woman who feels intellectually and culturally alienated from her white friends and associates allows her insecurities to create an image of herself as the mammy.

During slavery the mammy was identified by her physical characteristics as well as by her industriousness. The mammy was a buxom, matronly black woman with ebony skin. She was usually dressed in a loose-fitting shift that did not flatter her figure, an apron, and in some cases a white necktie and a cotton headscarf. The mammy, or "black mammy" as she was sometimes called, was responsible for overseeing and executing domestic duties such as cooking and cleaning, and in some cases she also worked in the fields. In comparison to other slaves, the mammy earned the respect of her slaveholders, to the extent that she was viewed as an important member of the family. Mammy was a maternal figure for whites, often raising children who later became her master and mistress. She was also a confidant to the mistress and a surrogate mother to the master's children. The mammy was above all loyal and trustworthy.

Over time the mammy "became an imaginary figure created in the minds of those who never possessed a 'mammy'" (Parkhurst 351). And as Patricia Turner's study *Ceramic Uncles & Celluloid Mammies* reveals, "by the turn of the [nineteenth] century mammy images had secured a permanent place in American pop culture" (51). Turner explains that the mammy became an iconic figure whose image was captured on artifacts such as cookie jars, planters, and potholders: "When she entered the discourse of commerce, however, she became an indestructible American icon, as pervasive as she is perverse" (Tucker 161). Some southern whites were so enamored by the mammy that in the early twentieth century the Daughters of the Confederacy petitioned Congress to erect a statue to be displayed in the nation's capital. After slavery the mammy became a popular figure appearing in movies like *Gone with the Wind* and *Mammy*. Literary works have also depicted a longstanding legacy of mammy figures. Nineteenth-century works such as Joel Chandler Harris's *Tales of Uncle Remus*, William Faulkner's *The Sound and the Fury*, and Toni Morrison's *Bluest Eye* feature mammies (Tucker 15). Even today the mammy remains ingrained in our culture. In *Yearning*, feminist scholar bell hooks referred to talk-show host Oprah Winfrey as a "beloved black 'mammy' icon" (91). hooks suggests that Winfrey was a modern-day mammy who caters to the emotional needs of her mainly white female audience.

Kiki serves as *On Beauty's* mammy figure. Kiki is a middle-aged African American woman married to Howard Belsey, a self-absorbed white patriarch who fails to sustain his marriage and his academic career. For three quarters of the narrative Kiki plays the role of submissive, silenced wife. She allows Howard to impose his own views of art, politics, religion, and ethics upon both herself and the entire family. Almost immediately readers can recognize Kiki's mammy traits. When we are introduced to Kiki she is in the kitchen, one of the main areas of the house that the mammy occupied. Like the plantation mammy of old, Kiki has dark skin, a southern accent (though somewhat inauthentic), and a no-nonsense attitude. And although Smith's updated version of the mammy is bereft of her apron and white head scarf, in keeping with tradition Kiki wears shapeless dresses and wraps her hair in "flame-coloured headwraps." Kiki's overweight status also meets the requirements for the mammy figure. Weighing in at two hundred and fifty pounds Kiki literally rounds out another requirement for the black mammy. The narrator's description of Kiki's breasts is another confirmation of Kiki's mammy status:

> The size was sexual and at the same time more than sexual: sex was only one small element of its symbolic range. If she were white, maybe it would refer only to sex, but she was not. And so her chest gave off a mass of signals beyond her direct control: sassy, sisterly, predatory, motherly, threatening, comforting—it was a mirror world she had stepped into in her mid forties, a strange fabulation of the person she believed she was. (47)[4]

Smith's characterization of Kiki's mountainous breasts as "sisterly," "comforting," and "motherly" once again associate Kiki with the mammy. Kiki's "threatening" breasts serve as a reminder that "all the functions of the mammy are magnificently physical. They involve the body as sensuous, as funky, the part of woman that white southern America was profoundly afraid of" (Christian; quoted in Collins 73–74). The detailed description of Kiki's breasts raises questions about black female beauty and sexuality. Kiki's black and overweight body renders her invisible and undesirable. Like the mammy, she is an asexual being whose sexuality is overshadowed by her maternal characteristics. In "The Other Side of the Looking Glass: The Marginalization of Fatness and Blackness in the Construction of Gender Identity," Andrea Shaw suggests "the fat black female body" performs "triple duty as an inverse signifier, the fat black woman's body is triply removed from the West's conceptualization of normalcy is situated beyond the outskirts of normative boundaries, which makes its incorporation into the body politic an impossible undertaking" (9). In *On Beauty*, Kiki's black fat body stands at the margins of white America's standard of beauty. As the narrator states, if Kiki were white her breasts might intimate sexuality, but because she is black, her breasts symbolize something different: power and comfort. Kiki's asexuality is later confirmed in a passage describing her thoughts about being deemed sexually invisible: "When you are no longer in the sexual universe—when you are supposedly too old, or too big, or simply no longer thought of in that way—apparently a whole new range of male reactions to you come into play" (51). As the mammy Kiki is stripped of her sexuality.

According to the narrator Kiki comes from a long line of mammy figures: "Kiki's great-great-grandmother, [was] a house-slave; great-grandmother, a maid; and then her grandmother, a nurse" (17). Reaching back to slavery, Smith illumines that catering to the emotional and physical needs of whites is a role black women have always played. Others have also recognized Kiki's mammy image. Susan Fischer's article in this collection refers to Kiki as a mammy and a reviewer of *White Teeth* titles their piece, "Black, Fat, and Feisty." Typically, the mammy was so devoted to her master's family that her own family was often neglected. After spending the majority of her time in the big house away from the field slaves, the mammy often felt detached from other blacks in the slave community. Harris observes that the

> the true southern maid is the mammy whose ineffective compromise in the home of the white mistress causes her to identify completely with the status quo; she believes within her heart in the rightness of the established order of which she is part. She has lost her black cultural identity (*if* she ever had one) and all sense of spiritual identification with black people. (24)

Kiki is definitely disconnected from her cultural heritage. Living in Wellington, New England in an upscale white community she is surrounded by erudite intellectuals with whom she has nothing in common. During an argument with Howard she expresses her frustration with her alienation: "Everywhere we go, I'm alone in this...this *sea* of white. I barely *know* any black folk any more, Howie. My whole life is white. I don't see any black folk unless they be cleaning under my feet in the fucking café in your *fucking* college" (206). Thus Kiki recognizes that she is *in* but not *of* this Wellington community. Kiki is not only isolated in her environment, but she feels stifled by Howard's notions about art and politics. Howard's dominant views silence Kiki. Later, when Kiki does finally becomes empowered she confronts Howard's dictatorship, asserting, "everyone's scared to speak in case you think it's clichéd or dull—you're like the thought police" (393). Like the mammy, although Kiki runs the household or "big house" all the real decisions are dictated by Howard, the master of the home.

While the narrator provides readers with ample proof to align Kiki with the mammy, Kiki also confirms her mammy role. On more than one occasion Kiki says she believes whites see her as the mammy. For example, when reflecting on the fact that white men no longer see her as a sexual object she says, "I'm the Aunt Jemima on the cookie boxes of their childhoods, the pair of thick ankles Tom and Jerry played around" (51).[5] Further along in the narrative while playing hostess for her anniversary party she imagines that to her white guests she looks like a maid: "Sometimes you get a flash of what you look like to other people. This one was unpleasant: a black woman in a head wrap, approaching with a bottle in one hand and a plate of food in the other, like a maid in an old movie" (98). From these examples it is clear that Kiki is affected by the mammy stereotype. Kiki's insecurities about her overweight body (which make her other to white women) and her discomfort among her husband's intellectual colleagues leads her to believe that the whites she interacts with do not see her as an equal. Kiki's application of the mammy stereotype to define herself reinforces the danger of stereotypes. Although she is a successful upper-middle class educated woman she associates herself with an image that is demeaning. This mammy image impacts how Kiki views herself and how she believes others view her. Smith's reference to *Tom and Jerry* and black and white movies in relationship to the mammy should not be overlooked. In *The Autograph Man* Smith revisits the mammy figure, this time making the point that Hollywood is partially responsible for promoting the mammy image. In the *Autograph Man* Smith historicizes the celluloid mammy figure. During the narrative the protagonist Alex Li Tandem learns that the mammy was a creation of white America. Alex discovers that when African American actress Louise Beavers, who appeared in movies such as *Imitation of Life*, was first hired for her role she did not meet the fat, black, feisty traits required of the mammy. Before filming began she had to be transformed into the mammy: "she wasn't fat naturally, so she had to eat all the time, you know, to get fat? She wasn't Southern, either, so she had to fake a Southern accent, and when she played Aunt Delilah someone had to teach that poor bitch to make flapjacks" (203). Although this passage is humorous Smith highlights the reality of racism: in order to secure employment Louise Beavers had to conform to a stereotype that probably compromised her dignity.

At first it is hard to see Kiki beyond the mammy stereotype, but toward the end of the text Kiki's character evolves, and the traits that associate her with the stereotype are abandoned. As the narrative concludes, Kiki stops catering to Howard's needs, and her loyalty to her family is traded for her own self-empowerment—she abandons both Howard and her children and begins a new life. Finally Kiki removes herself from the white world that she found so stifling. At the end of the narrative it is clear that of all the characters, Kiki makes the most change. Ultimately, by saving herself from a life of invisibility Kiki becomes a heroic figure. Harris's examination of mammies in black literature demonstrates that black writers have often transformed mammy figures into militants who "manipulated popular stereotypes of maids to make certain points" (xiv). With Kiki, Smith joins the ranks of other black writers who reject the mammy stereotype and creates a complex black female character.

While Smith is able to remove Kiki from the stereotype, Hortense Bowden in *White Teeth* never transitions from her portrayal as a tongue-lashing matriarch. According to Tucker, after slavery the mammy evolved into the sapphire/black matriarch. Patricia Bell Scott explains that "the term 'Sapphire' is frequently used to describe an age-old image of Black women. The caricature of the dominating, emasculating Black woman is one which historically saturated both the popular and scholarly literature" (Bell Scott 85). The sapphire's "assertive demeanor identifies her with Mammy, but unlike Mammy, she is devoid of maternal compassion and understanding" (Gray-White; quoted in Tucker 162). Like the matriarch, Hortense is a strong, independent, domineering black woman who rules her husband and daughter with an iron hand. Hortense's independence is established by a passage that describes her decision to travel to England. The narrator recounts that after waiting in Jamaica for fourteen years for her husband Darcus to return for herself and their daughter, Hortense finally refuses to wait for Darcus any longer. Taking the initiative, she decides to "make the journey under her own steam. Steam was something she had in abundance" (26). Hortense "arrived on the doorstep with the sixteen-year-old Clara, broke down the door in a fury and—so the legend went back in St. Elizabeth—gave Darcus Bowden the tongue-lashing of his life. Some say this onslaught lasted four hours..." (26). Unlike Kiki, Hortense is far from passive or silent. Breaking down the door and verbally attacking Darcus reinforces Hortense's aggressiveness. In this same passage Hortense's emasculation of Darcus is also established. After her tongue-lashing, Darcus reportedly "slumped deeper into the recesses of his chair.... Then he said just one word: Hmph. Hmph was all Darcus said or ever was to say after" (26–27). In contrast to *On Beauty* where Kiki is silenced, here it is the male character who is reduced to a muted state. Darcus is an insignificant presence in the Bowden home. Hortense is the head of the household and like the mythical black superwoman she rears their daughter alone and takes on the role as breadwinner for the family. In addition to her domineering personality, similar to the matriarch, Hortense is neither affectionate nor nurturing. In response to her daughter's marriage to a white male she refuses to speak to her daughter again. This image of the overbearing matriarch who silences her husband is evident in a number of black novels. Paule Marshall's *Brown Girl Brownstones*, for example, also features an aggressive West Indian matriarchal figure that emasculates her husband and becomes estranged from her daughters. The main problem with Smith's characterization of Hortense is that she is a one-dimensional flat character. Hortense's relationship with Clara never changes and her interaction with Darcus remains antagonistic. In contrast to Kiki, Hortense's character never deviates from the stereotype and so it is difficult to remove her from the matriarchal image Smith conveys.

The final stereotype portrayed in Smith's novels is the jezebel. Where the mammy and matriarch are disassociated from their sexuality, the jezebel is defined by her hypersexuality. Wallace and other black feminist scholars have noted that during slavery white males created the sexually deviant image of the slave woman because they needed "to supply the labor force" (Wallace 138) and justify their own violation of black women's bodies.[6] Mythologies about black female sexuality set up binaries between black and white women, with white women being defined as moral and chaste and black women being characterized as immoral and promiscuous. During the nineteenth century African American writers like Harriet Jacobs and Pauline Hopkins used their literature to debunk the image of the hypersexual black woman. In *Incidents in the Life of a Slave Girl* and *Contending Forces,* Jacobs and Hopkins demonstrate that the white men who promulgated the sexual deviancy of black women were the very individuals responsible for sexually violating these women and forcing them to compromise their virtuousness. Similar to the mammy and matriarch figures, the jezebel is still a stereotype attributed to black women.

The jezebel character appears in *The Autograph Man* as well as in *On Beauty*. In *The Autograph Man* Smith's jezebel is loosely based on real-life, infamous prostitute Divine Brown.[7] In 1995 Brown became the subject of scandal and media frenzy when she was arrested for having oral sex in public with British actor Hugh Grant. The encounter gave Brown five minutes of fame until she disappeared into obscurity. Smith transforms Divine Brown into Honey Richardson, a former prostitute who decides to sell autographs instead of selling her body. Honey befriends fellow autograph trader Alex Li Tandem and helps him in his quest to locate his favorite movie icon, Kitty Alexander. Honey's jezebel image is established from the reader's initial introduction to the character. When Alex first sees Honey she's wearing glossy red lipstick and a red dress. Honey's name (reminiscent of a porn star) and the color and fit of her dress associate her with the jezebel. Although Honey trades in sexual favors for the buying and selling of autographs, she is never completely able to divorce herself from the prostitute image. She is described as "the most famous whore in the *world*" (210). Like the prostitute who is scorned by others, Honey is subject to disapproving looks and lewd sexual gestures from those who recognize her; and when Alex's friends learn of his association with Honey they immediately bring up rumors that Honey is still turning tricks. One of Howard's friends reports that a fellow trader claimed that after trading an autograph she "did him under the bloody table…" (210). In another passage the narrator conjures an image of Honey performing fellatio. While drinking from a wine bottle "Honey took her bottle and put it to her mouth in such a way that one couldn't help but have thoughts" (211). Honey welcomes the attention she receives from those who recognize her. She seems unconcerned with the public's perception of her—in fact she confides in Alex that not being recognized is disturbing: "the weird thing is if nobody looks, I notice" (218). Fortunately, Smith allows readers to see beyond Honey's sexualized image. Honey's relationship with Alex offers readers a different view of Honey. Readers learn that Honey has her own desires and is loyal, intelligent, and vulnerable. Incidentally, Smith seems to trade Honey's jezebel image with character traits reminiscent of the mammy. Like an impatient mammy figure, Honey fusses over Alex and takes care of his emotional needs. In one scene Smith actually describes Honey giving Alex a "maternal pinch to his cheek" (216). In another instance Honey spoon-feeds Alex, and when Alex fumbles with his coat, "Honey, bored by the performance, gripped him firmly by the toggles, zipped him to the neck and brought the huge bear hood…over his head" (216). Finally, when it is apparent that Alex lacks the courage to track down his childhood icon, Honey boosts his ego and behaves like the overprotective mammy who takes on the responsibility of safeguarding her white charge. Though Honey has both the jezebel and mammy traits, Smith makes the effort to show that Honey is not just another recognizable, predictable character type.

Where Honey Richardson fails to maintain the jezebel image, in *On Beauty* Victoria Kipps affirms the jezebel stereotype. Initially, Victoria Kipps is featured as an intelligent, conservative black woman. She is a devout Christian who promotes moral values such as respect, virtue, and honor.

Midway through the novel Victoria transforms from a conservative good girl to a sexual super freak that seduces Kiki's husband and engages in pornographic-like sexual encounters. Like the jezebel, she is the sexual deviant who unabashedly sleeps with other women's men and uses her powers of seduction to entice willing male partners. At her mother's funeral Victoria initiates a sexual tryst with Howard. She jumps on his lap and reenacts her version of a scene from Nabokov's *Lolita*, or, as the narrator says, "maybe she had learned from Mrs. Robinson too" (315).[8] She "flickers her tongue in the top of his mouth while keeping a zealous and an uncomfortable grip on his balls (315). This highly amusing scene displays Victoria's sexual immaturity, as clearly her notions about sex have been influenced by what she has read and seen on television. Howard is so desperate and pathetic that he goes along with the act. As the sex scene continues the language becomes even more erotic: "She had already turned on her stomach, her head pressed against the bed as if an invisible hand were restraining her with a plan to suffocation, her legs splayed, her shorts off, her hands either side of her buttocks pulling them apart" (316). This passage is problematic, not because of the graphic nature of the sex described, but because of the vulgarity of Victoria's actions. The spreading apart of her buttocks and her wild gyrations reinforce the image of the sexual freak. Pornographic images of black women have had a detrimental impact upon black women's sexuality. Collins explains that pornographic images of black women were established in the nineteenth century, when Saartjie Baartman (venus hottentot), an African woman, was exhibited to the public because her buttocks and genitals were considered abnormal, thereby establishing "notions of racial purity" (137). Collins also notes: "Black women's portrayal in pornographic movies and magazines also depicts black women displaying animal like savage behavior that is symbolic of an unbridled female sexuality" (Collins 139). Victoria's insatiable sexual appetite is featured again when she invites Howard to engage in another sexual affair. Before the encounter Victoria sends Howard sexually explicit emails that are as pornographic as her previous sexual encounter. In the emails Victoria tells Howard that she wants to "Suck it. Suck it. Suck it" (379). She also emails Howard "images of orifices and apertures that were simply *awaiting* him" (380). Again, these emails reinforce Victoria's sexual deviancy and the representation of black women as sexual deviants. Finally, when Victoria meets Howard for their second rendezvous, she wears a trench coat, dressed underneath in a "Corset, stockings, G-string, [and] *garters*"

(380). Like Honey's red dress, this provocative outfit associates Victoria with an image of the prostitute. After the affair between Howard and Victoria dissolves and Victoria's hypersexuality is irrelevant and for the remainder of the narrative like Hortense character Victoria does not evolve. Fortunately Smith's humorous depiction of the sexual encounter allows readers not to take Victoria's character too seriously, but it does not change the fact that she is another black female character who is defined by her sexuality.

Clearly with characters like Hortense and Victoria Smith reinforces the mammy and jezebel stereotypes. The flatness of these characters makes it difficult to see the characters as anything more than the caricatures they represent. Fortunately, these characters are juxtaposed against other female characters that defy the mammy, matriarch, and jezebel stereotypes. In *White Teeth*, Hortense's daughter Clara is a nurturing mother and supportive wife who does not adopt any of her mother's aggressive traits. And in *On Beauty*, Victoria's sexual deviancy is contrasted with Zora's virginal demureness. By presenting alternative portrayals of these black female characters Smith saves herself from promoting only negative characterizations of black women. Perhaps when Smith becomes comfortable with writing from the female perspective she will create a black female protagonist who eludes the stereotypes and who is as complex and as round as the white male characters she creates.
[9]

## Notes

[1] See Patricia Hill Collins, *Black Feminist Thought: Knowledge, Consciousness, and the Politics of Empowerment.* 2nd ed. New York: Routledge, 2000.

[2] From 2005 Condeeleza Rice has served as Secretary of State. Nobel prize winner Wangari Maathai is the Kenyan ecofeminist who developed the Green Belt Movement, an environmental organization.

[3] For a more comprehensive discussion, see Donald Bogle's *Toms, Coons, Mulattoes, Mammies, and Bucks* (New York: Continuum, 1989).

[4] Susan Fischer and Maeve Tynan comment on Kiki's breasts
[5] Susan Fischer also comments upon this passage.

[6] See Collins, Angela Davis, bell hooks, and Felly Simmonds.
[7] Brown's real name is Stella Marie Thompson.

[8] In the 1967 movie *The Graduate*, Mrs. Robinson teaches her younger lover the art of love-making.

## Works Cited

Acocella, Joan. "Connections: Race and Relations in Zadie Smith's New Novel." *The New Yorker*, October 3, 2005, 99–101.

Bell Scott, Patricia. "Debunking Sapphire: Toward a Non-Racist and Non-Sexist Social Science." In *But Some of Us Are Brave*, edited by Gloria T. Hull, Patricia Bell Scott, and Barbara Smith, 85–92. Old Westbury, NY: Feminist Press, 1981.

"Black, Fat, and Feisty." *Economist*, September 10, 2005, 81–82.

Bogle, Donald. *Toms, Coons, Mulattoes, Mammies, and Bucks: An Interpretive History of Blacks in American Films*. 2nd ed. New York: Continuum, 1989.

Carby, Hazel V. *Reconstructing Womanhood: The Emergence of the Afro American Woman Novelist*. New York: Oxford University Press, 1987.

Collins, Patricia Hill. *Black Feminist Thought: Knowledge, Consciousness, and the Politics of Empowerment*. 2nd ed. New York: Routledge, 2000.

Freeman, Hadley. "Words Smith." *Vogue*, October 2005, 355+.

Hampton, Dream. "Confessions of a Hip Hop Critic." *Step into a World: A Global Anthology of the New Black Literature*. Ed. Kevin Powell. Hoboken, NJ: Wiley, 2000. 105-107.

Harris, Trudier. *From Mammies to Militants: Domestics in Black American Literature*. Philadelphia: Temple University Press, 1982.

hooks, bell. *Yearning: Race, Gender, and Cultural Politics*. Boston: South End Press, 1990.

Horsburgh, Susan. "Of Roots and Family Trees: A Young First Novelist Writes a 'Big Book' About the Rules We Live By." *Time*, May 8, 2000, 94.

Marshall, Paule. *Brown Girl, Brownstones*. New York: Feminist Press, 1981.

McGarty, Craig, Vincent Yzerbyt, and Russell Spears. "Social, Cultural and Cognitive Factors in Stereotype Formation." In *Stereotypes as Explanations: The Formation of Meaningful Beliefs about Social Groups*, edited by Craig McGarty, Vincent Yzerbyt, and Russell Spears, 1–15. Cambridge, UK: Cambridge University Press, 2002.

Parkhurst, Jessie W. "The Role of the Black Mammy in the Plantation Household." *The Journal of Negro History* 23, no. 3 (1938): 349–69.

Shaw, Andrea. "The Other Side of the Looking Glass: The Marginalization of Fatness and Blackness in the Construction of Gender Identity." *Social Semiotics* 15, no. 2 (2005): 143-52

Smith, Zadie. *The Autograph Man*. New York: Random House, 2002.

———. *Martha and Hanwell*. London: Penguin Books, 2005.

———. "Mrs Begum's Son and the Private Tutor." In *The May Anthology of Oxford and Cambridge Short Stories*, edited by Martha Kelly, 89–113. Oxford and Cambridge: Varsity Publications, 1997.

———. *On Beauty*. London: Hamish Hamilton, 2005.

———. *White Teeth*. New York: Random House, 2000.

Squires, Claire. *Zadie Smith's White Teeth: A Readers Guide*. New York: Continuum International, 2002.

Tucker, Veta Smith. "Reconstructing Mammy: Fictive Reinterpretations of Mammy's Role in the Slave Community and Image in American Culture." Ph.D. Diss., University of Michigan, 1994.

Turner, Patricia A. *Ceramic Uncles & Celluloid Mammies: Black Images and Their Influence on Culture.* New York: Anchor Books, 1994.

Wallace, Michele. *Black Macho and the Myth of the Superwoman.* New York: The Dial Press, 1979.

# CHAPTER VIII
## From the Dispossessed to the Decolonized:
## From Samuel Selvon's *The Lonely Londoners* to Zadie
## Smith's "Hanwell in Hell"

*Sharon Raynor, Johnson C. Smith University*

> Women loving women
> Is the hardest place to be
> Experiencing, learning them knowing
> The games of patriarchy
> Don't deliver us from our
> Colonization as women
> So easily…
> Each independent woman
> Finds herself policed,
> Policing herself and others of our kind
> Lest we stray too far
> Spilling over the boundaries
> Into Truth—
> Such a frightening place to be
> Alone—outside the colony,
> Will you come with me?
> I'm sick of living lies.
>
> —*Shadida Janjua, "Will You"*

> "People in this world don't know how other people does affect their lives."
>
> —Sam Selvon, *The Lonely Londoner*

In the tradition of Samuel Selvon's *The Lonely Londoners*, Zadie Smith, in her short story "Hanwell in Hell," creates characters who are both culturally alienated and displaced. Both are tales of "dramatic reversals of fortune" (Smith 113)—those in London, whether native or stranger, are dispossessed. The stories introduce such female characters as Tanty Bessy, Laura, and Claire, who are even further dispossessed and alienated than their male counterparts; their very existence depends upon the men's ability to achieve acceptance and to adapt to change within their environment. For both Selvon and Smith, a well-defined narrative structure articulates the stories of all of these characters, but especially the female characters. For characters like Tanty Bessy, Laura, and Claire, "migration creates the desire for home. Home can only have meaning once one experiences a level of displacement from it" (Davies 113). Through a postcolonial perspective, their race, their culture, and their identity clash with their host society; their lives on the mere margins of society are revealed within the narrative structure. In "Hanwell in Hell," Smith allows the reader to journey with two men, Clive and Hanwell, through their individual anguish and pain, as they form a friendship in such a dissolute place as London. For Selvon, the characters feel colonized and dispossessed because they are West Indian immigrants looking for a home in London, whereas the dispossession of the Londoners in "Hanwell in Hell" evolves from a place of isolation, whether self-inflicted or imposed upon them by others, is revealed through their stories, their voices, and their togetherness. Their identity within their loosely constructed global community becomes fragmented by their circumstances. The decolonization process for both the men and women sometimes involves a process of violence, whether emotional or physical, inflicted upon the women by the men, and somehow the women evolve out of their own tragedies—suicide, abandonment, domestic abuse, sexual exploitation, and loss of place—to circumvent their own situations and rediscover their home. Their existence is silenced and often sacrificed in the midst of the story for the survival of their own cultural counterparts.

The characters in both *The Lonely Londoners* and "Hanwell in Hell" are what Booker and Juraga would call, "racial and cultural outsider[s]" (64), and in order to survive, all of the characters, but especially the women, must deconstruct home and learn to live, according to Carole Boyce Davies, as strangers-outsiders (103). The women in the stories are so dispossessed in their home/lands because their desire for cultural and familial homes interferes with their abilities to adapt to their newer environments. For Zadie Smith's characters, perhaps the most alienated and dispossessed are Hanwell's daughter, Claire, who is desperately seeking anyone who knew her father, and her mother, Laura, who committed suicide with the tie cord of a bathrobe. For Selvon's characters, perhaps the loneliest of the Londoners is Tanty Bessy, who as an West Indian elder travels to London to be with and take care of her family. The stories of these secondary characters reveal the depth of their dispossession and alienation and are only told through the lives of the main male characters and the demise or exploitation of other female characters. References within these stories to people, places, events, and memories often trigger emotional displacement within the characters. This displacement can be viewed as a form of colonization in which the characters feel genuinely removed and ostracized within the dominant culture, thereby creating a dichotomy of oppression.

Colonization is a form of oppression. According to Paulo Freire, "the oppressed must be their own example in the struggle for their redemption. In their alienation, the oppressed want at any cost to resemble the oppressors, to imitate them, to follow them" (37). Throughout both stories, the characters allow their behaviors to emulate that of the white society in which they live. The theoretical basis for postcolonial studies reveals that characters are struggling with the tradition of colonial rule—those who attempt to possess and oppress them—as they attempt to develop their own national or global identity. Their place, location, economic exploitation, and identity are intertwined as they begin to move through their own cultural alienation. Both Selvon and Smith take a critical look at the lives of characters who now "belong" to the streets of London. Decolonization which "sets out to change the order of the world, is, obviously, a program of complete disorder. [It] is the meeting of two forces, opposed to each other by their very nature" (Fanon 36). They are ultimately marginalized and silenced throughout the decolonization process because they are both displaced from home and exploited in their current situation.

According to Carol Boyce Davies, the female characters' ideal of home is shattered when they are forced to identify with it from a distance:

> The decentering of home and exile advances the critique of labeling, place, origin, home/lands. It is a recognition that because of their history, Black women themselves have to redefine the contours of what identity, location, writing, theory and time mean, and thus redefine themselves against Empire constructs. In this context, when the colonizers have an epistemic position in defining "post-colonial" dynamics, this work recognizes the persistence of struggle. (96)

Home, in many regards, evokes resistance within those most longing for its familiarity and comfort. The acceptance that lies within creates cohesiveness and a sense of belonging, especially for the female characters who are experiencing rejection from within. According to Seodial Deena in *Canonization, Colonization, Decolonization: A Comparative Study of Political and Critical Works by Minority Writers,* "silencing and marginalization on the basis of gender are not only features of colonialism, but, more recently, also of the traditional literary canon" (21). The female characters are at first silenced and then sacrificed within the narrative. In their hopes of redemption, they must find themselves through the interaction with and knowledge of others.

In *The Lonely Londoners*, a sense of birth of a Caribbean identity is addressed in the novel where a West Indian community settles in the heart of England. This establishment causes England, to use Louise Bennett's phrase, "to be colonized in reverse" (Selvon 4), and this decolonization is present throughout the novel in various themes of displacement, fragmentation, alienation, objectification, identity, escape, home, and migration. When the characters settle in London, there exists an urge within them to identify with the things furthest from them—aspects of their culture that remind them of home. Even though the main character, Moses Aloetta, who is "sustained by a sense of Caribbean identity" (Paguet 445) and emerges as the natural leader of the immigrants, it is Tanty Bessy who manages both to evoke the feelings of and to remind "the boys" of home. Although it is the experiences of the boys that lie at the center of the novel, Tanty's alienation within her own family pushes her to the margins of her own existence and happiness in London. The West Indian men have difficulty accepting their own women within their new society, because they instantly become obsessed with being with white women—the exact opposite of women like Tanty. As Booker and Juraga note,

> A motif that runs throughout Selvon's work, in which West Indian men, feminized by their subaltern positions within the colonial system, seek empowerment through sexual exploitation of women. In Selvon's novels of immigrant life, this usually means white women, the sexual mastery of whom provides West Indian men with a measure of revenge for their own depersonalization and objectification by white society, as well as a measure of validation of their own manhood. (Booker and Juraga 70–71)

Throughout the story, the boys measure their success and ability to adapt to their new environment mostly by their sexual exploits with the white women of London and the skills they use to keep their jobs. Even though the boys admire Moses, he attempts to initiate them to London very differently than Tanty Bessy. While Moses attempts to guide them through this desolate place, Tanty reminds them of their lives at home. She maintains the role of the elder among the transplanted West Indians, even though they have the tendency to discredit her knowledge. The fellow expatriates' marginalization of Tanty results in their own displacement within their new society. She remembers who she is and where she is from, and throughout the narrative she is never afraid to display this brazenness. She is a bold and sassy character whose good intentions are often undermined by the boys because they see her as an embarrassment to their new lives.

Tanty's appearance in the novel is in total opposition to that of the boys. Tanty's abrasiveness and colorfulness seem alien to her new location. Her disposition is marked by her ironic words, "You cant take me alone. You have to take the whole family" (32). This sentiment becomes poignant to Tanty's place and presence in London. She becomes stereotyped as just another Jamaican immigrant because she evokes the images of the West Indies—the very place the boys wanted both to escape and forget. The underlying premise of her existence is marked by Shabnam Grewal's notion, "when a white person asks a Black woman where she comes from, the implicit assumption is that she does not belong here" (11). Further, the term "immigrant," with which many people in large European centers are marked, is a term which, Stuart Hall asserts, "places one so equivocally as really belonging somewhere else. 'And when are you going back home?' is the completing rhetorical gesture" (quoted in Davies 114). The female's identity is closely connected to her own perception of home in Trindad, not Jamica, unlike the male characters who migrated to London as well. Tanty has yet to establish her place among the other West Indians.

Despite her alienation, Tanty still attempts to serve her community as if she were still residing in the West Indies. She gives domestic advice to her fellow battered West Indian women while also advising the men about the perils of white women. Tanty's personality is either well-liked or hated within the community. Tanty's biggest influence on the community was the creation of a traditional West Indian community of trust and acceptance in London. In the Caribbean it is commonplace for store patrons to purchase groceries and other items on credit. Tanty convinces the apprehensive English shopkeeper to adopt this practice of selling merchandise on credit. With every intention of only humoring Tanty by just giving her credit, the shopkeeper learns about doing business her way. Tanty makes further attempts to become a part of the larger city and move beyond Harrow Road by having enough courage to take the tube or bus to travel into London. Even with a successful trip into the city, she feels empty and out of place. Tanty knows that she can be very self-sufficient living in London, but she still faces the reality of not being wanted there by her own people. Her feelings of displacement permeate the narrative. The men are continuously replacing and substituting their own people for those of their newly desired home.

The process of decolonization is evoked as the women are soon forgotten as the men replace them and continue on with their lives. Tanty's intuitiveness somehow protects the other women within their community who had initially migrated with their men but were soon exploited for the promise of London. Because the men are emasculated by their current situation within the white society, they inflict this same objectification upon the women. Their womanly exploits run throughout the novel and continue to infuriate Tanty. She tries to warn the boys about white girls: "You better watch out and don't get in no trouble. White girls is what sweeten up so many of you to come to London. You own kind of girls not good enough now, is only white girls. White girls! Go on! They will catch up with you in this country" (73). The mere thought of the West Indian men choosing other women over their own is appalling to Tanty. This very act by the men amplifies Tanty's sense of displacement and dispossession. She and other West Indian women are not wanted and are barely accepted by their own. Tanty's last appearance in the storyline takes place at a fete hosted by a fellow West Indian. She, according to her cultural counterparts, creates an embarrassing scene at the dance which causes them embarrassment and humiliation. She is called names, stared at, mocked, and ignored by others. While feeling further alienated and alone, Tanty soon grows tired and wants to go home (119). Midway through the narrative Tanty disappears from the storyline, as if her existence does not count or even make a significant difference to those in her community. Selvon's authorial decision to allow Tanty to fade into the shadows speaks volumes to the decolonization process for her. She is ultimately substituted, silenced and sacrificed for the survival of the others.

Tanty's desire for her home in the West Indies creates her alienation and longing for those aspects of familiarity. Even though she is within a familiar setting, she still finds herself on the outside of its existence. This newly established West Indian community within London is a fictitious creation of home. Even the West Indians are considered outsiders by the locals and still live among themselves in communities segregated by race, ethnicity, and class, their attempt to exist within their host society is based on the premise that they can have sex with women outside of their race. Thus, according to Davies, "the rewriting of home becomes a critical link in the articulation of identity. It is a play of resistance to domination which identifies where we come from, but also locates home in its many transgressive and disjunctive experiences" (115). Tanty's ideals of home become intertwined with what she hopes her new home will become for her despite the mass depersonalization by the host society. Because she was not born there, she will only ever exist on the outskirts of that society. The West Indian men are not even attempting to acculturate or even assimilate within that society but to achieve empowerment through sexual mastery over white women and abusive behavior and exploitation of their own women. This behavior pushes both the men and the women further to the margins of acceptance and belonging, thus rendering Tanty's character dispossessed and in search of home and unavailable to help those other women who suffer at the hands of their own men.

The decolonization process for Selvon's characters, like Zadie Smith's, begins and ends with their attempt to create a place in which they can truly feel compassion for each other and achieve a certain level of acceptance. In both stories, the male characters' lives are dictated by how they respond to their own particular circumstances and how this response changes their lives from ones that were once intertwined with loving and supporting women to a life that is destitute because of the absence of those same women. Zadie Smith portrays this dilemma through characters who suffer grave tragedies, and their traumatic lives are altered beyond repair or redemption, just a glimmer of hope. "Hanwell in Hell" is a paradoxical story of catastrophe and hope that lies in a daughter who, in hopes of discovering lost memories of family, is seeking to find anyone who knew her father when he lived in the Bristol area from 1970 to 1973. The lives of the female characters in the story are described so subtly that careful attention must be paid to their own personal tragedies and objectification before they completely disappear from the storyline.

"Hanwell in Hell" could easily read as a story about masculinity, class, and place, but for the purpose of this comparative analysis it is being read as a story of cultural alienation and the displacement of the female characters their loss of home, family, and each other. Unlike, Selvon's characters, the daughters, due to certain circumstances of their mother's death, believed that they were not wanted by their father not knowing his plans for them. What is similar to Selvon's novel is the notion that the male characters are not suitable to live with. The narrative speaks to the colonization of the men while charting the decolonization of the daughters. All are removed from their homes/homeland and in search of a newly established life elsewhere. The daughters are living elsewhere, in search of the home/land from which they were not just displaced but also estranged. Davies notes,

> Home is often portrayed as a place of alienation and displacement. The family is sometimes situated as a site of oppression for women. The mystified notions of home and family are removed from their romantic idealized moorings, to speak of pain, movement, difficulty, learning and love in complex ways. Thus the complicated notion of home mirrors the problematizing of community/nation/identity that one finds in Black women's writing from a variety of communities. (21)

Their existence as strangers-outsiders have them seeking answers to perhaps unspeakable memories that their father has yet to articulate and ascribe meaning.

Hanwell's daughter, Claire, is seeking answers as to why she and her sisters were left with relatives in London. Her letter solicits information from anyone who may have known her father. It is also the story of women's lives lost to feelings of abandonment, displacement, utter hopelessness, and despair. Her correspondence receives a response from Clive Black, whose interesting encounter with Hanwell, thirty-four years earlier, provides the premise for the short story. He is drawn to Hanwell's dreary and miserable existence because they both served in Normandy, France, during World War II in 1944. The irony of Hanwell's name as a location of significant disastrous bombings during World War II is also a direct reflection on Hanwell's own character and his difficulty in adapting to his own environment. The letter is an attempt to find closure for a situation that seemed beyond anyone's control, but Clive attempts to provide Claire with some closure and convince her that they were complete opposites because Hanwell "valued the domestic and lamented its loss; women, the home, family" (113). Clive's own self-pity is doubly burdened because he desired the company of women but could only find solace in a place like Barry Franks and the memory of Hanwell who is also lost in despair as he attempts to explain, during their strange encounter, the loss of his wife and his estrangement from his daughters. Clive not only empathizes with Hanwell because of their service in the war but also because they were both down on their luck. Clive who had lost his home, business, and family connected with Hanwell rather quickly but never shared his own circumstances. It seems that only his newfound friend, Clive, can hear the desperation in his story because of the commonalties with his own. In order to completely hear the stories of the women in the narrative, the togetherness of the men must be established within the story line. Laura and Claire are all but invisible and voiceless in the narrative while one other unnamed woman makes a brief appearance but is then sacrificed for the survival of their male counterparts.

The decolonization process for Clive and Hanwell includes substituting each other for the women they desired to have in their lives. Even though Clive desired the company of women, he cannot remember the name of the girl who accompanied him the night he met Hanwell. He can, however, remember her appearance. Within his remembrance of beauty, he objectifies her:

> Her name is lost to me, but the outline of her chest is not—huge, carefully wrapped and cantilevered, like a present on a shelf which she had not yet decided to give away. She was thirty years my junior and also a diluted Italian, although she was still taking her Catholicism neat. I had spent the better part of five hours that evening—in my flat, in my car, in the cinema, and in a park—persistently trying to get my hand to go where she would not have it go. (Smith 117)

Her presence in the narrative is based more on her body and the sexuality insinuated in her movements and gestures than her actual presence. Her objectification by Clive quickly leads to his disgust for her as she becomes fascinated by Hanwell's stories. Clive alienates her even further by only conversing with Hanwell until she completely loses interest and departs. Instead of becoming irritated with Hanwell for attracting her with such intriguing stories, he further blames and isolates her. As with the West Indian men in *The Lonely Londoners*, the women are being silenced and then substituted for others. In this particular case, Clive substitutes Hanwell for his female companion, who remains nameless during her short appearance, within the narrative. The strange togetherness hinges on the mere premise that they are both women-less men, who no one will miss, not Clive's unnamed companion nor Hanwell's wife, who he says is in London.

After the girl's departure, a conversation about her appearance and the ideal of beauty leads to Hanwell's remark, "It makes me feel better knowing there are women as beautiful as that in the world. [It is] a signal that that the world is good. Beautiful women help you know that" (Smith 118). Like Tanty, this female character disappears from the story just as quickly as she entered. Her presence has to be sacrificed for the progression of the men's narrative. Her beauty alone is not enough to sustain her presence within their lives, even though they long for such beauty. Because this beauty is in the form of a woman, she, like the others within the narrative, is sacrificed for

Clive and Hanwell's survival. Hanwell's comments foreshadows his longing and desire yet alienation of his own family.

The nameless girl becomes just a symbol for both the men; she is the unobtainable object of the male gaze. Her silencing and disappearance from the storyline is immediately followed by the appearance of a wailing fox collapsed in a hedge. This ironic scene leads directly to the mystery surrounding the suicide of Laura, Hanwell's wife, and the eventual abandonment of his daughters. The narrative includes the girl only as a symbolic juxtaposition to a wounded animal that is ultimately killed by Hanwell. In order to silence its suffering, the fox had to be killed. The fox had been displaced from its home, wounded, left unattended and sacrificed, so others will not have to hear the sounds of its anguish. The wailing moves Hanwell to action. Not being able to bear the sound of suffering, he ends the fox's misery with one quick gesture (Hanwell broke its neck with his boot). Poignant to the narrative is the insinuation that Hanwell feels responsible for ending the suffering of his family, or at least that of his wife. The appearance of the animal was remarkable because it did not look as if it was suffering. Their perception of the wounded animal was in complete opposition to the reality of its suffering. The fox, like the unnamed girl, was alienated from where it truly belonged and at the moment of its departure from the narrative, was also seen as an object of beauty:

> Pretty thing, I said and I can remember now what a deliberate understatement that was. It was, in truth, extraordinary to be standing this close to something so wild, so usually elusive, so slender-legged, so orange-tailed, so yellow-eyed, so unexpected. We were face to snot with the animal. There wasn't a mark on it. It was as spotless as it if had been stuffed and it was perfectly serene apart from this terrible screaming. (Smith 119)

Clive was shocked by the instant death of the fox. The beauty of the fox/unnamed girl is parallel to their disappearance from the narrative so both Clive and Hanwell could continue forth with their night. The significance of this scene is essential to understanding the story. This scene precedes what is revealed of Laura's suicide, and it also implies that even though Hanwell was not directly responsible for it, Hanwell did nothing to prevent it from happening. Seeing Hanwell kill the fox physically sickens Clive, and despite Hanwell's concern, Clive remembers: "He did not make any move to help me. Men like us don't know how to comfort each other. We need women for that. I felt a little throb of despair pass through me; the absolute certainty that there would be no one waiting for me tonight, no matter what time I came home" (Smith 120). Ironically, this is what they have been doing all night—comforting each other.

Just like Hanwell and Clive discover the wounded fox, he reveals that he also discovered his wife's body in a somewhat discreet location: in the stairwell on the way to the cellar. The location her suicide proves significant because of the discovery. The premise that her neck was broken from being hanged is significant to Hanwell freely being able to kill the wounded animal. Very little is ever said about the wife's suicide or the circumstances leading to it within the story; however, much is implied. Hanwell feels ultimately responsible for his family's demise, but despite his many efforts, he is unable to keep them together. The killing of the fox also parallels what Hanwell perceives he did to his family. They think they need women but they both have the tendency to rid their own lives of the women who loved and needed them or at least those who found them interesting: Laura, Claire, and Clive's unnamed female companion. Hanwell, allowed his wife's possessions to remain in the flat as if she still lived there. He lived with both her presence and absence. The narrative insinuates that his alienation from his family seems forced by others, or perhaps it was brought on by the war. While the narrative only offers room here for speculation, it is, however, a point of departure that cannot be overlooked, particularly as it relates to how it could have affected the lives of the women.

This same loneliness and despair that had Clive and Hanwell headed to Hanwell's flat in a near-drunken stupor in the pouring rain is still tainted by the absence of women. Clive's self-pity continues as the night progresses. He feels completely comfortable blaming Hanwell for his anguish and despair. He remarks, "I had the keen sense that this was the lowest moment of my decline, that there would be nothing beneath this. Time has proven this instinct correct. Two wet strangers, outdoors, without women, at night, and with death curled up nearby" (Smith 121). Hanwell does not know how to communicate his own despair or need. These men are drawn together because of a stroke of hellish misfortune and circumstance.

Hanwell's living environment reveals that he actually has, or a least, had, a family which seems to surprise Clive. This correspondence, sent to Claire, has to dispel any notion that Hanwell never thought of his family. He mentions the photographs of Emily, Carol, and Claire. Once Hanwell shares with Clive the story of Laura's suicide, they both sit "quiet for a minute, considering death in the incompetent way that people do" (Smith 121). As they continue to sit and drink Clive soon discovers that Hanwell is painting a room intended for his daughters in a hellish red color, a color that Hanwell believes is the color of sunset, Deepest Sun. Clive's facial expression obviously leads Hanwell to think the paint is wrong. In a moment of despair, Hanwell begins to talk about his daughters, blaming himself for their mother's death. The more he talks about his family, the more the narrative reveals about the lives of the women. His first concern is that the room is too small for three girls of their age (seventeen, sixteen, and fourteen) who are currently living in Bromley with their aunt and uncle. He admits that he writes to his daughters but that they never write back. His failed attempts to contact his family moves Clive to help him paint the room without ever telling him that what he thought was sunshine yellow is actually deep red. The painting of the room creates a sense of accomplishment for both Hanwell and Clive who remarks, "I thought it extremely unlikely that any daughter of Hanwell's would ever spend a night in this room as we just had, but again I held my counsel" (Smith 123). Clive is able to sense Hanwell's desperate loneliness because of his own. They share the same sentiment of abandonment and alienation, which for these two characters have been self-imposed. Claire's curiosity about her father and eventually her mother is only natural because of the estrangement she experiences.

The question of who abandoned whom seems significant at this point in the narrative. Did Hanwell abandon/neglect his family, or did his family have no other choice but to abandon him? While Hanwell's existence and environment seem to suggest that his daughters abandoned him, Claire's correspondence suggests just the opposite. Perhaps this is why they were not suitable to be lived with. While Claire is in search of her home, Hanwell and Clive seem to be alienated from theirs. Earlier in the narrative, it is revealed that Clive, even though he spends a "humiliating amount of time with women," because of his job, he prefers the company of men because they are emotionally simpler (Smith 113). They "sniffed out the other's catastrophe" (113) by realizing that they both spent time in France and then arrived on the beach in Normandy at different times. Their connection was instantaneous. While Clive attempts to figure out if Hanwell was either a butcher's son, a schoolteacher's son or a civil servant's son, they became civil and talked. One significant question Clive asked of Hanwell when he learned that he used to work in Soho: "what in God's name are you doing in this hellhole?" (116) greatly affects Hanwell's demeanor about his own situation.

As the daughter tries to piece together this puzzle, she openly asks the question why she and her sisters were left in London. Clive's original sentiment to Claire was that Hanwell must have left his family against his will because "no one would choose the life that Hanwell had" (Smith 113). He wants her to know that Hanwell was the type of man who made plans for his family to be with him. Because Clive can offer very little solace to Claire, he offers her gestures of remorse and his apologies instead:

> More and more, I suspect that men of our generation were not to be lived with. We made people unhappy because we ourselves were unhappy in irrevocable ways. My own daughter takes great pleasure in knowing the measure of me, of judging and convicting me, and maybe she is right, and maybe you are, too. These days, everyone passes the blame backward—but we couldn't do that. We kept blame close, we held it tight. I'm sorry your father made you so unhappy. Maybe the other replies you receive will help you put the blame in the right place and "come to terms," as people say now. But when I saw your request in the paper my first thought was of a man likable enough to remember—this is no small feat. (Smith 123)

Clive holds Hanwell in very high regard; he confesses, "everyone I met back then I'd rather forget" (Smith 123). His admiration for Hanwell allows for the further scolding he gives to Claire. "I think you are too hard on him. And I think you were wrong to think that he knew all the time you and your sisters wouldn't come, or that he didn't want you to. Hanwell had a beautiful way of hoping. Not many men can hope red yellow" (Smith 123). The storyline reveals that the daughters never went to stay with Hanwell; hence the need for the correspondence. According to Jason Jawando, "the story does, indeed, avoid using the characters to symbolize grand themes. Instead, a tiny detail, colour-blind Hanwell's accidental painting of his daughter's bedroom 'hellish deep red,' symbolizes the human tragedy of both characters, separation from their families. This detail is perfectly placed and weighed within the narrative, giving it genuine poignancy" (Jawando).

Several questions remained unanswered, but other details are revealed about Hanwell. He never lost hope of his daughters' return and never seemed to forgive himself about Laura's suicide, which makes him a sympathetic character, especially for Clive—the mirror image of himself. Laura, who never makes a physical appearance within the narrative construct, manages to become an integral part of the story. The daughters' estrangement and eventual abandonment, as it seems by their father, stems from his inability to cope with his wife's suicide. For the daughters, but especially for Claire, the narrative "produces [a] daughter caught in between the cultural demands of home and the larger society, producing a profound multiplying of experiences and the construction of new identities" (Davies 129). Claire is "caught on the borders between two culture areas and between exile and home, movement and fixity. She is in search of a home that she barely remembers but longs to possess. Because Claire does not know enough to blame the mother for taking her own life, Laura "attains symbolic importance in terms of definition and redefinition" (128). For this mother and daughter, their lives remain intertwined with each other (Hirsch 178) even in death, while Hanwell plunges into the depths of disillusionment about his own life and displacement within his own home/land and culture. Laura's existence was sacrificed for their survival in London. The family's cohesiveness and longevity is severed by the tragedy of the suicide. Prior to that, their lives were jeopardized because they could not help each other survive their hopeless state of being. The women have once again been sacrificed for Hanwell's survival, which results in his idealistic state of hope for things yet to happen. The loss of their families to unfortunate circumstances details their own existence.

In both "Hanwell in Hell" and *The Lonely Londoners*, in order for the men to bond and move toward understanding their own dispossession and fully comprehend their existence, the women have to be pushed to the margins (of the narrative)—removed from their current circumstances. These women—Clive's unnamed female companion; the dead mother, Laura; the estranged daughters, Claire, Carol, and Emily; and Tanty Bessy—become sacrificial elements in the decolonization process of "the boys," Hanwell and Clive. The narrative progresses toward renewal for some and redemption for others only after the female characters are alienated into their own separate worlds that are no longer written about within the narrative construct. Their self-definition is not complete because, within both stories, their existence hinges on the renewal and acceptance of their culture by the patriarchal society. Their place becomes ambiguous, thereby further displacing and alienating them. They experience a level of abandonment by their own.

The hope only seems to live within the male characters' abilities to "change the order of the world" for their own survival and existence. The importance of the women in this transformational process of decolonization is witnessed through the narratives of the male characters. Selvon's novel ends with the boys congregating together thinking about women. "It was a summer night: laughter fell softly: it was the sort of night that you wasn't making love to a woman you feel you was the only person in the world like that" (141). For Clive, his encounter with Hanwell somehow changes him. He remarks, "When you feel lost in the world, there is some joy to be gleaned from exact imitations of familiar things" (Smith 113). Their renewal and redemption rest on the premise that their experiences have moved them a bit closer to cultural and personal fulfillment, despite the looming feeling of loneliness. For Clive, he loses Hanwell but holds on only to his memory in order to convey it to his daughter. For the boys, they long for the women they push beyond the margins of forgiveness. In the tradition of Selvon, Zadie Smith writes the lives of characters living in states of apparent disrepair. While they are not completely hopeless in their living, they are attempting at least to begin their decolonization process despite their struggle to survive.

## Works Cited

Booker, Keith M., and Dubravka Juraga. *The Caribbean Novel: An Introduction*. Portsmouth, NH: Heinemann, 2001.

Davies, Carole Boyce. *Black Women, Writing and Identity*. New York: Routledge, 1994.

Deena, Seodial F.H. *Canonization, Colonization, Decolonization: A Comparative Study of Political and Critical Works by Minority Writers*. New York: Peter Lang, 2001.

Fanon, Frantz. *The Wretched of the Earth*. New York: Grove Press, 1965.

Freire, Paulo. *Pedagogy of the Oppressed*. New York: Continuum, 1996.

Grewal, Shabnam, et al. *Charting the Journey. Writings by Black and Third World Women*. London: Sheba Feminist Publishers, 1988.

Hirsch, Marianne. *The Mother/Daughter Plot: Narrative, Psychoanalysis, Feminism*. Bloomington: Indiana University Press, 1989.

Jawando, Jason. "Martha and Hanwell by Zadie Smith." 2005. Review. www.birminghamwords.coik/ content/view/497/82/.

Selvon, Samuel. *The Lonely Londoners*. London: Longman, 1956.

Smith, Zadie. "Hanwell in Hell." *The New Yorker* 80, no. 28 (9/24/2004): 113-23. http://www.newyorker.com/printables/fiction/040927fi_fiction.

# CHAPTER IX
## Red and Yellow, Black and White: Color-Blindness as Disillusionment in Zadie Smith's "Hanwell in Hell"

*Lexi Stuckey, University of Central Oklahoma*

Zadie Smith burst onto the literary scene in 2000 with her sprawling opening salvo, *White Teeth*. Beloved by critics and readers alike, the book helped brand its twenty-four-year-old author as the spokesperson for a new literary subgenre: the postmillennial multicultural novel; multicultural in the sense of many diverse cultural groups living within a single society, but also in the sense of differing cultural groups living within a single family. Smith's positive portrayal of her multicultural characters, who pinball through their lives in urban London but ultimately find peace and a sense of home, helps to account for *White Teeth*'s success. As Smith herself said in an interview, "It's optimistic, I think" (quoted in Gerzina 271).

*White Teeth* began to attract more attention in great part because of that optimistic tone, and Smith built upon it, continuing to spread a bright vision of the future while doing press for the novel's release. In an interview with Kathleen O'Grady, she said that a North London school and its racially heterogeneous student body "really lifts your spirits. It is amazing. And you just want to drag certain people to the school and say, 'Look at this, look at how well it can work. Look at how these people are doing'" (quoted in O'Grady 106). Though Smith's novel suggests that she is a proponent of multiculturalism, after the publication of *White Teeth*, Smith felt her own ideology shift. In a number of interviews Smith conveyed her apparent weariness with her role as the literary world's poster child for multiculturalism. In an interview with the *Kansas City Star* toward the conclusion of *White Teeth*'s long publicity campaign, she preemptively and with gentle humor warned interviewer John Mark Eberhart against using certain critical buzzwords:

> Before we begin, there are certain words that make the author very tired. These words are: multicultural, post-colonial, archetype, stereotype, post-millennial, literally, identity, zucchini. The author is not responsible for her own mental shutdown should she come across these words in the course of scrolling down this e-mail interview. In all other respects, however, she will be sweetness and light personified. (quoted in Eberhart F1)

By the time her short story "Hanwell in Hell" appeared in *The New Yorker* just four years later, Smith's outlook had definitively changed. The mild combativeness Smith revealed to Eberhart in 2001 was now a full-blown hostility toward the multicultural genre that put her on the literary map. As Molly Thompson notes, Smith "is in accordance with many post-colonial critics and theorists who have contested the term [multiculturalism] and who believe it may obscure a different reality—one with more sinister connotations" (123). Unlike *White Teeth*, this short story explores the alienation that results from racial hybridity. By examining the title character's literal and metaphoric condition, color-blindness, one can see how the condition can be read as symbolic for a bleak, failed conception of multiculturalism within a family.

*White Teeth*, in the seven years since its publication, thus garnered an enormous amount of popular publicity but a surprisingly small amount of more scholarly analysis. Even less serious critical work has been done on "Hanwell in Hell." At the time when this article went to press, in addition to the article in chapter six of this anthology and an on-line article, the only other criticism to date is a complimentary mention in a *Harper's Magazine* article. The brief review argues that the story represents a departure from what some critics deride as Smith's penchant for "mimicry" of other, more idiosyncratic writers: "Hanwell" allows readers to experience "Smith doing no one, at last, but Smith" (Mason 88). Without placing undue emphasis on a single critical opinion, it may be meaningful at least to entertain the possibility of "Hanwell in Hell" being Smith's first mature work, one that conveys more of her own voice, personal experience, and agenda than previous works. When examined in this light, the short story reveals Smith to be less enamored of her characters' tangled roots than critics at first thought.

In the story, readers follow a solitary British man, Hanwell, through one night, as remembered by a casual acquaintance, Clive Black. As the evening progresses, Hanwell is revealed to be a widower with three estranged daughters, trying and failing to pull his life and his home together for them. Before plunging into analysis, one must first establish that the Hanwells are indeed a multicultural family with "tangled roots," a metaphor familiar to Smith's readers in that "roots" were a major preoccupation for the characters in *White Teeth*. The short story is somewhat ambiguous in its evocation of a potentially multicultural family. The Hanwells are not explicitly identified as multicultural, but there is a definite difference between the ways the father and his daughters are described. Hanwell is "pink," "sandy-haired," the archetypal Briton; readers can assume he is Caucasian. His three daughters, however, are described as "dark" and as having their mother's beauty ("Hanwell" 120–21). This is significant given that in Smith's two novels, the biracial characters have Caucasian British fathers and black mothers.

Evoking the "sinister" implications of multiculturalism, Hanwell is described as having "managed to plummet beneath acceptability" ("Hanwell" 113), a phrase with potentially unsavory connotations. Hanwell's lack of "acceptability" may be an experience he shares with Archie Jones of *White Teeth*, who is awkwardly uninvited from a company function because his Jamaican wife makes his co-workers feel uncomfortable, and Belsey, whose father disapproves of "the exotic manner in which Howard has chosen to continue the Belsey line" (*On Beauty* 18). In addition to the textual evidence, one must consider the past works and the authorial idiosyncrasies of the author. Smith has alternately admitted to and denied incorporating elements of her own life into her fiction. At the 2006 Orange Prize party, at which she was honored for *On Beauty*, Smith confirmed that the object of a *White Teeth*'s character's affection—a classmate named "Nicky Laird"—was in fact a reference to her own university classmate and now-husband, poet Nick Laird (Rifkind 13). While the character appears too briefly to determine whether he is in fact based more closely on Smith's husband Laird, the fact remains that she used his name as a way of connecting individuals in her life to her fiction.

Similarly, Smith connects her own personal experience and that of her characters. She is not so obvious as to name any major biracial character "Zadie," but her ties to her biracial characters are strong, suggesting that they may be significantly self-referential. Smith herself is biracial, the daughter of a Jamaican mother and a Caucasian British father. At least one reviewer argues of *White Teeth*, "Although [Smith] insists the book is not based on her own life, the central character of Irie is largely autobiographical" (Chittenden 13). In fact, each of Smith's major works—*White Teeth*, *The Autograph Man*, and *On Beauty*—showcases at least one character of mixed race, and, in two of the three novels, this character is the child of a black mother and a white father. It would be unsurprising, then, to find Smith including other biracial characters in her fiction, including Hanwell's daughters.

Situated between the confident *White Teeth* and the skeptical *On Beauty*, "Hanwell" occupies the median point between the poles of Smith's representation of multiculturalism. "Hanwell in Hell" is unique in that it incorporates significant stylistic elements and characterization from both novels, allowing the reader to see Smith's internal struggle with her subject matter. Hanwell's story is the definitive tipping point from a family relatively content in its multicultural existence to a family at the brink of collapse for the very same circumstance.

Hanwell should be the hero of the story, but instead he is consistently presented in ambiguous or contradictory lights: innocent and wary, domestic but cruel, hopeful yet defeated. Hanwell's clashing characterizations make sense because he is the marker of an ending and a precursor to a new beginning, the representation of Smith's churning sea change on the topic of the multicultural family. The "innocent" glimmers of personality recall Archie Jones, who has an open, friendly face, an almost peacefully childlike nature, and no bigger dreams than to work, drink a pint, and love his family. But Hanwell has uglier qualities. He can too quickly turn wary or coy, or completely "shut up shop" on that eager pink face, leaving "Hanwell" narrator Clive Black to wonder "whether his innocence went all the way down" ("Hanwell" 116). These are markers of the character-yet-to-come: Howard Belsey, who feels "hustled by circumstance" into sacrifices for his family and quickly resorts to lying, cheating, and deceiving that family. Hanwell separates Archie's story from Howard's.

Hanwell as a character owes much to his predecessor Archie Jones. The softer qualities of Hanwell—his youthful coloring, his innocence, and his indefatigable lack of guile when it comes to the sticky issue of race—all recall Jones. Good. Jones, despite being at least twenty years past "youth," has "the physiognomy of innocence" (*White Teeth* 60), looking "pink-faced and polished" (71). Despite the novel's emphasis on the quiet battles between people with white and black and brown and yellow skins, Archie, at the book's heart, believes "people should just live together, you know, in peace or harmony or something" (159).

Archie's seemingly more desperate plight in the first chapter of *White Teeth* signals the despair that will soon haunt Hanwell. Following his divorce, Archie laments, "[I]t was infinitely easier to leave all baggage here on the roadside and walk on into the blackness" (*White Teeth* 9), a blackness that evokes the space Hanwell inhabits, a lonely flat that "points nowhere but into a void, a dark place that leaves a bright light in a reader's mind" (Mason 88). In *White Teeth*, "blackness" is a loaded and duplicitous word: Archie eventually does leave his life's baggage and walk into a marriage with Clara, a vision of exotically beautiful "blackness." But Clara should not be compared to the blackness of death, the image Smith appears to invoke with her word choice. Instead, *White Teeth*'s use of "blackness" is one of renewal and beginnings. In the case of the Hanwell family, however, blackness has no connotations save for negative ones: the disintegration of the family is brought about by the friction between darkness and lightness of skin, the unbridgeable difference between an unlike father and daughter. The Hanwells can hope for no possibility of renewal, only an unchangeable end.

Both Jones and Belsey are defined by the breakdown of their families or, as Clive Black tactfully describes such events, "dramatic reversals of fortune" ("Hanwell" 113). It is only in the outcomes that the reader can see Smith's differing approaches to the multicultural family: Archie, in embracing his multicultural family, thrives, but Hanwell and Howard Belsey, in failing to embrace (intentionally or not) their multicultural families, destroy those families and themselves. Archie is introduced to the reader as middle-aged and suicidal, broken by his divorce from a now-mad Italian woman he met while serving as a soldier. *White Teeth* is, in part, the tale of his redemption through Clara and Irie. Howard travels in the opposite direction, experiencing a slow, painful decline punctuated by Kiki's abandonment of him and their children. How does Hanwell connect the two? What does he tell us as he mediates between the subject positions occupied by the sweetly naïve Archie Jones and the steadily decaying Howard Belsey?

The Belsey family in *On Beauty* continues along Smith's newly bleak path toward an unhappy ending, carrying on the narrative theme begun in "Hanwell." But "Hanwell" itself draws much from *White Teeth*. Why does Smith link the themes of two novels in a work of short fiction? She crafts "Hanwell" to bridge the gap for her readers, using Hanwell's color-blindness. His pointedly emblematic condition emphasizes that, despite ignoring or being unable to see color, a neatly clear euphemism for the more complex term of "race," differences still exist among individuals of different colors. Hanwell's color-blindness is revealed to Clive and the reader at the moment when they realize that his wife is dead and his children are alienated from him, cementing its symbolism. If a multicultural relationship evolves into a multicultural family, there will be three colors and three identities to consider, the third of which wholly matches neither one parent nor the other. In a multicultural family, the parents and children become isolated from one another since, as in most families, personalities differ, and in their case, the

most basic shared physical and cultural characteristics are tenuous or contradictory. An examination of real and euphemistic "color-blindness" reveals
truths that transform hope into disillusionment. A belief in color-blindness,
no matter how admirable, ultimately sets the multicultural family up to fail.
This transition can be traced in the defining colors of Smith's works: the
white of *White Teeth*, the red of "Hanwell in Hell," and the yellow of *On
Beauty*.

Here, it would be prudent to address Smith's use of color as symbol, particularly as symbolic of race. This technique is a convention of Western literature, going as far back as the sixteenth century and Shakespeare's famous
"dark lady." Color symbolism is an especially popular tool for critics of the
novel: investigations have been undertaken into the works of authors as diverse as Fitzgerald and Melville, and Dante and Proust. Structuralists have
developed a semiotics of color to study just such codified literary relations
between color and symbol, signifiers and signified. Of course, color is a slippery theoretical construct, prone to historical and cultural factors, evidenced
in *White Teeth* through Smith's play on blackness as both redemptive (as seen
in Clara) and shameful (as seen in Irie), not to mention the sometimes in-
consistent, opposing conceptions of color between works, like in *White Teeth*
versus in *On Beauty*. Any and all of Smith's works would lend themselves to
in-depth analyses of their use of color symbolism. Seeing as that is a significant critical undertaking lying just outside the scope of this essay, I will not
attempt it; rather, I hope to highlight a select few of Smith's employments of
color as signifier.

Smith drops stylistic hints, all tied to pigment, that tie together these
three men and their flaws. For instance, Jones and Hanwell share that English pinkness of skin, while Belsey is described as "a dying sun his family
were orbiting" (*On Beauty* 338), a simile that recalls another colorful celestial
entity: the harsh and horrifying "Deepest Sun" paint Hanwell uses to spruce
up Claire's room. A fox also appears in both works, giving a "piteous wail"
("Hanwell" 119) and "keening" (*On Beauty* 308); the fox is so distinct that its
inclusion cannot be anything other than intentional. The fox figures promi-
nently in "Hanwell in Hell," serving as a bright spot of color that wails in
pain although it has no marks on it, signaling that its wound is somewhere
on the inside. Considering that everything in the story that is specifically described in terms of color can be read to comment on the state of the multicultural family, the fox can be interpreted as a being of color, hurt internally,

broken. Hanwell brutally and unexpectedly snaps its neck under his boot, claiming that it is "Better to put it out of its misery" ("Hanwell" 119). In *On Beauty* the fox's howl also comes at a pivotal point in the narrative, when Howard Belsey begins a journey that will lead to an encounter with his student, a long-building and deliberate sexual affair that definitively breaks his marriage and his family apart. Hanwell's shocking action marks another definitive break: of Hanwell snapping his tether from Archie and connecting instead to Howard. Hanwell's wounded fox represents of the internally crippled multicultural family; like Howard, Hanwell would rather kill it outright than attempt to discover what ails it.

In addition to the fox, *On Beauty* contains one of Smith's most knowing passages on color, race, family, and home—the summation of the Jones-Hanwell-Belsey descent. What first appears to be a throwaway paragraph about the Belsey house offers a painful insight into the families' struggles in all three narratives:

> The sole original window is the skylight at the very top of the house, a harlequin pane that casts a disc of varicolored light upon different spots on the upper landing as the sun passes over America, turning a white shirt pink as one passes through it, for example, or a yellow tie blue. Once the spot reaches the floor in mid-morning it is a family superstition never to step through it. Ten years earlier you would have found children here, wrestling, trying to force each other into its orbit. Even now, as young adults, they continue to step round it on their way down the stairs. (*On Beauty* 16)

This description, which occurs within the first twenty pages of the novel, deftly sums up the problem: while color cannot be changed, it can change everything. The "harlequin pane" of the Belsey home is a window into every mixed-race home. These families skirt the color; its presence is scarcely acknowledged and studiously avoided. Howard concedes as much when he admits that he "dislike[s] and fear[s] conversations with his children that [concern] race" (*On Beauty* 85).

In scientific terms, color may be, as one *On Beauty* character claims, "An accidental matter of pigment" (44), or, like the windowpane, a trick of light, but Smith's characters do not live in a perfect, rational world. They already recognize what Hanwell must painfully discover in his story and in his own mixed-race family: despite wishes to "hope red yellow" ("Hanwell" 123), color cannot be changed. So, is this just a continuation of what happens with the Chalfens and the FutureMouse Project, in that there are multiple mutations of the same thing that cancel out absolutes? Regardless of what he personally may not see because of his color-blindness, the hellish red paint cannot and will not become a sunny yellow simply because he wishes it to. The same can be said for his children and for Archie's and Howard's: No matter how much they wish to be categorized as white or black, their color will not change. Instead, they are caught in a cultural "no-man's land" of feeling, simultaneously belonging to and alienated from both of the groups from which they come.

Hanwell's distance from Jones is made even clearer by his color-blindness. Within the context of Smith's previous works and her personal statements, color-blindness should appear as metaphorically positive, suggesting tolerance, but it is presented in "Hanwell" as an affliction. The "major preoccupation" in *White Teeth* was, obviously, teeth, because of their roots (Thompson 124). In "Hanwell in Hell" and in *On Beauty*, the focus shifts upward to the organs of sight: the eyes. No longer is Smith interested in "speaking" what she hopes to be the truth about the complicated realities of life as a mixed-race individual in a world unsure about its burgeoning multi-culturalism, both in the fact that it is becoming multicultural and in how to respond to this development. Instead, she is showing readers what she "sees"—the sometimes beautiful but sometimes incredibly ugly reality of being not-black but not-white. As a reviewer notes of *On Beauty*: "Tears run freely for many of this novel's characters. It is as if the ideological detritus that hinders their ability to see life and each other must be washed from their eyes" (Fisher 31). No longer a spokesperson for any agenda, Smith has become a lens, albeit a lens with its own focus and capacity to distort.

This interpretation raises an important question, given that both Hanwell and the Belsey family are afflicted with vision problems. Interestingly, Hanwell, the white member of his family, has the problem of color-blindness, while Kiki and the Belsey children, the black or half-black members of their family, have the problem of myopia (*On Beauty* 64). Smith does not clearly place this issue of a faulty worldview on one side or the other of the color line. *On Beauty*'s matriarch Kiki Belsey comes close to conceding a failure of vision when she thinks "that if her family could only speak the truth, together they would emerge, weeping but clear-eyed, into the light" (60); later Carlene Kipps tells her, "[T]he eyes and the heart are directly connected" (268). For both Hanwell and Kiki Belsey, the inability to see the truth about troubled mixed-race families leads to disillusionment, shattered expectations, and broken hearts. Clearly, in these two works, Smith has rejected her earlier positive conception of multiculturalism and, using the metaphor of color-blindness, instead presents a much bleaker vision of the multicultural family.

Is there meaning to be drawn from the fact that a white character is color-blind, while a black character is myopic? Hanwell, in his attempt to be "color-blind," actually neglects his family by refusing to accept that there are any differences among himself, white, his wife, black, and their children, who are at the same time both and neither race. Conversely, Kiki Belsey is too shortsighted. She cannot perceive the complications within her home until the problems grow so large that even her weak eyes must see the enormity. Embracing multiculturalism leads to the ruin of her family, but her eyes do not allow her to see this happening until it is too late. This theory has larger implications in Hanwell's case. Smith describes Hanwell as the prototypical British man: "Men in England have looked like Hanwell since the days of King Raedwald; there are hundreds of Hanwells in that fearful mound in Sutton Hoo" ("Hanwell" 120). Readers may extrapolate that this one man's story signals a wider cultural issue when narrator Clive Black exposes his own paternal relationship, divulging, "My daughter takes great pleasure in knowing the measure of me...and maybe she is right." He continues by noting that "Everyone passes the blame backward" ("Hanwell" 123), an illumination of a burgeoning problem between parents and their children. Are there thousands more Claires isolated and alienated by the actions of their parents? How many more children find themselves trying to "piece together the jigsaw" ("Hanwell" 113), while the chorus of cheers for multiculturalism rises around them? Cheers like the ones for *White Teeth* and its "feel-good" depiction of multiculturalism (Chittenden), the cheers that Claire Berlinski scorns as "wishful thinking" (quoted in Chittenden). Perhaps Berlinski's criticism is a fair one, when comparing Smith's idealized picture to the difficult realities of living as a biracial individual.

Since "Hanwell in Hell" is the story of Hanwell and not of his daughter, the reader is given little more information about Claire. This makes it difficult to analyze the ways her father's metaphorical color-blindness may have affected her sense of self. Claire, as the child of a Caucasian English father and a black mother, shares the same family makeup as Irie Jones and the three Belsey children, and she may also share some of the same life experiences of the author. First there is Irie, without her mother's "European proportions" (*White Teeth* 221), saddled with too much hair, too much weight, too much butt: her "brown bulges" (222). Her Jamaican physique haunts her because it sets her apart. She feels invisible, non-existent, "*wrong*" (224): "There was England, a gigantic mirror, and there was Irie, without reflection" (222). Smith makes a point to set Irie apart as a mixed-race child and not simply a diasporic subject, since Magid and Millat, while still experiencing the indignity of being labeled with the one-size-fits-all epithet for Indo-Asians ("Pakis"), look "less racially ambiguous," and this helps them establish their identities as both Bengalis and as the children of their uniformly Bengali parents (Thompson 129). In other words, Magid and Millat have fewer identity issues because they share physical, religious, social, and cultural characteristics with Samad and Alsana, while Irie cannot claim such identity in her genes or her home with Archie and Clara. Even though at the outset of the novel the twins reject their Bengali heritage, adopting various personae as they mature, they have a stable identity to which to return, a luxury Irie does not share.

Irie, with her concept of identity constantly in flux, swings back and forth between racial extremes, alternately embracing her Jamaican characteristics and trying to suppress them to integrate into the predominantly white British society. This identity confusion can be seen in the Belsey children as well, also as a result of their mixed race. Jerome, the eldest Belsey, finds that he has "fallen in love with a family [the Kippses]" (*On Beauty* 44). He does so because they are the "un-Belsey" (44), a "family who wanted to spend so much time with each other" (5). Little separates the Belseys and the Kippses: both fathers are university professors, both mothers are homemakers, and the children are all high-achieving students. But the Kippses are not a mixed-race family, and they believe that "Multiculturalism [is] a fatuous dream" (44). Theirs is a homogenous family, one that has no internal differences that will slowly but surely pull the family apart.

Zora Belsey fares no better in her effort to form an identity for herself. She recognizes how, because her body carries one-half of Howard's genes, she differs from Carl, the African American street poet she befriends: "His well-madeness as a human being made her feel her own bad design" (*On Beauty* 134). Zora fails to relate wholly to Carl, since she is half-white, but she also fails to relate wholly to her Caucasian schoolmates, since she is half-black. These disparate genes cause her to be never whole, neither fully "black" nor fully "white" to herself or to others. Readers hear echoes of Irie as, unable to find her place, Zora begins to lose all sense of herself:

> She found it difficult, this thing of being alone, awaiting the arrival of a group. She prepared a face—as her favorite poet had it—to meet the faces that she met, and it was a procedure that required time and forewarning to function correctly. In fact, when she was not in company it didn't seem to her that she had a face at all.... (*On Beauty* 209)

Zora is not alone in feeling her displacement. In a moment of anger, Carl reveals his true thoughts about Zora and her brothers: "You people aren't even black any more, man—I don't know *what* you are" (418).

Even young Levi is lost, affecting urban American clothing and speech in order to create an identity to replace the uncertain one into which he was born. Despite his desire to appear reckless and street-savvy, Levi actually craves a sense of belonging. He happily works for minimum wage at a blandly corporate music store overseen by a global conglomerate, feeling that he "wanted to be a part of it" (*On Beauty* 180). He discovers security, camaraderie, and answers in this structure rather than in his own family. Like Jerome and Zora, Levi unconsciously understands that he is somehow isolated from others by "Not being an anything" (*On Beauty* 354).

Since Claire is in the same situation as Irie and the Belsey children, one could presume that she too is plagued by feelings of displacement and "unbelonging." As she reveals in her letter, she is trying to puzzle together the realities of her family, her past, her identity, and her life. Those gnarled and far-reaching roots within *White Teeth* create a sense of internal isolation, with the biracial characters lacking a clear sense of identity, and external antagonism, with black and white characters viewing the biracial characters as somehow not fully a part of either racial and cultural group.

While Smith communicates disillusionment with multiculturalism using her adult characters, she does seem to retain hope for a sense of community and shared belonging among the children. For them, being not-black but not-white leads to a perceived lack of personal identity, as well as the sense that others are unable to identify them as members of specific racial or cultural groups. Yet there is always "such a shelter in each other" (*On Beauty* 93), in siblings. Howard Belsey expresses what Hanwell likely feels, that his children, obviously a product of himself, are unique and independent beings, not even the same color as he. Howard's son Jerome similarly does not find comfort or reflection in his father or mother, only in his brother and sister:

> Looking at them both now, Jerome found himself in their finger joints and neat conch ears, in their long legs and wild curls. He heard himself in their partial lisps caused by puffy tongues vibrating against slightly noticeable buckteeth. He did not consider if or how or why he loved them. They were just love: they were the first evidence he ever had of love, and they would be the last confirmation of love when everything else fell away. (*On Beauty* 235–36)

He does not extend this love to his parents because neither is quite like him; he is only like his siblings. Tellingly, the children's parents are still struggling at novel's end, but the last vision of the three children is as a group, moving forward in a journey, both literal and symbolical. Despite the escalation of disillusionment over the course of Smith's work—from the relatively untroubled Joneses of *White Teeth* to the estrangement of the Hanwells of "Hanwell in Hell," to the spectacular downfall of *On Beauty*'s Belseys—a glimmer of hope remains in Smith's vision of multiculturalism.

"Hanwell in Hell," read in relation to Smith's two other major works, reveals a significant shift in Smith's presentation of multiculturalism. Smith's more recent works show how multiculturalism has failed and may possibly be doomed to fail in instances where families of different colors and cultures try to come together. For a writer whose early work cemented her status as an example of and advocate for multiculturalism, "Hanwell in Hell" reveals an unexpected degree of dissent and uncertainty. Yet Smith does not appear completely to have given up her original hope for a society that embraces multiculturalism, even if her writing no longer reflects that hope. As she revealed in a 2006 interview, "There's a line that Katharine Hepburn says in *The Philadelphia Story*: 'The time to make up your mind about people is never.' I love that" (quoted in Leddy 23). The question still unanswered is, with a part of her sense of optimism still intact, what sparked Smith's radical change of heart on the issue of multiculturalism? Looking at her career, one event stands out above all others as a potential culprit: September 11, 2001. The terrorist attacks resulted in a xenophobic fear of the same "dun-colored" (*White Teeth* 145) individuals about whom Smith writes. The implication is that in the Western world, particularly in Britain and America, non-white members of society are immediately considered a threat and suspect. The world became a very different place on that day, and perhaps in its change

Smith found that it could no longer accommodate men like Archie Jones and stories like *White Teeth.*

Percy Bysshe Shelley once observed that "Poets are the hierophants of an unapprehended inspiration; the mirrors of the gigantic shadows which futurity casts upon the present...." As one of the most recognized and influential voices on today's British literary scene, Smith's new take on multiculturalism may change much more than her own writing. Not only will fellow authors, readers, and critics have to wait for her future works to see where her mind may come to rest, but also her narratives may be prophesizing coming movements on the issue of multiculturalism in our larger geopolitical sphere.

## Works Cited

Chittenden, Maurice. "Award-Winning Book Accused of Papering over Britain's Racial Decay." *Australian,* February 20, 2006, 13.

Eberhart, John Mark. "British Author's Novel Reflects the Melting Pot That Is London." *Kansas City Star,* July 5, 2001, F1.

Fis[c]her, Susan Alice. "The Shelter of Each Other." *Women's Review of Books* 23, no. 2 (March–April 2006): 30–31.

Gerzina, Gretchen Holbrook. "Zadie Smith." In *Writing Across Worlds: Contemporary Writers Talk,* edited by Susheila Nasta, 266–78. London: Routledge, 2004.

Leddy, Chuck. "Zadie Smith's World View." *Writer,* February 2006, 20–23.

Mason, Wyatt. "White Knees." *Harper's Magazine,* October 2005, 83–88.

O'Grady, Kathleen. "White Teeth: A Conversation with Author Zadie Smith." *Atlantis,* September 2002, 105–11.

Rifkind, Hugo. "Zadie Smith." *Time,* June 8, 2006, 13.

Shelley, Percy Bysshe. "A Defence of Poetry." *Bartleby,* August 15, 2006. http://www.bartleby.com/27/23.html.

Smith, Zadie. "Hanwell in Hell." *The New Yorker,* September 27, 2004, 113–23.

———. *On Beauty.* New York: Penguin, 2005.

———. *White Teeth.* New York: Random House, 2000.

Thompson, Molly. "'Happy Multicultural Land'? The Implications of an 'Excess of Belonging' in Zadie Smith's *White Teeth.*" In *Write Black, Write British,* edited by Kadjia Sesay, 122–44. Hertford, UK: Hansib, 2005.

# CHAPTER X
## The Root Canals of Zadie Smith:
## London's Intergenerational Adaptation

*Kris Knauer, Morley College, London, UK*

Zadie Smith's 2000 bestseller *White Teeth* was often described in Britain as a novel truthfully exploring ideas of "Britishness" at the turn of the millennium, and although the London-born writer certainly captivated the British public with her in-depth analysis of the multiethnic stage of postcolonial Britain, the younger generations of her characters in her novels go well beyond the conventional ways of envisaging identity in relation to their nationality, religion, race, or ethnicity. Understanding the British colonial past, which the sagas of the (Jamaican) Bowden and the (Bangladeshi) Iqbal families are shaped by, Zadie Smith has a knack for scrutinizing and illustrating what is new; the social and cultural changes occurring in postwar Britain are the backdrop to all three of her novels, and although *On Beauty* is predominantly set in New England, the reader is invited to participate in Mrs. Kipps's funeral in London, the city which provides a sharp contrast to the ethnic relations in America. What has to be observed is Smith's refreshing take on issues and controversies surrounding identity, ethnicity and nationality in the contemporary world is not merely this still-young writer's manifesto or anything of the sort. The ease with which she creates characters "who are different to herself" in terms of ethnicity, religion, or age (her protagonists are white English, black English, Jewish, black Jewish, Chinese-Jewish, British South Asian, South Asian, Caribbean, white American, African American, mixed race, and of different generations) must be viewed as a result equally of her acute power of observation and sensibilities, her upbringing, and of what Paul Gilroy calls "intergenerational adaptation."

While not denying Smith's uniqueness or talent, we have to note that scores of young London writers are largely responsible for a certain shift in viewing cultural belonging, which is reflective of the physical reality of London's unsegregated schools, residential areas, housing estates, and entertainment venues, as well as streets and often homes. The recent successes of writers such as Meera Syal (whose *Life Isn't All Ha Ha Hee Hee* was adapted for television), Monica Ali (whose 2003 *Brick Lane* proved to be another hit), Andrea Levy (whose *Small Island* won the Whitbread Award in 2004),

Diana Evans (Orange Prize for *26a* in 2005), and the publication of novels like *Disobedience* by Naomi Alderman, *Londonstani* by Gautam Malkani, or Mike Phillips's *London Crossings: Biography of Black Britain*, to name just a few, confirm that the multicultural British public had finally begun to enjoy tackling the ruptures and raptures of the multiethnic state. The trend toward a new understanding of the changing realities of identity, ethnicity, and belonging, punctuated by both the winning of the 2012 Olympic bid and the London bombing the next morning in July 2006, seems to have caught on.

The concept of "intergenerational adaptation," which captures the cultural adaptation of generations of Londoners living, working, and growing up together in the same neighborhoods in this diverse city, helps understand Zadie Smith's work, just as W.E.B. DuBois's term "double consciousness" helps understand the formation of African American identities and, thanks to Paul Gilroy's re-interpretation, the condition of being English/British and black.[1] Far from idealizing race relations in Britain, Gilroy nonetheless admits that the "mainstream Britain has been required to become fluent in the anthropological idiom of official multiculturalism"(xxii), a claim that is so abundantly illustrated by artists of various backgrounds in the boom of their exquisitely original work of the early twenty-first century. In *On Beauty*, Zadie Smith relates the Belseys' trip to London, the home town of the father of the family, Howard, who works at an American university in Wellington. Howard is married to Kiki, an African American, with whom he has three children. Their reflections on North London's ethnic makeup and the social mixing, which they observe during Carlene Kipps's funeral, are truly typical of newcomers to the British capital:

> 'Every kind of person,' whispered Jerome, because everybody was whispering. 'You can tell she knew every type of person. Can you imagine a funeral—*any* event—this mixed, back home?'
>
> The Belseys looked around themselves and saw the truth of this. Every age, every colour and several faiths; people dressed very finely—hats and handbags, pearls and rings—and people who were clearly of a different world again, in jeans and baseball caps, saris and duffle coats. (282)

Despite differences between various localities in London with respect to wealth and ethnicity of the inhabitants, the way the city is laid out is preventing ghettoisation as blocks of council flats had been built even throughout the richest boroughs. Mike Phillips noted that "London denied us [the black community] the economical strength and physical space to shut ourselves off.

Ironically, inside the inner-city bubbles of territorial and cultural comfort we created we couldn't help including a white population which was more numerical than ourselves." Consequently, both geographical and cultural space in the capital was shared, and "the unshackled looseness of the space created by this process made it possible to reclaim black identities, independent of blackness," he writes. That, in turn, resulted in a number of transformations and new hybrids of cultures and styles springing up throughout the capital. "In the present day, the ferment which marks the centre of London makes it possible to imagine identities which are mobile and adaptable, formed by a variety of circumstances in which ethnicity is only one of a list of priorities" (203-204).

The mix of guests at Carlene's funeral (she was from one of the smaller islands in the Caribbean—"St Something or other" in Jerome's words—and domiciled in London) forces even the youngest of the Belseys, Levi (fascinated by the American urban street culture), to think: "Seriously...this is *weird*," said Levi, and yanked his stiff shirt collar from his neck with a hooked finger. It was Levi's first funeral, but he meant more than that. It did seem a surreal gathering, what with the strange class mix (noticeable even to as American a boy as Levi)" (284). Not surprisingly, no matter how "weird" this looks to many a visitor, this specificity of London's life fills the majority of its inhabitants with pride. Having left the funeral, Howard walks around the area on the way to his father's house, musing:

> Cricklewood is beyond salvation: so say the estate agents who drive by the derelict bingo halls and the trading estates in their decorated Mini Coopers. They are mistaken. To appreciate Cricklewood you have to walk its streets, as Howard did that afternoon. Then you find out that there is more charm in half-mile of Cricklewood's passing human faces than in all the double-fronted Georgian houses in Primrose Hill. The African women in their colourful kenti cloths, the whippet blonde with three phones tucked into the waistband of her tracksuit, the unmistakable Poles and Russians introducing the bone structure of Soviet Realism to an island of chinless, browless potato-faces, the Irish men resting on the gates of housing estates like farmers at a pig fair in Kerry.... At this distance, walking past them all...flaneur Howard was able to love them and more than this, to feel himself, in his own romantic fashion to be one of them. We scum, we happy scum! From people like these he had come. To people like these he would always belong. (292)

Belonging to such multiethnic communities provides protagonists of many London novels with a moral center not only in Zadie Smith's work.

Atima Srivastava starts her second novel from a description of the West End busy life, and in the first paragraph she makes her narrator, a young British Indian writer named Mira, make the following remarks: "All around me, people were babbling in different languages.... I'd told Luke all about the corners of London, full of different cultures, introduced him proudly to places that he had only heard about as he was growing up by the sea"(1). And Diran Adebayo's protagonist in *Some Kind of Black*, British-born Dele (of Nigerian parentage) describes the way he grew up in the eastern part of North London: "But growing up where he did, there were Asians, Africans, Caribs, Jews, pure Greeks up Palmers Green, Cypriots down Stokey, Orthodox Jews in Stamford Hill and reformed down Crouch End, Irish most everywhere, and a guy could do most things with most people" (104). Such descriptions of the city's life have recently become far from rare and too numerous to quote in a short essay. They nonetheless confirm Paul Gilroy's thesis that there occurred dramatic changes in Britain between the time he first published his *There Ain't No Black in the Union Jack* in 1987 and the turn of the millennium. London's landmark quality is perhaps that its diverse communities are porous and not sealed off from each other: they interact and influence each other, and their individual members not infrequently find themselves crossing borders and lines without terms like "crossover" coming to mind.

> This has been the century of strangers [in Britain], brown, yellow and white. This has been the century of the great immigrant experiment. It is only this late in the day that you can walk into a playground and find Isaac Leung by the fish pond, Danny Rahman in the football cage, Quang O'Rourke bouncing a basketball, and Irie Jones humming a tune. Children with first and last names on a direct collision course.... It is only this late in the day, and possibly only in Willesden, that you can find best friends Sita and Sharon, constantly mistaken for each other because Sita is white (her mother liked the name) and Sharon is Pakistani (her mother thought it best—less trouble). Yet, despite all the mixing up, despite the fact that we have finally slipped into each other's lives with reasonable comfort...there are still young white men who are angry about that; who will roll out at closing time into the poorly lit streets with a kitchen knife wrapped in a tight fist. (327)

One of the reasons for terms like "crossover" not being applied to the cultural phenomena in London is because many writers and critics realize that the cultural changes in the capital are of much deeper character, for it is not only the immigrant who adjusts to the new surroundings, but it is also the society into which they came that undergoes profound transformations as well. Although, as Zadie Smith observes, there are racist environments and thus racially motivated crime (infamously recognized by the British police only in 1999 as the aftermath of the Stephen Lawrence's death, which led to the investigation of the Metropolitan police and the finding that it followed practices of institutional racism as revealed in Macpherson's Report), the other side of the coin is marked by "creolisation" of London's streets, culture, and speech. Fashion, food, music, and entertainment industry are traditionally flagged up as the most emblematic illustrations of the impact of the twentieth-century immigrant populations on the lifestyles of British host communities. These are the most spectacular examples, which one cannot fail to notice even on the streets where reggae met punk; sari blouses are matched with boots, and curry goes with chips (English fries). Tikka has been celebrated as the Indian dish invented in Britain; the Bristol sound of Trip Hop of such artists as Morcheeba, Massive Attack, Tricky, Portishead, or Dido utilize any genre from electronica, hip hop, reggae, jazz, rock, and pop, while at least half the population of under-eighteens in urban Britain wants to look American and sound Jamaican. Contemporary literature, media, and even academic texts are full of informative and occasionally humorous accounts of innumerable "mix-and-match" fashions of which Meera Syal writes in *Life Isn't All Ha Ha Hee Hee* and which are exemplified in most of contemporary literary London-based texts.

Listening to his sons, Hanif Kureishi in *My Ear at His Heart* reflects: "Britain is such a melange of accents now.... When my sons return from school they can sound Jamaican. 'Hush your mouth there, bwoy,' they say,' but at other times their English is so RP that he was alarmed when he overheard one of their au pairs imitating their middle class accents"(21-22, 26). Likewise, Zadie Smith makes a similar point when she relates one of the exchanges between the younger generation of kids in *White Teeth*, when Irie Jones, Magid, and Millat Iqbal are about ten years old: '*Cha*, man! Believe, I don't *want* to tax dat crap,' said Millat with the Jamaican accent that all kids, whatever their nationality, used to express scorn" (167). Like languages, cultures keep evolving, inscribing themselves on the physicality of the city with every new generation, which in a multiethnic environment often finds their "cultural genetic inheritance like an extra shoe—whoa!"(31) as Zadie Smith observes in *The Autograph Man*, significantly adding to our sense of wonderment at the world. In *26a*, the half-English/half-Nigerian twins ask their mother whether they can be Nigerian once they have arrived in their mum's motherland. When Ida replies that they can be as Nigerian as they like because she is their mum, Georgia and Bessi engage in elaborate calculations resulting in a decision that they need to learn Edo language to be a *bit* Nigerian, but they cannot become utterly Nigerian to be able to return home to England in four years (58). The appearance of large African communities in the 1990s—Somali, Sierra Leonean, Nigerian—changed "black politics" in Britain, which had been previously shaped by the combative decades of the American and Caribbean civil rights movements, decolonization, and black power, as Gilroy wrote in 2002.[3] Difference was acknowledged within racial groups, which did not create communities based on Western racial designations, and it is culture rather than race to be flagged up in Britain as the reason for celebrating difference. Given the porous formation of London's communities, ethnic essentialism and ethnic absolutism is on the wane because the younger generations of the city have frequently much more in common with each other regardless of their background than with the elders of the communities from which they came, as the Commission on the Future of Multi-Ethnic Britain found in 2000. The commission called them "skilful cultural navigators,"[4] and from Zadie Smith's novels and other contemporary London texts we can learn how they operate. The city (being an existential realm where immediacy of contact with the others sharing the same crowded space) calls for unmediated ways of relating to one's surrounding and to each other—unmediated by theories, politics and media inasmuch as everyday physical proximity results in sometimes even surprising new bonds and ties developing across the traditional divides. Ever-changing London's cityscapes do not encourage separateness or fixing one's mind once and for all, becoming therefore fertile playgrounds for the "cultural navigators" of all persuasions.

Let's have a look at these at work in Zadie Smith's first novel:

> Everyone at Glenard Oak was at work; they were Babelians of every conceivable class and colour speaking in tongues, each in their own industrious corner, their busy censer mouths sending the votive offering of tobacco smoke to the many gods above them (Brent Schools Report 1990: 67 different faiths, 123 different languages)....
>     And everybody, everybody smoking fags, fags, fags, working at the begging of them, the lighting of them and the inhaling of them, the collecting of butts and the remaking of them, celebrating their power to bring people together across cultures and faiths, but mostly just smoking them. (292)

Glenard Oak is a secondary comprehensive school in Willesden Green, North London, where Irie Jones and Millat Iqbal, the "second generation" of characters in *White Teeth*, attend with various degrees of academic achievement and where they smoke fags. Irie, a heavy-set daughter of a lower middle-class English "war hero," Archibald Jones, and Clara Bowden Jones, a Jamaican by birth, "swallowed an encyclopedia and a gutter at the same time,"(241), according to Millat's mother, Alsana. Meanwhile, Millat indulges in his popularity: the leader of the Raggastani crowd, "to the cockney wide-boys in the jeans and the colored shirts, he was the joker, the risk-taker, respected lady-killer. To the black kids he was fellow weed-smoker and valued customer. To the Asian kids, hero and spokesman. Social chameleon" (269). Glenard Oak is also a school to which Millat's twin brother Magid was *not* sent, since he had been sent "back" to Bangladesh[5] a few years earlier by their father Samad Iqbal, when the latter was experiencing religious torments and identity problems, lamenting the weakening of faith in the Muslim living in the West. (The deed that Alsana could never forgive him for, because it was a betrayal of her London home.) Glenard Oak is one school among many similar schools in London or Britain in general: there is nothing exceptional about it, apart from the fact that it is the one so famously described by Zadie Smith. It is a school whose representation in a nationally acclaimed novel and in its subsequently televised dramatization takes part in the changing perspective on Britishness and on national identity or on contemporary culture as such. It is a school in which the word "difference" is not a demonized mumbo jumbo that we somehow have to incorporate in our curricula to show how liberal and progressive we are, but it is part of *lived experience* of the young crowds. Difference, understood this way, escapes definitions and defies holistic approaches to class, race, ethnicity, or gender inasmuch as it reveals itself in non-essentialist ways, quite often much to the surprise of the interested parties and much to the delight of Zadie Smith's reader. The youngsters with all the "many gods above" find new bonds even if these are merely "fags" with their "power to bring people together across cultures and faiths."

That intergenerational adaptation was not, however, an easy process can be demonstrated by other fragments from the book, starting with a scene where the children are younger and attend the Manor School. Zadie Smith gives us an example of how the "official multiculturalism" Paul Gilroy mentions was being introduced and how difficult it was for the older generations to liberate themselves from their essentialist views. During orchestra practice, the music teacher Poppy Burt-Jones announces her intention to "try to experiment with some *Indian* music," when one of the schoolboys replies: "what, you mean that EeeeEEEEAAaaaaEEEeeeeAAOoooo music?" To which "the class let out a blast of laughter," giving Poppy Burt-Jones a chance to take up her role as a fine educator:

> 'I don't think—'.... 'I DON'T THINK IT IS VERY NICE TO—' and here her voice slipped back to normal as the class registered the angry tone and quietened down. 'I don't think it is very nice to make fun of *somebody else's culture.*'
>
> The orchestra, unaware that this is what they had been doing, but aware that this was the most heinous crime in the Manor School rule book, looked to their collective feet.
>
> 'Do *you?* How would *you* like it, Sophie, if someone made fun of Queen?'...
>
> 'Wouldn't like it, Miss.'...
>
> 'Because Freddie Mercury is from *your culture.*'
>
> Samad, who was waiting for his son in the audience, remembered at this point that he heard rumours 'that this Mercury character was in actual fact a very light-skinned Persian named Farookh, whom the chef remembered from school in Panchgani, near Bombay. But who wished to split hairs.' Once Poppy Burt-Jones regained composure and control over the ten-year-olds, she tried to pursue the idea of respect being due to different cultural belonging:
>
> 'For example, what music do you like, Millat?'
>
> Millat thought for a moment, swung his saxophone to his side and began fingering it like a guitar. 'Bo-orn to ruuun! Da da da da daaa! Bruce Springsteen, Miss!...'
>
> 'Umm, nothing—nothing else? Something you listen to *at home*, maybe?'
>
> At this point Millat, troubled that his answer seemed somehow wrong, looked at his father, who started gesticulating wildly to convey head and hand movement of bharata natyam, a dance from the subcontinent. Elated Millat shouted:
>
> 'Thriiiii-ller!'...believing he had caught his father's gist. Thriii-ller night! Michael Jackson, Miss! Michael Jackson!'
>
> Samad put his head in his hands. (154-156)

Far from negating the importance of "cultural belonging," Zadie Smith engages us in re-imagining the term through its practical manifestations. Samad and Poppy Burt-Jones seem to share a certain "code" or knowledge that Millat does not seem to have access to. For both Samad and the teacher, the idea of Millat's "home" is irreversibly connected to the subcontinent, although for Burt-Jones it is India, while for Samad it is his Bangladeshi home in Willesden Green. This is exactly why Magid gets sent to Bangladesh a few months later, and simultaneously this is why Poppy wants to "experiment with *Indian* music," being quite impressed with the young Iqbal's intelligence and manner but, above all, their "difference." Samad was the only one to understand her question about the type of music Millat listened to at home *correctly*. Millat, at least at ten, did not share this knowledge of belonging with them. His idea of "home" was "inhabited" by Bruce Springsteen's music just as well as Michael Jackson's, regardless of what anyone might expect him to listen to. His attentiveness to his elders and his initial distress caused by the teacher's disappointment should also be of key interest here, because it will mean that Millat might "learn" one day what is expected of him, and which results in the protagonist joining a fairly radical Muslim organization a few years later, having renounced his white girlfriends, albeit reluctantly at first.

Samad's and Poppy's knowledge is based on essentialist assumptions, as if of moderate ethnic (and, in Samad's case, religious) absolutism, according to which Freddie Mercury is part of white English culture (for Poppy), while Millat should identify with Indian/Bangladeshi music more than with Michael Jackson or Bruce Springsteen. Both Samad and Poppy are clearly upset that Millat *does not know that*. Samad puts his head in his hands, while Poppy has to back down, not having proven her point for tolerance and cultural diversity among her pupils. Although Samad knows that Freddie Mercury is of Persian origin and participated in the mainstream British culture with such success (and thus we would have to see Samad as aware of ethnic lines not being impassable), it does not shake his conviction of the lines being drawn there not to be crossed. Even as he himself engages in adultery with Poppy Burt-Jones, the more frustrated he becomes with a vision of his son's future in the morally loose West. His perception of his own moral and religious decay makes him send Magid to Bangladesh in hopes that at least one of his sons will bring him credit in the eyes of Allah. Ideally, he would have sent both of his sons had it not been for lack of adequate financial resources.

Poppy Burt-Jones (although unaware of Freddie Mercury's Asian roots) is clearly the one to work hard to instill respect for cultural diversity in her pupils, however misguided some of her attempts are. She shows herself as a "true liberal" who would go as far in promoting the steady flow of multicultural exchange as to connect with the parent of her "multicultural kids" in ways going way beyond mere understanding and respect. What is more, as a

person suffering from the "fascination with the Other" syndrome, she becomes liable to be misled in her gullible way, as in the case of Samad invent-
ing Muslim customs for her to cover his embarrassment with Magid's strike
of not speaking. Samad tells Poppy it is *Amar durbol lagché*—'closed mouth
worship of the Creator,' to which she wows and replies: "I don't know.... To
me, it's just like this *incredible* act of *self-control*. We just don't have that in
the West" (159-160).

The kids are *different* to the generation of their parents, though—at least
in some ways and for some time as they change with the changing times. At
Manor School, they all know they have to respect "other cultures," although
the phrase has a slightly inane tinge to it. "Difference" has to do with their
parents more than with anything else. The older generations of their parents
and strangers on the street know more about constructs such as "otherness"
and "difference." During the old Druid festival of harvest, in accordance with
the school's tradition, the children were sent to visit elderly people in the area
and offer them their charity of simple goods prepared by their parents. On
the way to see a Mr. J.P. Hamilton of Kensal Rise, Irie, Magid, and Millat
board a bus and inspect their offerings. After the first round of argument
about whether "old people like raisins," and whether raisins are dried (Irie) or
dead (Millat) grapes, Magid asks: "What else have you got?"

> Irie reached into her bag. 'A coconut.'
> 'A coconut!'
> 'For your information,' snapped Irie, moving the nut out of Millat's reach, 'old peo-
> ple *like* coconuts. They can use the milk for their tea.'
> Irie pressed on in the face of Millat retching. '*And* I got some crusty French bread
> and some cheese-singlets and some apples—'
> 'We *got* apples, you chief,' cut in Millat....
> 'Well, I got some *more* and *better* apples, *akchully*, and some Kendal mint cake and
> some ackee and saltfish.'
> 'I *hate* ackee and saltfish.'
> 'Who said *you* were eating it?'
> 'I don't *want* to.'
> 'Well, you're not *going* to.'
> 'Well, good, 'cos I don't *want* to.'
> 'Well, good, 'cos I wouldn't let you even if you *wanted* to.'
> 'Well, that's lucky 'cos I *don't*. So *shame*,' said Millat....
> 'Our stop!' cried Magid, shooting to his feet and pulling the [bus's] bell cord too
> many times.

'*If you ask me,*' said one disgruntled OAP to another, '*they should all go back to their own*...[countries].'(162-163)

More than ethnic or religious difference, Irie, Millat, and Magid experience the difference of age. On hearing "ackee and saltfish" on Irie's list, Millat is not picking on the national dish of Jamaica, but he is simply disrespecting anything Irie mentions at that moment. The fellow passengers, however, who are seemingly adult, single out the kids' ethnicity as the cause of their argument and childish behavior. The contrast between the racialized world of adults and the world of Irie, Magid, and Millat, who are being socialized into it, is amplified by the scene of the encounter with the said J.P. Hamilton, who greets them at his door with: "Please, I must ask that you remove yourselves from my doorstep. I have no money whatsoever; so be your intention robbing or selling I'm afraid you will be disappointed" (169).

After much pleading from behind the door, which was shut even though the children tried to explain the purpose of their visit, Hamilton finally lets them in. During a pleasant exchange that follows, he explains that he cannot have any of the things they brought as he has no teeth, and after a pleasant exchange on the importance of brushing teeth, which an adult might have with ten-year-olds, Mr. Hamilton imparts a different truth about *clean white teeth*:

'But like all things, the business has two sides. Clean white teeth are not    always wise, now are they? Par exemplum: when I was in the Congo, the only way I could identify the nigger was by the whiteness of his teeth, if you see what I mean. Horrid business. Dark as buggery, it was. And they died because of it, you see? Poor bastards. Or rather I survived, to look at it in another way, do you see?'(172)

I still remember reading this passage for the first time. "Conrad!" I said to myself aloud on the bus in Hackney, East London. "So well meaning (perhaps), and so nasty!" As a result of the older man's words, Irie starts to cry, but Mr. Hamilton is in his element:

'Those are the split decisions you make in war. See a flash of white teeth and bang! as it were... Dark as buggery. Terrible times. All these beautiful boys lying dead there, right in front of me, right at my feet. Stomachs open, you know, with their guts on my shoes. Like the end of the bloody world. Beautiful men, enlisted by the Krauts, black as the ace of spades; poor fools didn't even know why they were there, what people they were fighting for, who they were shooting at. The decision of the gun. So quick, children. So brutal. Biscuit?' (172)

Such a supreme example of Conradian understanding of the world! The African, whether portrayed by an anti-imperialist Polish English liberal at the turn of the twentieth century, or by a British soldier of World War II, is always passive, never knowing, always pitied for the misery of his "condition," and even his "clean white teeth" or his "beauty" are eventually the reason for his doom. Mr. J.P. Hamilton takes the kids on a Conradian journey into the Congo, into Darkness and "grinning teeth," into the horrid times of dead black (as the ace of spades) bodies lying at his feet. Dark as buggery. These "beautiful black men," these "poor fools" and their "white teeth" are somehow always somewhere fresh and at hand in British memory. The root canals of Irie Jones, Magid, and Millat Iqbal are inextricably *rooted in* and *routed through* the history of the British Empire. Up to their teeth, as it were. But, on this occasion of the harvest festival celebrated by their school, they were also "routed" through an imperial memory of a toothless and forgotten "older man," who wasn't fluent enough in the contemporary "official idiom of multiculturalism" to tell his story other than in Conradian terms.

Although "mainstream Britain has been required to become fluent in the anthropological idiom of official multiculturalism," we should not assume that everybody in Britain is or wants to be fluent in it, to which the example of the passengers on the bus saying "they should all go back to their own countries" attests. Furthermore, analyzing Hamilton's exchange with the kids, one should note his "there were no wogs as I remember—though you're probably not allowed to say that these days are you?" which suggests that he was not unaware of what he was saying, that he was not completely oblivious to the multicultural idiom, but just chose to ignore it at home in his private space. For the distinction between the public and the private sphere is focal when it comes to any "official" idiom, which one has to pay heed to while in public and can forget when unmonitored at home. Simultaneously, far from idealizing the world of the child, in that we all remember *The Lord of the Flies*, and far from suggesting that "children are innocent and pure," there is a lot more to be said about the specific context of Manor School, Glenard Oak, and Willesden Green kids and youth. The initially perceived otherness of J.P. Hamilton for Irie, Magid, and Millat lay in his age and not in his ethnicity or race. For the kids *they were all the same* (to a certain point and to a certain degree of course)—*everyone in Willesden Green was the same*, which became apparent in one of Irie's conversations with her mom, when she was trying to get permission from Clara to take a year off, after her A-levels and before taking up dentistry, which would make her the first Bowden or Jones ever ("by the Grace of God, fingers crossed") to enter university. The problem with the idea was that not only did Irie want to take a year off but she wanted to take it in the Indian subcontinent and Africa, to which Clara strongly objected ("Malaria! Poverty! Tapeworm!"). After three months of warfare and after all the mediators were sent back empty-handed (*Why can't she go to Bangladesh if she wants to? Are you saying my country is not good enough for your daughter?*—Alsana) (376), Irie says to Clara:

> 'I don't just *want* to have a year off, I *need* one. It's essential—I'm young, I want some experiences. I've lived in this bloody suburb all my life. Everyone's the same here. I want to go and see people of the world....(377)
>
> But Clara was adamant, even though she could hardly speak without her false teeth, and when Irie pressed on for her permission, she lost her temper:
>
> 'Permishon for *what*? Koo go and share and ogle at poor black folk? Dr. Livingstone, I prejume? Iz dat what you learnt from da Shalfenz? Because if thash what you want, you can do dat here. Jush sit and look at me for shix munfs!'
>
> 'It's nothing to do with that! I just want to see how other people live!'
>
> 'An' gek youshelf killed in da proshess! Why don' you go necksh door, dere are uvver people dere. Go shee how dey live!'(377-378)

Apart from the comical value of this short exchange, what captivated me in this scene was its play on the idea of "sameness" and "difference." Paul Gilroy, analyzing the "official multiculturalism" of the last two decades or so in Britain, quite interestingly observes, "all parties...have come to share an interest in magnifying racial, cultural and ethnic differences so that a special transgressive pleasure can be discovered in their spectacular overcoming"(xxii). I suppose this scene, like many others in Zadie Smith's novel, could be understood in these terms, as a moment of "overcoming" difference. (Zadie Smith's novel as such and especially its phenomenal reception in Britain constituted such a spectacular moment as well). However, this context of "spectacular overcoming of difference" in this scene works on many levels insofar as Zadie Smith plays on the idea itself. If, as Gilroy explains further, "these social and political divisions [in Britain] are presented as unbridgeable gaps"(xxii), then Irie realizes that this is only a matter of representation, and her "practical" knowledge of her surroundings does not prove the popular belief that ethnic, racial, or class differences are so unbridgeable. What Irie can see beyond the spectacular manifestations of difference is "sameness" shared by the inhabitants of Willesden Green, their "uniformity" in their being "different," in the way they perhaps "carry" it around. She is so familiar with the "difference" of the people of Willesden Green that it does not seem "different" to her at all. She knows them all, whether they are white and solid middle class like the Chalfens, whether they are Bangladeshi and struggling, or mixed, or black, or "what have you"—they are *all* Willesden Green lot.

However, Zadie Smith does not stop at this first "complication." She has still got Clara Bowden Jones at hand, and although I started from the kids and Irie and their "different" to the older generation outlook on the world, especially as race and ethnicity are concerned, it is Clara's responses to Irie's intended quest that interested me here just as much. Naturally, on the one hand, one could possibly argue that her arguments have nothing to do with what she actually *says* because her primary concern is for her daughter's safety. We might presume that she does not really care what she sounds like and what she says as long as she can manage to dissuade Irie from going away. On the other hand, however, she seems to have ulterior motives that she did not voice overtly although quite explicitly nonetheless. It seems that Clara positions herself much more consciously as part of "us" and part of "them" at the same time during these arguments with her daughter. First, she accentuates malaria, poverty, tapeworm, etc., somewhat stereotypically of the Western citizen, perhaps. Later, however, she turns the tables and makes Irie sound like an early anthropologist voyeur and suggests that her daughter should not really need to go as far as Africa, as she has her own mum to "ogle at." Aware of the ambivalence of her own presence in Britain, in a way, she is also trying to remind Irie about the nature of some "liberal" gestures. Has Irie become a "liberal" like the Chalfens, who took such a voyeuristic pleasure from "being around" and getting into the lives of their Others (Irie and Millat)? Perhaps Clara could not have known that Joyce Chalfen was enchanted and enthralled with her Muslim Asian favorite (Millat), while Marcus, the scientist, took such great pleasure in giving Irie an educational chance while admiring her breasts, but she surely must have known the type. Therefore, comparing Irie to Dr. Livingstone seems to be more laden with meaning, and it appears to carry a bit more weight than the assumption that it could be just a funny line. Clara does recognize certain differences that her daughter has yet to learn, and vice versa: Irie has adapted to the surroundings of her birth in a way that is too far-fetched for her mum to comprehend.

However distinct the two generations in Zadie Smith's novel are, and whatever sociological vocabulary we could deploy to delineate the second generation's world, whether we would choose to theorize it in terms of syncretism, hybridity, acculturation, intersystem, integration, or the "fusion of horizons," one can argue for sure that it is not about color-blindness and that intergenerational adaptation was at work. In his brilliant *Liquid Love*, Zygmunt Bauman, a domiciled-in-Britain, Polish-Jewish academic, writes:

> It is in the city that the strangers who confront each other in global space as hostile states, inimical civilizations or military adversaries meet as individual human beings, watch each other at close quarters, talk to each other, learn each other's ways, negotiate the rules of life in common, cooperate and sooner or later get used to each other's presence and on an increasing number of occasions find pleasure in sharing each other's company. (117)[7]

This new predicament in London's life has recently been brought into focus by numerous young writers like Zadie Smith who, like the Commission on the Future of the Multi-Ethnic Britain, portray the city as the *community of communities*, whose rights should be recognized but balanced with the rights of individuals to move away from their community, thus proposing to also see the society as the *community of citizens*. Whether we think of the Bowdens, the Joneses, or the Iqbals; the guests at Carlene Kipps's funeral or Alex-Li Tandem from *The Autograph Man* (who detested groupings of "all kinds—social, racial, national or political—he had never joined so much as a swimming club")(167); Adebayo's Dele; Hanif Kureishi's sons' linguistic navigation; Alderman's Ronit (who has a few bones to pick with the Orthodox Jewish community of Hendon, North London, in which she grew up); or white English teenager Jas/Jason of Malkani's *Londonstani* (who joins a "desi" [South Asian] non-Muslim gang), we are bound to realize how porous London communities are and how "liquid," to use Bauman's concept, contemporary London has become. And this fluidity of social formations in the British capital, along with its inhabitants' intergenerational adaptation, is often the subject and the backdrop of Zadie Smith's inspired work. Creolization of this city's life and other social changes enabling Londoners to live together and create new values and styles are her root canals.

## Notes

[1] Paul Gilroy, *The Black Atlantic: Double Consciousness and Modernity* (Cambridge, MA: Harvard University Press, 1991).

[2] Meera Syal, *Life Isn't All Ha Ha Hee Hee* (London: Black Swan, 2000), 43–44.

[3] Gilroy, *There Ain't No Black.*

[4] The Commission on the Future of Multi-Ethnic Britain, *The Future of the Multi-Ethnic Britain: The Parekh Report* (London: Profile Books, 2000), 28–29.

[5] Magid was born in London.

[6] Samad's thoughts: 'Literal translation: *I feel weak.* It means, Miss Burt-Jones, that *every strand of me feels weakened by the desire to kiss you.'*

[7] Zygmunt Bauman, *Liquid Love: On the Frailty of Human Bonds* (Cambridge, UK: Polity, 2003), 117.

## Works Cited

Adebayo, Diran. *Some Kind of Black.* London: Abacus: 1997.
Bauman, Zygmunt. *Liquid Love: On the Frailty of Human Bonds.* Cambridge, UK: Polity, 2003.
Commission on the Future of Multi-Ethnic Britain. *The Future of the Multi-Ethnic Britain: The Parekh Report.* London: Profile Books, 2000.
Evans, Diana. *26a.* London: Chatto & Windus, 2005.
Gilroy, Paul. *The Black Atlantic: Double Consciousness and Modernity.* Cambridge, MA: Harvard University Press, 1993.
———. *There Ain't No Black in the Union Jack.* London and New York: Routledge, 2002.
Kureishi, Hanif. *My Ear at His Heart.* London: Faber and Faber, 2004.
Phillips, Mike. *London Crossings: A Biography of Black Britain.* London: Continuum, 2001.
Smith, Zadie. *The Autograph Man.* London: Penguin Books, 2003.
———. *On Beauty.* London: Hamish Hamilton, 2005.
———. *White Teeth.* London: Penguin, 2001.
Srivastava, Atima. *Looking for Maya.* London: Quarter Books, 1999.
Syal, Meera. *Life Isn't All Ha Ha Hee Hee.* London: Black Swan, 2000.

# CHAPTER XI
## Fundamental Differences in Zadie Smith's *White Teeth*
### Z. Esra Mirze, University of Tampa

The increase in academic attention to religious identity can perhaps be attributed to the tragic events of 9/11, but even before the threat of terrorism, there was an ongoing conversation, particularly in Europe, regarding how to interpellate the immigrant population—especially those of Muslim descent—into a Christian Euroculture. The rise of Islamic fundamentalism has undoubtedly intensified such discussions and has drawn new attention to the orientalist presentation of the ostensible split between the East and the West as a clash of civilizations. Preoccupied with the question of religious affiliation and its impact on political consciousness, novelists including Salman Rushdie, Hanif Kureishi, Monica Ali, and Zadie Smith have been contemplating whether "a European Muslim identity" is a plausible form of self-identification (Alibhai-Brown xiii). Smith's *White Teeth*, in particular, investigates the way in which religion has become a form of identification that impacts the way other traditional components of identity (race, class, gender, and nationalism) are constructed within the Muslim immigrant community. What used to be about race, Smith suggests, is now being replaced by a discourse of religion.

The novel focuses on the different attitudes of first- and second-generation immigrants toward religion and examines the correlation between national belonging and religious seclusion: the more the immigrant embraces Islamic values as a way of life, the more s/he is alienated from the national sphere. Smith implies that religion is a coping mechanism, uniting those marginalized Muslims living in Britain who are systematically ostracized from the center; at the same time, it remains an impediment that endangers the interpellation of the migrant as a citizen. The novel ultimately raises the question of what it means to be a multicultural society; Smith reasons that multiculturalism must be understood not as "a euphemism for 'non-white,'" but as a movement that embraces both racial and religious diversity (Alibhai-Brown 107).

Focusing on the lives of two nontraditional British families living in London—Archibald and his Jamaican wife Clara, along with Bengali-Muslims Samad and Alsana—Smith investigates how the domestic sphere is projected to the national level, impacting the definition of Britishness. The two families are a study in contrast. Archibald and Clara's interracial union suggests that, despite the disapproval of a small minority, racial differences are no longer insurmountable obstacles within the cosmopolitan, postcolonial setting. After a turbulent divorce from his first wife, Archibald handles his midlife crisis by asking the strikingly young and beautiful Clara, twenty-eight years his junior, to marry him. Clara, who is brought up as a Jehovah's Witness, regards this marriage proposal as a chance to sever her ties with her fanatical mother and her faith. With Archie, she hopes to embrace secular Englishness as an antidote to religious fanaticism. Samad and Alsana, on the other hand, are moderate Muslims who have far greater difficulty in negotiating national identity because of their racial and religious separation from the national sphere. Over the years, Samad's financial and personal failures have caused him to adhere to his religious convictions more vehemently. His increasing attachment to faith, however, is not motivated by a desire for righteousness; rather he latches on to religion as a spiritual remedy to fight off his disenfranchisement as an immigrant. Years later, when the two families have teenage children, they observe that religion is no longer a private, spiritual matter, but rather a public, political movement. When Archie and Clara's atheist daughter, Irie, moves in temporarily with her estranged grandmother, still actively recruiting young people to join her faith, her parents fear that she is getting caught up with "religion, that nasty disease" (Smith 330). The same is also true for Samad and Alsana's British-born twins. Despite all his efforts, Samad fails to set a strong example for his sons, Magid and Millat, who end up adopting extreme viewpoints: Millat finds his calling in KEVIN, "Keepers of the Eternal and Victorious Islamic Nation," an organization dedicated to the Islamization of England, while Magid, who is sent "back home" to Bangladesh to escape from "cultural corruption," comes back as a militant repudiator of religion. Through this irony, Smith seems to suggest that geographical estrangement is secondary to religious identification in the Muslim's efforts to establish a strong sense of identity in a multicultural society. By contrasting the attitudes of the two generations toward Islam, this essay will analyze an ideological shift in the definition of otherness. As a term, otherness is no longer limited to the colonial designation of racial difference, but can include those born in postcolonial England whose religious values seem to be irreconcilable with Britishness (itself a term increasingly defined according to religion). *White Teeth*, in this sense, is an exploration of how to redefine immigrant subjectivity in the light of the mutual rise of religious militarism and religious intolerance.

As a first-generation migrant, Samad has to struggle with the task of reconstructing a home for himself in the West. Through his example, Smith exhibits the complex nature of an identity that consists of a range of seemingly contradictory affiliations. As a Bengali serving in the British Army during World War II, Samad negotiates his racial and national attachments by acknowledging this diversity as the condition of colonial subjectivity. He fully embraces his racial identity while also identifying with the British Empire, which has endowed him with a colonial education and a sense of patriotic duty. During his service in the military, his racial difference marks Samad as an atypical soldier, but not as an outsider. Samad rarely questions his presence in the squad and is determined to prove himself, vowing that he will "show the English army that the Muslim men of Bengal can fight" (75). He believes he was promoted to the fight in Europe because of his merits ("Samad Miah Iqbal, Samad, we are going to confer on you a great honor. You will fight in mainland Europe—not starve and drink your own piss in Egypt or Malaya" [75]), and he is determined to live up to the expectations. For Samad, this war is an opportunity to achieve greatness, which he ironically recognizes in the actions of his heroic great-grandfather, Mangal Pande, who "shot the first bullet of the mutiny" in 1857 (84). By replicating the courageous actions of his ancestor against Britain, he now hopes, by fighting *for* Britain, to inscribe himself in British history books. Samad's desire to please the empire reflects the extent of his colonial subjectivity. As Caryl Phillips explains in *New World Order,* Samad represents a mind frame that reflects the parent child dynamic of the colonial style of thought: "They expected from Britain in the same uncomplicated manner in which a child expects from the mother. They expected to be accepted, but they hoped to be loved. They expected to be treated fairly, but secretly they yearned for preference" (264). Samad hopes to earn that preference by being heroic. His crippled hand, however, causes him to be assigned to the "bridge-laying division of His Majesty's Army," which is guaranteed to see minimum action. He initially protests his role: "I should not be here…I mean, I am educated. I am trained. I should be soaring with the Royal Airborne Force, shelling from on high!" (Smith 74). Yet despite his sporadic outbursts, Samad quickly accepts his limitations, and gradually uses his physical handicap as a justification of his inaction: "If it wasn't for this buggery hand…, this shitty hand that the useless Indian army gave me for my troubles, I would have matched his achievements" (75). By the end of the war, he feels cheated by his fate and regrets his lack of involvement: "Like a bus, Jones," he nags his friend Archibald, "We have missed the bloody war" (88). He feels insignificant, knowing that he will not be able to bequeath to his children the reputation he longs to possess. He rightly fears that his trivial role in the war will be an inescapable curse, one that will beget other failures. His fear eventually turns into self-loathing, and he holds on to religion in his later years as a means of accepting his weaknesses.

Samad's transformation from being a moderate to a sanctimonious Muslim takes place only after he relocates in London. Before, he had rarely referred to himself as a Muslim, although he was quick to reveal his racial background. While he considered himself a believer, he did not hold strong convictions about the Islamic faith; in fact, he appeared to embrace a secular notion of religion that emphasizes morality without extremism: "our actions...define us. And it makes no difference whether you are being watched by Allah, Jesus, Buddha, or whether you're not" (87). His fellow soldiers had assigned him nicknames inspired by his racial difference; at the time, however, Samad feels that this banter is motivated less by racism than by naïveté. When called "Sultan" because of his attractive physique and posh English accent, Samad takes it upon himself to correct them:

> Sultan... Sultan... Do you know I, I wouldn't mind the epithet...if it were at least *accurate*. It's not historically *accurate*, you know. It's not even *geographically* speaking, accurate. I am sure I have explained to you that I am from *Bengal*. The word *Sultan* refers to certain men of the *Arab* lands—many hundreds of miles west of Bengal. To call me Sultan is about as accurate, in terms of the mileage, you understand, as if I referred to you as Jerry-Hun fat bastard. (73)

At the same time, Samad largely ignores the ways in which the racial labels reflect the trivializing attitude of the English, who both eroticize and ridicule the colonial subject. While Samad is blind to it, the squad senses the captain's homoerotic infatuation with Samad's exoticism, noting that his superior "was in a passion over Samad's arse (but not only that; also his mind; also two slender muscular arms that could only make sense wrapped around a lover; also those luscious light green/brown eyes)" (72).

Samad is not always patient with racial epithets when he feels his identity is under attack. He does not display such tolerance when Archie addresses him as "Sam." To hear his name Anglified causes him to react with revulsion: "Don't call me Sam.... I am not one of your English matey-boys. My name is Samad Miah Iqbal. Not Sam. Not Sammy. And not—God forbid—Samuel. It is *Samad*" (94). Samad's reaction can, first of all, be understood in terms of the sensitive balancing act of identity. He takes the Anglicization of his name as a verbal assault on his identity. His outburst suggests that while he can negotiate the coexistence of national and racial affiliations as interdependent categories, he refuses the erasure of one for the sake of the other. Therefore, he gives precedence to the category which he feels is under attack. This attitude justifies his early identification with Britishness against the enemies of the empire, and his later determination to defend his Bengali background against the ignorance of the English. It is crucial for him to keep his identity compartmentalized in order to avoid the nullification of one or the other. His tempered responses to the old wives' tales about India he frequently hears nevertheless reveal his agitation with the epistemological violence exerted on his culture. At one point, he begs Archie to be aware of the deceptive nature of stereotypes:

> If you are told "they are all this" or "they do this" or "their opinions are these," withhold your judgment until all the facts are upon you. Because that land they call "India" goes by a thousand names and is populated by millions, and if you think you have found two men the same among that multitude, then you are mistaken. It is merely a trick of the moonlight. (85)

Samad's sensitivity indicates his determination to construct an identity that allows his racial and national affiliation to coexist without merging entirely. He does this by differentiating between Britishness and Englishness, terms that implicate different projections of nationalism: Britishness allows for the preservation of racial heritage, while Englishness tends to homogenize its members either by eradicating or excluding difference. This fragmentation is essentially a political problem. Tariq Modood explains that Englishness "has been treated by the new Britons as a closed ethnicity rather than an open nationality. Hence, while many [minority groups] have come to think of themselves as hyphenated Brits, few yet think of themselves as English" (77). Samad includes himself under the umbrella of Britishness, an identity that absorbs racial difference, as opposed to Englishness, a term historically connected to oppression, world domination, and racism. Samad eventually acknowledges his hyphenated identity as a Bengali-British subject, a description that emphasizes racial diversity as well as his investment in

British nationalism, a dynamic that "asserts a natural bond between *all* the members of a nation" regardless of their racial difference (Kumar 44). Although Samad is able to sustain a balance between racial and national belonging by keeping both of his categorical identities intact, once religion figures into the equation as yet another category of difference, he loses his footing. The ultimate puzzle he needs to solve is how to triangulate his identity between race, nation, and religion in a way that will be compatible with Britishness.

After the war, when Samad is still leaning toward a conception of his identity as English rather than British, he faces a decision about where to build a home for himself: "What am I going to do...? Go back to Bengal? Or to Delhi? Who would have such an Englishman there? To England? Who would have such an Indian?" (Smith 95). He makes the decision to relocate in London, well aware of the challenges of being a minority at a time when "the rapacious Empire was becoming the toothless Commonwealth, Britain was having to adjust to a new relationship with countries such as India and Pakistan" (Phillips 271). As he predicts, his experience in London as a civilian is dramatically different from his days in the military; while his patriotism enabled him to be accepted by the squad as the colonial other, he finds that the civilian life after the decline of the empire is not as welcoming. As London transitions from a colonial metropole to a postcolonial cosmopolis, so does Samad have to refashion his identity from colonial to postcolonial subjectivity. The further compartmentalization of identity, Smith suggests, generates a crisis leading to a schizophrenic existence. Especially after he becomes a father, Samad's paranoia increases, and he starts viewing all things British as a source of corruption. To resist assimilation, he turns to religion as a defense mechanism. By clinging to his faith, he hopes to resist the changes around him: "I do not wish to be a modern man," he pleads, thinking that he can avoid conflict by burying his head in the sand (Smith 121). Samad is apparently guided by "an ethnic assertiveness, arising out of the feelings of not being respected or of lacking access to public space, consisting of counterposing 'positive' images against traditional or dominant stereotypes" (Modood 67). According to Modood, this assertiveness "is a politics of projecting identities in order to challenge existing power relations; of seeking not just toleration for ethnic difference but also public acknowledgement, resources, and representation" (67). He picks ideological fights as a way of solidifying his newly religious persona. Contesting the school board's decision to celebrate the Harvest Festival, Samad expresses his objections to the glorification of pagan traditions.

In reality, Samad has never been a devout Muslim. Rather, Islam is a facade he adopts to protect the roots that he is so afraid to lose. His co-worker, Shiva, is aware of Samad's conversion to Islam as a performance, and comments that he "should never have got religious" since it does not "suit [him]" (Smith 120). Samad's superficial transformation can best be understood as he gets into the habit of making "deals" with God as he tries to negotiate what notions of Islam can fit into his life:

> The deal was this: on January 1, 1980, like a New Year dieter who gives up cheese on the condition that he can have chocolate, Samad gave up masturbation so that he might drink. It was a deal, a business proposition, that he had made with God.... I am basically a good man. I don't slap the salami.... Can't say fairer than that.... (117)

Samad's religious practices are purely a way for him to settle personal moral crises. Giving up one impure act for the sake of another seems to him reasonable religious behavior. He readily pushes religion aside altogether when he resolves to commit adultery with a young, red-haired Englishwoman, Poppy Burt-Jones. Ironically, this affair commences at a time when Poppy is praising the Islamic notion of self-restraint and discipline. Samad, however, hardly resists temptation and "kick[s] the stool from under him like a man hanging himself, and me[ets] the loquacious lips of Poppy Burt-Jones with his own feverish pair" (133). From then on, rather than feeling repentance, Samad resolves not to mix sexual politics with politics of religion as the simplest way of avoiding further moral crises.

While religion does not give Samad the moral superiority he pretends to possess, it does give him a strong grounding regarding the upbringing of his children. Despite his own religious hypocrisy, he is determined to raise his children according to Islam, hoping that religion can act as an antidote to the disorientation brought about by the plurality of their attachments as second-generation migrants:

> Because immigrants have always been particularly prone to repetition—it's something to do with that experience of moving from West to East or East to West or from island to island. Even when you arrive, you're still going back and forth; your children are going round and round. There's no proper term for it—original sin seems too harsh; maybe original trauma would be better. A trauma is something that repeats and repeats, after all, and this is the tragedy of the Iqbals. (135–36)

Samad hopes to counter the trauma of being homeless by sending his sons back "home," a home he has abandoned years ago, and a home that is foreign to his sons. He believes that their re-placement in what has now become Bangladesh will allow them to connect with their roots and will enhance their relationship with Islam. However, he can only afford to send one son. After many nights of contemplation, he chooses Magid, his favorite, as opposed to Millat, who, in fact, is "the one more in need of moral direction" (163). When he sends his eleven-year-old son off to a distant relative, he truly thinks that he has made the right decision: "You'll thank me in the end. This country's no good. We tear each other apart in this country" (167). Samad hopes that in Bangladesh Magid will be able to refashion his identity in the absence of Western corruption and devote his life to God without being subject to discrimination. What Samad does not understand, however, is that Magid is not at home in Bangladesh, but rather has been sent into exile, just as out of touch with the new realities forced upon him as Samad was when he arrived in England. As a result, Magid, rather than turning Bangladeshi, becomes more "English" and secular.

Starting in their pre-teen years, Magid and Millat find themselves facing an identity crisis that distances them from their family. Millat finds his father's moral hypocrisy repulsive, while Magid often fantasizes about having another family that is more "English":

> Magid really wanted to be in some other family. He wanted to own cats, not cockroaches, he wanted his mother to make the music of the cello, not the sound of the sewing machine, he wanted to have a trellis of flowers growing up on one side of the house instead of the ever-growing pile of other people's rubbish; he wanted a piano in the hallway in place of the broken door off cousin Kurshed's car; he wanted to go on biking holidays to France, not day trips to Blackpool to visit aunties; he wanted the floor of his room to be shiny wood, not the orange-and-green swirled carpet left over from the restaurant; he wanted his father to be a doctor, not a one-handed waiter.... (126)

The passage demonstrates how Magid's desire for a more normal life is equated with mainstream Englishness. It is evident that Magid's dissatisfaction is partly due to his racial difference and partly due to class. Both of these components work to keep him away from the life he longs to lead. Because he is a second-generation migrant, his ties with his ethnic roots are much weaker; at the same time, he feels othered because he has adopted English notions of class. Magid does not follow his father as a model because he sees his father's class position as unacceptable. He is not interested in constructing a hyphenated ethnic identity, either, since he has no firsthand experience with his ethnic homeland. And when it comes to religion, which is presented to him as an antidote to assimilation, Magid rejects it instantly. He "swallows [England] as a whole" and is determined to build an alternative future to transcend his father's limitations as an immigrant (166).

For these reasons, Magid's removal from British soil does not create the outcome Samad anticipates. Magid becomes an exile, one whose subjectivity is still influenced by the values he was raised with rather than the ones that are imposed on him in Bangladesh. Being in exile shapes him as a free thinker, denouncing faith and fatalism on the basis of their escapist implications. Magid agrees with his new mentor, "the great Indian novelist" R.V. Saraswati's observations that "too often we Indians, we Bengalis, we Pakistanis, throw up our hands and cry 'Fate' in the face of history" (240). Samad is appalled by his son's association with this shady intellectual, whom he calls a "colonial throw-back, English licker-of-behinds," and erupts with anger, realizing that his master plan is actually backfiring (239):

> He learns nothing from a man who knows nothing! Where is his beard? Where is his khamise? Where is his humility? If Allah says there will be storm, there will be storm.... This is the very reason I sent the child there—to understand that essentially we are weak, that we are not in control. What does Islam mean? What does the word, the very word, mean? I surrender. I surrender to God. I surrender to him. This is not my life, this is his life. This life I call mine is his to do what he will. Indeed, I shall be tossed and turned on the wave, and there shall be nothing to be done. Nothing! Nature itself is Muslim, because it obeys the laws the creator has ingrained in it. (240)

Samad's anger is motivated by his recognition that he has been misled by the false notion of a pure identity. His chief aim in sending his son abroad was to raise him as "a real Bengali, a proper Muslim," without exposing him to the corruption of the English (179). He learns, instead, that "They're Englishifying him completely. They're deliberately leading him away from this culture and his family and his religion" (286). But Magid's newfound devotion to Western values is not the work of an abstract "them"; rather, it is Magid's own decision, his way of avoiding the mistakes of his father, who too readily accepted his limitations as an immigrant by taking refuge in religion. Because of this, Magid is now inclined to recognize religion as "the opiate of the people," an excuse to shirk social responsibility. Magid decides to dedicate his life to becoming a lawyer in order "to make the Asian countries sensible places, where order prevailed, disaster was prepared for"; in short, he is invested in the idea of Westernizing the East (239). Years later, when Samad reunites with his estranged son, eating a bacon sandwich, working on a genetic experiment with a Jewish academic, he sadly observes that Magid has become "more English than the English" (336).

Millat, on the other hand, cannot feel at home in England. His difference does not allow him to enter fully into the national sphere. This rejection, Modood explains, creates a crisis for the immigrant, who needs to live with an imposed sense of dual identity: one that he possesses, one that is inscribed on him as the other.

> They were not comfortable with the idea of British being anything more than a legal title; in particular they found it difficult to call themselves "British" because they felt that the majority of white people did not accept them as British because of their race, cultural background; through hurtful jokes, harassment, discrimination, and violence they found their claim to be British was all too often denied. (Modood 74)

Millat responds to this denial with anger; he "knew he had no face in this country, no voice in the country, until the week before last when suddenly people like Millat were on every channel and radio and every newspaper and they were angry, and Millat recognized the anger, thought it recognized him, and grabbed it with both hands" (Smith 194). It is this anger that pushes him to embrace his difference more intensely by joining the Muslim brotherhood. Like Samad, he hopes to use religion as a coping mechanism to counter his alienation from the center. However, while for Samad religion was a means of escape to the private sphere and avoidance of the public sphere, Millat is determined to use his religious persona as a way to make political statements. He participates in his first demonstration as a Muslim, rallying against Salman Rushdie's *Satanic Verses*: "It's a fucking insult!…We've taken it too long in this country. And now we're getting it from our own, man. Rhas clut! He's a fucking b dor, white man's puppet" (193).

Although Millat is quick to issue statements, he lacks a deeper understanding of what he is trying to propagate. For him, the assumption of a new identity is part of a game, an attempt to become more visible against the English nationalists who are determined to keep the "purity" of their nation. Millat and his Muslim friends had experienced this division on a day-to-day basis; they soon discover that it is easier to embrace this division and stop trying to fit in:

> People had fucked with Rajik back in the days when he was into chess and wore V-necks. People had fucked with Ranil, when he sat at the back of the class and carefully copied all teachers' comments into his book. People had fucked with Dipesh and Hifan when they wore traditional dress in the playground. People had even fucked with Millat, with his tight jeans and his white rock. But no one fucked with any of them anymore because they looked like trouble. (193)

Millat, rather than resisting his difference, comes to embrace it. He decides that as a Muslim he "had no face in this country, no voice in the country, until the week before last when suddenly people like Millat were on every channel and radio and every newspaper and they were angry, and Millat recognized the anger, thought it recognized him, and grabbed it with both hands" (194). Millat's anger and self-loathing lead him in a new direction, one which allows him to rechannel his destructive tendencies outward toward an external adversary. What better way to irritate the nationalists than by acting out as a radical Muslim? What better way to solve an identity crisis than by adopting the ready-made one his opponents are constantly trying to impose on him?

Millat joins KEVIN, "an extremist faction dedicated to direct, often violent action, a splinter group frowned on by the rest of the Islamic community; popular with the sixteen-to-twenty-five age group; feared and ridiculed in the press" (390). A militant group, KEVIN defines itself as "a radical movement where politics and religion were the two sides of the same coin" (390). They use religion as a unifying force to stand against the injustices of the white majority. Despite his lack of interest in the literature they produce and the discussion groups they establish to speak about the Koran, Millat feels that for the first time he belongs to a group that understands him. The gang mentality allows them to reverse the inferiority they feel about their religious difference; rather than accepting Islam as a marker of their difference that alienates them from the center, they treat it as a weapon to fight back. Embracing their religious identity, they aspire to gaining a legitimate voice in a society that tends to demonize them. For Millat, especially, religion is just a front—just as it had been a facade for his father. Theologically speaking, Millat "was neither one thing nor the other, this or that, Muslim or Christian, Englishman or Bengali; he lived for the in between, he lived up to his middle name, Zulfikar, the clashing of two swords" (291). What he

wants is a new forum to express the "anger inside him. Not the righteous
anger of a man of God, but the seething, violent anger of a gangster" (369).
Acting on his impulse, Millat joins KEVIN, solely because KEVIN was a
clan, and "because he loved clans" (365). His lack of intellectual commitment
is often questioned by his fellow Muslims: "You could be a great leader of
men, Millat.… But at the moment you're half the man. We need the whole
man," states Brother Tyron, criticizing Millat's promiscuous ways and encourages him to give up the worldly pleasures to commit himself fully to the
cause. For Millat, KEVIN fills a void in his life. This void, ironically, is not a
religious one. Rather, he compares being in KEVIN to "the real-life Mafia or
a Bond movie or something. Them both in their black and white suits, nod-
ding at each other. *I understand we understand each other*" (308). Caryl Phillips explains this need of belonging as a matter of distinguishing between "us
and them" (244). He observes that in societies in which there is hostility between racial groups, "Lines were not to be crossed. Those who transgressed
were to be severely punished by social ostracisation and random acts of violence" (244).

The image of the Muslim in the West is a threatening one. Indeed, Modood contends that "the prejudice against Asians is primarily a prejudice
against Muslims" (75). By participating in the formation of a Muslim Brotherhood, Millat hopes to be empowered. He is aware of the way he is perceived by others. Mrs. Chalfen thinks of him as a boy "filled with self-
revulsion and hatred of his own kind," possibly because "he had a slave mentality, or maybe a color-complex…or a wish for his own annihilation by
means of dilution in a white gene pool, or an inability to reconcile two opposing cultures" (Smith 311). To her musings Irie responds dismissively,
stating that Millat "hasn't got a disorder, he's just a Muslim" (358). One of
the misconceptions about Islam is its incompatibility with modernity. Mrs.
Chalfen believes that Millat cannot fit in with English society due to Islam's
insistence on purity and its intolerance of other religions. Lacking critical
consciousness, she fails to see that it also works the other way around, that it
is the English nationalists who are also adamant about purity that continue
to marginalize Muslim minorities, denying them access to the national domain.

*White Teeth* demonstrates that the second-generation migrant's relationship with Britishness differs dramatically from that of the previous one.
Unlike Archibald and Samad, the twins find multicultural friendship a much

more difficult challenge because racial hostility and religious intolerance, while always present in Britain, now exist in a different guise. The racial makeup of modern Britain is far more complex, as Smith points out: it is no longer a question of simply "white" and "other." Similarly, religious identity is increasingly fraught, as different religious experiences and rivalries exist even within Islam itself. Complicating matters further is the fact that while the twins, like their father, recognize the importance of fighting for a cause, they cannot draw upon the sense of imperial patriotism that inspired Archibald and Samad to serve in the military.

All of this leads to a sense of disorientation, one that cannot simply be solved by embracing a superficial form of Islam, as Samad did. After Magid's departure to Bangladesh, Millat feels lost: "he stood schizophrenic, one foot in Bengal and one in Willesden. In his mind he was as much there as he was here. He did not require a passport to live in two places at once, he needed no visa to live his brother's life and his own" (183). He decides to counter the duality he experiences by choosing one component of identity to dominate others. Like his father, he ultimately chooses Islam, but a form of Islam that offers no space for moral negotiation or individual agency. Magid, recognizing this, worries that his brother shuns him because of his repudiation of Islam: "He marks me as Cain because I am a nonbeliever. At least not in his god or any others with a name" (354). Yet regardless of their religious convictions, Magid and Millat eventually come to the realization that blind militancy (Islamic or atheistic) is not a solution. They cannot concentrate on one element of identity as a way of shutting out all other aspects of their existence in the national sphere. Rather than ignoring or repudiating their migrant identity, they ultimately confront and embrace it fully to come to terms with the challenges of making England home.

The twins' confrontation of their migrant identity is not done in the name of British nationalism or multiculturalism. Indeed, Smith encourages her readers to be critical of the nationalistic viewpoint which, from the view of the minority groups, has long failed to accept and assimilate different identities via the process of multiculturalism; the first generation was marginalized because of its race, the second because of its religion. Second-generation migrants respond to such marginalization by asserting their difference with more vigor. Orhan Pamuk has described the dangers of "the feeling of impotence deriving from degeneration, the failure to be understood, and the inability of such people to make their voices heard" (65).

Reading Smith, on the other hand, one can recognize a certain sort of Islamization as having a different sort of potential, as something that encourages a redefinition of Britishness—the concept that causes the alienation of minority groups in the first place

The ultimate argument of *White Teeth* is that a coherent national identity cannot be based on homogeneity—after all, complete homogeneity (racial, religious, philosophical) is an impossibility—but must rather be based upon a recognition of difference as a means of cultural enrichment:

> Self-realization and a sense of self cannot be sustained simply by creative activity or an identification with humanity…. What we find in people…is the need not only to be able to say what they can do but to say who they are. This is found, not created, and is found in the identification with others in a shared culture based on nationality or race or religion or some slice or amalgam thereof. Given this nature of our human nature, national consciousness and the forging and sustaining of a nation are extremely important to us whoever we are. (Nielsen; quoted in Miscevic 219)

In this context, one of Samad's early questions gains a larger significance: *"what kind of a world do you want your children to grow up in?"* (99). *White Teeth* is an attempt to formulate possible responses to Samad's question. Any kind of blind extremism—whether it be Millat's investment in violent Islamization or Magid's eventual willingness to discard ethics for the sake of science—creates a threat beyond reckoning. The ultimate defense mechanism to extremism, Smith seems to suggest, is the plurality of voices in a multicultural society.

## Works Cited

Alibhai-Brown, Yasmin. *Imagining the New Britain.* New York: Routledge, 2001.

Kumar, Krishan. "'Englishness' and English National Identity." In *British Cultural Studies*, edited by David Morley and Kevin Robbins, 41–56. Oxford: Oxford University Press, 2001.

Miscevic, Nenad. *Nationalism and Beyond: Introducing Moral Debate about Values.* Hungary: [?AU: what city in Hungary?] Central European Press, 2001.

Modood, Tariq. "British Asian Identities: Something Old, Something Borrowed, Something New." In *British Cultural Studies*, edited by David Morley and Kevin Robbins, 67–78. Oxford: Oxford University Press, 2001.

Pamuk, Orhan. "The Anger of the Damned." In *Striking Terror: America's New War*, edited by Robert B. Silvers and Barbara Epstein, 59–68. New York: New York Review of Books, 2002.

Phillips, Caryl. *New World Order.* New York: Vintage International, 2001.

Smith, Zadie. *White Teeth.* New York: Vintage International, 2001.

# CHAPTER XII
## Simulated Optimism:
## The International Marketing of *White Teeth*

*Katarzyna Jakubiak, Millersville University*

The January 2000 publication of *White Teeth* turned Zadie Smith almost overnight into the first global literary celebrity of the twenty-first century. Anyone attempting to follow closely the writer's career cannot help but feel overwhelmed by the enormous volume of publicity the novel and its author attracted internationally. In addition to the acclaim *White Teeth* gained in Great Britain and United States, the novel was translated into more than twenty languages, stimulating the interest of an unusually diverse group of international readers. In Great Britain itself, *White Teeth* was lauded in both newspapers designed for middle-class/intellectual readership (*The Guardian* and *The Times*) and popular tabloids (such as *The Evening Standard*). By comparison, in Poland, where the translation of *White Teeth* reached best-seller status, the novel's publicity ranged from glossy women's magazines (e.g., a Polish edition of *Cosmopolitan*) to highbrow literary magazines and cultural weeklies (e.g., *Tygodnik Powszechny*, an established Catholic sociocultural weekly). On the one hand, this high international visibility of a text by a Jamaican-British author, which engages in the subjects of immigrant identity, assimilation, and tradition, as well as racial and class conflict in the postcolonial world, sheds positive light on the contemporary global publishing market and its involvement in the most vital political issues of our times. On the other hand, however, one is tempted to ask about the reasons why such enthusiastic responses of the international media have greeted this particular novel.

Many postcolonial and cultural studies scholars have observed that when "minority" experience finds channels of representation in the dominant cultural institutions, problems are frequently bound to arise. For Gayatri Spivak and Sneja Gunew, one significant problem is that these representations almost always come with a stamp of "authenticity," a status of a voice that speaks for *all* "minority" experience. This status provides the cultural institutions with what Gunew calls a "secure alibi"; there is no need to hear other voices, because the minority experience has already been "covered" (60). Lori Ween problematizes the issue further when she argues that the perceived "authenticity" of a "minority" novel is usually the condition of the novel's ability to tap into the images and expectations that mainstream audiences already hold about the given "ethnic" community. Thus, Ween's perspective converges with Gunew's claim that the very notion of *authenticity* has been "constructed by hegemonic voices" (61). Because of that, Gunew argues, one has to tease "what is *not* there" out of postcolonial literature and its representations (61). One has to reflect on "what readings are not privileged, what is not there, what questions can't be asked" (61). This essay "tease[s] out what is *not* there": it investigates what is left out of the enthusiastic reviews of *White Teeth*, what readings prevail in the novel's transnational reception, and what questions on the novel's themes and structures are hardly ever posed. In this way, this essay explores the mechanisms of commodification, through which international book-marketing industries attempt to turn Smith's multidimensional novel into a "safe" and easily consumable product.

One popular interpretation of *White Teeth* that illustrates such mechanisms particularly well is the widespread misperception of the multicultural world represented in the novel as "optimistic." The reading of *White Teeth* as an "optimistic," at times even "utopian" view of race relations, unites critics regardless of their geographic location. One of the first British reviews of the novel, Alex O'Connell's article in *The Times*, describes it as "an incredibly optimistic portrayal of life in multicultural London in which immigrants battle it out to be heard above the traffic." Another British critic, Peter Childs, echoes this statement in his book on contemporary British fiction, calling *White Teeth* "a generally optimistic view of multicultural Britain" and a "fairy-tale" that expresses hopes for Britain's future "Happy Multicultural Land" (209–10). Also in American reviews the novel is perceived as optimistic, celebratory, and joyful. Anthony Quinn's *New York Times* article, for example, characterizes Smith's work as "a peculiarly sunny novel" that shows the readers that "there are reasons…to be cheerful" about the British multicultural society at the dawn of the twenty-first century. In some American reviews Smith herself is quoted as supporting "optimistic" readings of her novel. Another *New York Times* article, which features Sarah Lyall's conversation with the author, brings up Smith's claim that the book presents "'a utopian view' of race relations[; i]t's what it might be, and what it should be and maybe what it will be." A *Salon* journalist, Maria Russo, on the other hand, reporting on her interview with the author, cites Smith's concern that "the book's optimism about race relations [may] be perceived as some sort of nicey-nice obliviousness to the ugly realities of how prejudice operates."

An interesting take on the novel's "optimistic reading" can be found among Polish reviews. Calling the novel "a celebration of democracy" that gives a sense of freedom and belonging to all citizens, a well-known Polish journalist and long-time British correspondent, Adam Szostkiewicz, uses his critical response to *White Teeth* as an opportunity to promote his own political goals. Since the novel was published in Poland in October 2002, several months before the referendum in which Polish people would decide the fate of the country's membership in the European Union, Szostkiewicz quotes the book's portrayal of a multicultural society as a strong argument in favor of those political forces in Poland who support joining the union. According to Szostkiewicz:

> It is useful to read *White Teeth* also…as a book about Poland; the Poland in which we will live in a few years or a decade…when we will fully become a part of the multiethnic, multicultural Europe and the world. But it might also be a book about the Poland we will not have if we are dominated by those political forces which, claiming to guard the tradition and the defensively defined "culture," say they do not wish to see a "mish-mash of colors" in Poland. (Goźliński et al. 36).[1]

Szostkiewicz continues to argue that unlike the post-1989 Poland, where "[political] freedom" appears to bring more problems than benefits to young people, Smith's London, despite many problems and conflicts, is "a bearable" place to live"(Goźliński et al. 36).Szostkiewicz emphasizes that Smith's representation is more "sunny" than the British reality; in the real London, he explains, there is still xenophobia, still "a lot of work to be done by the future generations" (Goźliński et al. 36).

Szostkiewicz's argument admittedly illuminates important educational qualities of *White Teeth*; however, his unquestionably "optimistic" interpretation of Smith's vision makes him overlook the many ironies underlying the novel's representation of multicultural London. While the overall "optimistic" impression that *White Teeth* gives to its readers can be ascribed to abundance of humor and irony in the novel, a simple act of stopping and reflecting on the novel's plot immediately reveals the illusiveness of its celebratory tone. Studied without the comic elements that cushion the effect of disturbing messages, the events of the novel reveal themselves in their tragic rawness, and the depiction of race relations falls short of giving hope for British society's peaceful future. Although some optimism can definitely be derived from the unlikely friendship of white, working-class Archie Jones and the Bangladeshi immigrant Samad Iqbal, another potentially positive multicultural relationship in the novel, Irie Jones and Millat Iqbal's involvement with the Chalfens, a seemingly "perfect" family of white, middle-class liberal intellectuals, has quite tragic consequences. Millat gains little from his visits to the Chalfens beside the financial help, which he guiltlessly abuses. Rather than developing his "intellectual potential," as had been his school headmaster's plan, Millat grows more confused and strengthens his ties with a militant Islamic organization (whose ironic acronym, KEVIN, prevents us from taking its radicalism seriously). To make matters worse, angered by the questionable ethics of Marcus Chalfen's scientific experiments, Millat decides to assassinate Marcus's mentor during a public presentation of their genetic programming research. On the other end, Joshua Chalfen, who through close contact with the immigrant culture begins to notice the holes in his family's "perfect" image, in an act of rebellion joins an animal rights group and participates in the preparation for an attack on his own father.

Another problem of British multicultural reality clearly portrayed in the novel is the situation of minority women, one of the most vulnerable social groups. O'Connell's restaurant's "historic" acceptance of women as customers at the dawn of the twenty-first century is a pitiful sign of progress. The event's optimistic implications disappear when one realizes how often Clara Jones and Alsana Iqbal receive sexist or patronizing comments from their husbands, who spend more time with each other than with their wives. Clara, who seems happier, or at least more content, in her marriage than her Bangladeshi friend, never experiences any affection from her husband, and their touches are merely "virtual, existing only in the absences where both sets of fingers had previously been: the remote control, the biscuit-tin lid, the light switches" (Smith 167). Alsana's relationship with Samad is even more distant; it seems to continue in the manner it started: as an arrangement, a contract whose power lies not in mutual affection or even respect but in mutual investment in the business of everyday life, including household maintenance and child rearing. In fact, once the comedy through which the novel's portrayal of the Iqbal marriage is placed in the background, some of Alsana's experiences arise as the most heart-wrenching elements of the plot. Samad pointedly disregards his wife's feelings when, consumed with guilt after his illicit sexual affair, he sends Magid to Bangladesh as a way of protecting the boy against the Western "evil." When, upon discovering what had happened, Alsana takes action to bring her child back, her own powerlessness in the society becomes painfully obvious. Speaking to "the relevant authorities," she is dismissed by statements like: "To be honest, love, we're more worried about them coming *in*," or, "To tell you the truth, if it was your *husband* who ar-ranged the trip, there's not a great deal that we—" (177). Eventually, she re-signs herself to the status quo, hoping for the son's return in the future. Her only form of protest comes through language; she refuses to ever answer her husband's questions with a direct "yes" or "no," a method that seems hardly adequate to the gravity of hurt the separation from a son inflicts on a mother.[ii] Even though Magid is finally brought back to England, the decision of his return does not result so much from the mother's protest but rather from the apparent failure of the father's plan to make his "better" son em-brace the tradition and the ideals of Islam.

Even the strategies of promoting multicultural education in schools, sati-rized in the novel through the portrayal of Glenard Oak, leave one concerned about the condition of British society. The school's efforts to incorporate the traditions of many cultures into its curriculum seem to be more a matter of protocol than a drive toward genuine cross-cultural understanding. Instead of encouraging students' inquiry into Indian tradition, the music teacher's naive interest in Indian culture results in the aforementioned affair with the father of two of her students. On the other hand, the Harvest Festival, a new holi-day, which among other activities entails sending out students with gifts for elderly, predominantly white members of the community, shockingly exposes little Irie, Millat, and Magid to the community's racist mind-set. Mr. J.P Hamilton initially takes the "brown children" on his doorstep for either beg-gars or sellers, and shuts the door in their faces. When he finally remembers about the school project and invites the children in, he shares with them his memories of fighting in the Congo and shooting "niggers." After Millat in-forms him that his father also fought in the British Army in World War II, Mr. Hamilton dismisses his claim with a confident assurance that there were no "wogs" in the army (144).

In light of the above examples, it is clear that the world presented in the novel can by no means be called "incredibly optimistic." It can hardly be treated as the "utopian" environment, which would encourage an average Polish reader to rush for European Union membership. One is then com-pelled to ask: Where does the "optimistic" reading of *White Teeth* and the reading's international popularity come from? How did the novel's sarcasm become so unanimously translated among the international readership into a happy tale?

James Wood's essay from *The New Republic*, the first largely critical dis-

cussion of *White Teeth*, marks a good direction from which one may start answering the above questions. Wood places *White Teeth*, along with Salman
Rushdie, Don DeLillo, and David Foster Wallace's fiction in a category he
jokingly labels "hysterical realism." It is a style of writing, he explains, where
"the conventions of realism are not being abolished but, on the contrary, ex-
hausted, and overworked" (2). Novels like *White Teeth*, Wood continues, do
not lack reality but are "evasive of reality while borrowing from realism itself"
(2). The main mechanism of this kind of evasion is unstoppable storytelling,
which sprouts substories on every page, without leaving much room for moments of reflection. Wood quotes as an example the biography of one of
Smith's minor characters, Brother Ibrahim ad-Din Shukrallah, the founder
of KEVIN, which fails to be convincing not because of the unusual quality of
the events that compose it but because of the events' profusion. In one breath
Smith tells the story of Brother Ibrahim's origins as "the son of two poverty-
stricken barefoot Presbyterian dipsomaniacs," his conversion to Islam, his
flight to Saudi Arabia, his return to England, and his five-year period of local
media fame in Birmingham, where he locked himself in his aunt's garage in
order to study the Koran (Wood 3; Smith 389). Wood rightly claims that
however imaginative the biography, it stands microcosmically for the novel's
larger dilemma of excessive storytelling, which reduces the characters to caricature. For Wood, this biography is a good illustration of the deceptive quality of books like *White Teeth;* it shows the novel's skill in creating an illusion
of reality through a portrayal of "real people who could never...endure the
stories that happen to them"(2). Significantly, despite their participation in
myriad events, some of the characters never develop. They merely change lo-
cations and opinions. Thus, Wood concludes, in novels like *White Teeth*, the
profusion of information *about* the characters has replaced the buildup of the
characters' consciousness. The ultimate effect of this style of writing is "a
showy liveliness, a theatricality," which sometimes succeeds in hiding the fact
that the characters are not human (3).

    It is with one reservation that Wood's argument can be helpful in an-
swering the question about the origins of *White Teeth*'s optimistic readings.
While Wood's point of describing Smith's style as "showy liveliness" is well
taken, the theater reference could be more appropriately replaced with a reference to another kind of "show": the "show" of the television, Internet, and
computer games, the media that are responsible for the contemporary information overload. I believe it is exactly Smith's strategy of borrowing from
these media and from their patterns of evading a direct human-to-human in-

teraction that allows the marketing industry a convenient foothold for translating Smith's critique of multicultural society into a celebration.

It is interesting to pair the example from Wood's essay, cited above, with another excerpt that, again in a microcosmic way, illustrates *White Teeth*'s overall reliance on media discourse. Toward the end of the book we receive an account of one of the minor characters' problems. Mohammed Hussein-Ishmael, a local butcher, decides to join KEVIN. His immediate reason for joining is the increased violence he experiences running his traditional halal shop. Over the years, we are told, Mo got used to the "run-of-the-mill" physical attacks: "the numerous punches to the head, quick smacks with a crowbar, shifty kicks in the groin, or anything else that failed to draw blood" (391). Recently, however, Mo had encountered some "real" violence: "Mo had been knifed a total of five times *(ah)*, lost the tips of three fingers *(eeeesh)*, had both legs and arms broken *(oaooow)*, his feet set on fire *(jiii)*, his teeth kicked out *(ka-tooof)*, and an airgun bullet embedded in his thankfully fleshy posterior. *Boof*" (391).

The above passage indeed evokes Wood's thesis about the impossible profusion of possible events experienced by Smith's characters. However, it cannot escape anybody's attention that, with the exception of the last clause, the comic tone and thus also the "showy quality" of the disturbing account included in the passage rely entirely on the sound effects transcribed in the parentheses. A simple act of removing the parenthetical parts reveals the meaning of the account in its full horror: "Mo had been knifed a total of five times, lost the tips of three fingers, had both legs and arms broken, his feet set on fire, his teeth kicked out" (391).

What, then, are the sound effects that so drastically alter the above images? What do they imitate? Certainly, they could be sounds of a computer game, where violence occurs without any impact on the characters' feelings, while mutilated body parts and lost lives can always be replaced. They could be sounds uttered by cartoon characters, who blow themselves up with dynamite, fall thirty feet off a cliff, or get run flat into the ground by a car, only to rise without any injury. Finally, they can be sounds of a sitcom laugh track, which programs the viewers' reactions, makes sure they always know how to respond, and wraps any ambiguous turn of events in a protective layer of comedy. In other words, the sound effects included in parentheses are indicators that the world we are observing is virtual; the characters, despite their "real" appearance, never experience pain, no matter how much violence is inflicted on them; everything, including our reaction, has been prerecorded, and thus all choices are *a priori* limited.

Further proof that "virtual," or mediated, reality, which bars the reader from direct involvement, is the dominant mode of representation in *White Teeth* can be found in the abundance of images of film, television, and (less frequently) computer games found in the novel.[iii] Trying to understand their relationship to history, religion, tradition, or society, the novel's characters often refer to well-known scenes from popular culture. Samad Iqbal imagines his great grandfather's participation in anti-British mutiny through clips from *The Godfather;* his son Millat, on the other hand, tries to reinforce his involvement with Islam by substituting the word "Muslim" for "gangster" in the popular line from *GoodFellas*: "As far back as I can remember, I always wanted to be a gangster" (368–69). In another section of the novel, early into the plot, Millat, still a child of nine, appears wearing *Tomytronic* over his head, "a basic computer game that looked like a large pair of binoculars" (122). When his annoyed father pulls the game down his son's neck, Millat laments, "YOU KILLED ME!," watching his alter-ego explode in "a catastrophic light show" (124). An echo of this incident, which makes death appear to be no more than a light show, is introduced in the final chapter of the novel. Holding the gun with which he plans to assassinate Dr. Perret, Millat realizes that the experience of violence is not new to him; on the contrary, it is familiar and easy: "…there aren't any alien objects or events anymore, just as there aren't any sacred ones. It's all so familiar. It's all on TV" (436).

It is exactly in the final chapter of the novel that the image of television and the broader concept of "the mediated world" receive particular emphasis. The chapter, which focuses on Marcus Chalfen's public presentation of his genetically modified mouse, opens with the exclamation "It's just like on TV!" We soon learn that for different characters such a statement marks different modes of evaluation of reality. For Archibald Jones, a resemblance to a television show is "the most superlative compliment [he] can think of for any real-life event" (432); for Joshua Chalfen, the fact that his animal rights group's activities seem modeled on Jack Nicholson's movies is an indication of a lack of taste; finally, for Millat, television shares characteristics with Fate; like Fate, a television show is "an unstoppable narrative, written, produced and directed by somebody else" (436). Whatever their approach, however, for all the characters television is an important point of reference, and the phrase "What a performance" forms a refrain that returns throughout the chapter, linking diverse perspectives.

The refrain and the concluding section of the chapter openly suggest to the readers that Smith designs her narrative as a form that approximates television programs. The final scene of the novel, in which Archie Jones gets wounded protecting Chalfen's mentor, is described in a deliberately filmic manner, which again blunts the force of violence involved in the incident: "Everybody in the room watches with horror as he takes it in the thigh…spins around with some melodrama and falls right through the mouse's glass box. Shards of glass over the gaff. What a performance. If it were TV you would hear the saxophone around now; the credits would be rolling" (447). However, before she lets "the credits roll," Smith fast-forwards to the forthcoming episodes and presents a collection of clips from her characters' future. Significantly, while doing this, Smith lets the narrator engage in a metafictional description, which borrows its rhetoric from the media marketing discourse. In a self-mocking way the narrator wonders which elements of the plot would be of interest to particular "focus groups" (448); thus, the narrative appears as a self-consciously commercial product, written with an intention not of reflecting reality but of molding reality according to the viewers' expectations.

Interestingly, looking through the novel's reviews, one realizes that *White Teeth* is often described by its critics with the use of metaphors which refer to film media. *The Los Angeles Times*, for example, talks about "a clip of accents" and "mosaic of personal histories" that form "the Technicolor of *White Teeth*" (E3). A reviewer from the Polish daily *Gazeta Wyborcza*, on the other hand, labels the novel as "komiczna telenowela," which could be translated as "a comic television series" or "a sitcom" (36). Smith herself, in a much-cited, ironic self-review, characterizes her novel through references to popular icons of child performers (Shirley Temple, Bonnie Langford) and calls *White Teeth* "the literary equivalent of a hyperactive, ginger-haired tap-dancing 10-year-old" (Russo 1). Smith's review brings to mind the minstrelsy tradition,[iv] indicating that the author is quite conscious of the "masking" strategy she employs in the novel to make the immigrant experience "consumable" for the publishers' preferred audience. However, even when Smith makes her self-consciousness visible in *White Teeth*'s conclusion, this does not prevent the novel (and Smith herself) from becoming appropriated by the marketing industries. Despite the visibility of the novel's self-consciousness as a commercial "show," with the exception of Woods' article, in British and American reviews there is never any suggestion that *White Teeth*'s perceived optimism might be a result of the virtual quality of suffering and violence represented in the book.

Further interesting connections between Smith's use of media images and the international reception of *White Teeth* could be drawn from Paul Gilroy's comments on the relationship between technology and African diaspora cultural production. In *Against Race*, Gilroy argues that while technology, by conquering distance, compressing time, and soliciting novel forms of identification between creators and users of culture, allowed for easier global circulation and translation of African diaspora expressions, at the same time it exposed these expressions to the risks of misappropriation and manipulation. By failing to reproduce African diaspora cultures' "ethical investment in face-to-face, body-to-body, real-time interaction," the use of technology led to "simulation" of cross-cultural encounters rather than to the boosting of real communication (*Against Race* 252). The "solidarity of proximity" yielded to "the faceless intersubjectivity," abolishing "the distinctive privilege accorded to the process of performance" (252). Moreover, the use of recycled cultural products (which is exactly what Smith's use of media discourse is in the novel) has led to the "loosening of proprietary claims" and has made it easier for African diaspora cultures to be "plundered and appropriated" by what he calls "the corporate multiculturalism" (252). "The culture industry,'" explains Gilroy in a section devoted to the corporate world's recent interest in "difference," is prepared to make "substantial investments in blackness," provided that "blackness" is rendered in a "user-friendly, house-trained, and marketable 'reading' or translation" (242). The celebration of difference is then merely "simulated"; rather than serving as a tool of cross-cultural communication, technology reveals itself in service to capitalism, enabling the creation of "a tame version of…cultural disaggregation to work as part of marketing operations" of "corporate multiculturalism" (252). David Palumbo-Liu in *The Ethnic Canon* calls such "taming," or in his words "stabilizing" methods, which the mainstream applies to minority cultural production, a part of today's "management techniques" through which capitalism tries to create an "illusion of participatory democracy" (13).

In the light of Gilroy and Palumbo-Liu's remarks, it becomes possible to attribute the international popularity of *White Teeth*'s "optimistic" reading to global capitalism's power to stabilize or "translate" the text into a user-friendly, marketable version. To a large extent, this power draws from the book's reliance on structures and themes borrowed from film and electronic media. Marketing industries exploit the way in which the novel replaces the bodily performance and its openness to improvisation with a predetermined set of relations between recorded images; it persuades the readers to enter the simulated, and thus (by virtue of containing only what is expected) safe world merely for the purpose of being entertained. What is predominantly lacking from the marketing strategies designed for *White Teeth* is a clear invitation to reflect on the ironic dimensions of the novel and on the ways in which the novel's disembodied world refers to material relations hidden behind simulated images.

Interestingly, marketing industries' need to control the text of *White Teeth* results also in media attempts to regulate the authorial persona of Zadie Smith herself. This happens because, as Ween describes, the authorial persona is always a "paratextual element," which although located outside of the proper literary text, creates meaning and influences readers' interpretations. "The author's political goals, personality and even style of dress are important to the significance of the work of literature," explains Ween (96). Even a casual glance at *White Teeth*'s reviews makes it clear that the international popularity of the novel's optimistic interpretations depends greatly on the marketing of the author. In these reviews Smith's biography is usually presented as a joyful extension of the novel, an amazing success story of a working-class Jamaican immigrant's daughter. Thus, to Smith's own protests (she explains that her family class status has changed over the years), many reviews present her as a person of "humble beginnings" whose experience converges with that of her characters. British and American critics in particular highlight the fact that until her recent financial success Smith lived with her mother and siblings in Willesden, north London, where most of her novel takes place. Smith's physical attractiveness, age, and ethnic origins get exploited in a similar way. *The Guardian* journalist Simon Hattenstone describes Smith as "the perfect demographic: young, attractive, black, female," and this statement is echoed by other journalists and reviewers, who repeatedly refer to the writer as "ethnically interesting," "stunning," or "a stylist's dream." Hattenstone in fact reveals a desire to force Smith into an "exotic" image when he expresses regret that Smith decided to discard her Afro and wore straight hair to their interview. In the end, however, he assures the readers that the writer's "makeover" is just "a passing phase." The on-line *BBC News*'s Chris Jones similarly draws attention to Smith's exoticism when he emphasizes the "oriental turban" the writer wore to the reception of the Whitbread Awards. A full-page picture of Smith in a turban appears also in

*Wysokie Obcasy*, a Polish weekend supplement to the largest national daily paper. In addition to Smith's "exoticism," there is much fascination with the amount of money she received upon signing her two-book contract with the British publisher Hamish Hamilton. The figure of £250,000 is often placed right next to her age in the by-lines or opening paragraphs of *White Teeth*'s reviews.

The above eagerness to highlight the "wondrous" qualities of Zadie Smith's biography and personality goes hand in hand with the tendency to trivialize the significance of her expressions of dissatisfaction, which seem to occur quite frequently during her interviews. O'Connell describes his impression of the writer: "However likeable one finds Smith (and she is) you find yourself constantly biting back the urge to tell her to cheer up a bit. For a young woman who has landed on her feet, without so much as scuffing up her heels, she is strangely sedate…" (2). Lynell George from *The Los Angeles Times*, on the other hand, spends several paragraphs describing Smith's grim attitude and impatience with the U.S. tour only to dismiss it in the end as "thorniness" and sum it up with a patronizing description: "She's as prickly as a blooming succulent—if you want to inspect the flower close up do so with trepidation" (E3). It is clear from the above examples that, just as they coerce *White Teeth* into optimistic interpretations, the reviewers also try to force Zadie Smith into an image of a successful, happy, and complicit "ethnic" author. Thus, marketing industries' attitude toward the writer is a component of a larger intent to deny that what appears as the novel's celebratory, entertaining tone is in fact a simulation of a successful society.

Fortunately, attempts at managing the author in the same way her book is managed are not always successful; the tensions between the writer's and the market's perspectives leave many reviews of *White Teeth* ridden with contradictions. Shortly after comparing Smith to a "blooming succulent," George (a black writer himself) unconsciously questions his own approach by citing the author's concern about people who "fixate on her" instead of paying attention to the novel itself. Moreover, at the end of the article George quotes the Dominican-born writer Junot Díaz, who criticizes the very attitudes George exhibits at the beginning:

> The European and the U.S. press are far more eager to welcome a riotous book about immigrants than they are the immigrants themselves…. I believe that Ms. Smith's book is being viewed in much the same way certain desirable immigrants are being viewed by the country in which they have arrived…as a welcome addition— just don't cause any trouble. (E3)

In a similar way, O'Connell, however mystified by Smith's sedateness, never draws a connection between the writer's mood and her anecdote he quotes at the very opening of his article: "...a writer, who shall remain nameless, said he was dreading reading my book because he'd heard it was a 'multicultural novel.' Then he read it and said he wanted to tell me how he'd really enjoyed it, despite everything" (1). There are also a few articles in which Smith's voice can be heard clearly, without her interlocutors' interference. Although her comments are often framed to appear as cutesy modesty, a series of consistent attitudes emerges, which reflect Smith's overall position on the publicity craze inspired by her first book. Thus, one finds out that she does not necessarily like *White Teeth*, or at least does not consider it "her great book," and regards the attention it attracted to be excessive (Eberhart 2; Lyall 2). Moreover, she protests the role the publicity immediately bestows on her—one of a spokesperson for women and minorities—which she sees as deriving directly from gender and race prejudice ("a white male writer is never asked to be a spokesman for anything; he has complete artistic freedom") (Hattenstone 3). Finally, she objects to the commodification of her own persona, demanding the right for a woman writer to be treated as an author, "not the thing who is being looked at or judged or observed by other people" (O'Grady 2). Another proof of Smith's resistance to commodification is her decision to sell the film rights to *White Teeth* to the BBC and the Independent Company Television, despite more lucrative Hollywood offers.

Smith's articulate resistance to the commodification of her first novel suggests that despite their "taming" strategies, international marketing industries do not deprive *White Teeth* of its agency. Significantly, in *Against Race*, when Gilroy discusses the "taming" practices that "corporate multiculturalism" applies to African diaspora expressions, he refers to them, among other terms, as "translations" (242). It is useful to reflect on this term in the context of *White Teeth*. Contemporary translation theories, represented, for example, by Lawrence Venuti and Jacques Derrida, claim that the processes of translation always reveal incompleteness of hegemonic projects, even when translation is used specifically to support these projects. Sanctioning one reading of a text, translation always indicates a possibility of another. Most important, translation demonstrates that the definitive reading of a text (and thus the totality of a project) is arrived at only when some elements are banished to the outside. As Derrida repeats in numerous essays, a text always "calls for" translation because only through translation can it "live on" in the constantly renewable condition of possibility.

While marketing industries translate *White Teeth* into a "tame, user-friendly" version, the process of translation, paradoxically, points toward other possibilities of interpretation. It is important to notice that the impulse for translation does not derive solely from the international publishing markets; this impulse is inscribed in the themes and structures of the novel itself. In *White Teeth* translation emerges, side by side with the media discourse, as a major figure that defines the experience of the characters. To evoke Gilroy again, who defines translation as a "routine" condition of life in postcolonial societies (77), for the characters of *White Teeth* translation is a major way of coping with the contradictory cultural systems in which history has placed them. If Millat can enter an Islamic organization only by imagining its activities as a plot from *GoodFellas*, it is because he tries to translate his supposedly "original" tradition (Islam) into the tradition he has been familiar with since his childhood (American popular culture). If Magid comes back from Bangladesh "more English than the English," it is because he buys into the way that colonial India was historically encouraged to translate itself into the mimicry of a British culture. Also, Irie understands "wires" of Shakespeare's Dark Lady as "kinky hair" because she wants to translate British literary tradition into something meaningful for herself. Finally, Archie Jones can understand Marcus's genetic programming demonstration only as a television show, because television is the predominant mode through which genetic programming has thus far been translated for his working-class world. In these contexts, one can find another explanation for the abundance of television and media images in *White Teeth*. Television and popular media discourses seem to be the only languages through which *White Teeth's* diverse characters (and readers) can reach at least a semblance of communication. Thus, television and popular media at the same time create an effect of simulation *and* function as a means of translation in the novel.

In "The Work of Art in the Age of Mechanical Reproduction," Walter Benjamin, the "father" of contemporary translation theory, states that once a work of art is reproduced it becomes "the work of art designed for reproducibility" (224). *White Teeth*—a work composed of reproduced/borrowed/recycled elements—also appears to be a novel "designed for reproducibility." However, as my discussion above shows, the form of reproduction which the novel "calls for" is not a copy (a replica) but a translation. As a result, if a "taming," commodifying reading of *White Teeth* is one response to the call for translation, the reading does not have the power of excluding other interpretations. The discourse of the novel, with its emphasis on translation, invites multiple perspectives and opens the text for constant reinterpretation.

To illustrate *White Teeth*'s openness to reinterpretation, it is worthwhile to summon, by way of conclusion, another reference to the novel's "life" in Poland. In Poland, as in the United States and Great Britain, *White Teeth* has not avoided slipping into the trap of commodification and reductive readings. Małgorzata Szczurek, the fiction editor of Smith's Polish publisher, Znak, admitted in our email correspondence that in addition to aesthetic qualities of *White Teeth*, the decision to translate and publish the novel in Poland relied strongly on the image of the author as "a young, trendy, black woman writer." Emphasizing the marketability of the novel, Szczurek suggested that one of the project's driving forces was a desire to *repeat,* on Polish territory, the financial and media success the novel achieved in its original linguistic context. However, despite its focus on profit and media success, one element of *White Teeth*'s Polish marketing campaign enabled the novel to demonstrate its ability to transcend "stabilizing" translations. One of the many ways in which the Polish publisher decided to promote *White Teeth* was by organizing a public panel discussion, with participation of both journalists and scholars. In her email the fiction editor explained this marketing strategy in the following way:

> We hoped that if we invite journalists from important media, they will write something about the book afterwards. It turned out to be true, Szczuka who at the time worked for the TV program *Dobre książki* [Good Books] mentioned the book on TV. The whole panel discussion was published afterwards in *Gazeta Wyborcza* [the largest national daily].

Szostkiewicz's pro-European Union (EU) argument, which I cited earlier, comes exactly from this panel discussion. Thus, as shown earlier, although some panelists supported the "tame" readings of *White Teeth*, the discussion overall managed to draw attention of the wide readership (via the national daily) to some of the most thought-provoking qualities of the novel. Among other things, the panelists stressed the novel's criticism of xenophobia and its ability to expose the dangers of unquestioning reliance on tradition; they pointed toward the novel's warning against the potentially entrapping fetish of history; finally, they discussed the ways in which the novel undermines ideas of "cultural purity."

As Szostkiewicz's evocation of the EU membership suggests, these were

the very topics that required the most urgent attention at the historical moment of *White Teeth*'s publication in Poland. Interestingly, among the panelists these issues were raised with a simultaneous lament that contemporary
Polish writers lack an interest in them. The general attitude of the discussion
can be summarized by a half-envious sigh: "if only our writers could do that!"
Szostkiewicz confessed: "I am sorry that among the generation of Polish
twenty-something-years-old writers one cannot find a novel of this rank"
(Goźliński et al. 36). Szczuka articulated the problem more explicitly:

> The Polish novelistic tradition is still awaiting its post-xenophobic or post-anti-
> semitic era, which would be the equivalent of the Western post-colonialism. So far
> our contemporary literature simply evades these problems, showing the world, which
> is not exactly free from prejudice, but homogenized, indifferent and idealized.
> (Goźliński et al. 36)

Inevitably, then, Szostkiewicz was not the only commentator who drew a
direct link between the issues raised in *White Teeth* and the Polish reality.
Jarniewicz, for example, observed: "The novel states some obvious truths,
though in our setting they are constantly worth repeating: that pure English
or pure Pakistani people do not exist, just as there are no pure Poles. We are
all mixed. Purity is a dangerous myth" (Goźliński et al. 36). Małgorzata
Olszewska, the journalist of a local Kraków newspaper, echoed this remark in
her later review of the novel: "...Zadie Smith clearly emphasizes that in the
contemporary world, to some extent everybody is an immigrant.... And everybody experiences the immigrants' conflicts in their own way. It is worthwhile to be aware of that; even here, in a country that seems homogenously
pale, it is worthwhile to recognize and accept diverse colors, shades and positions" (n.p.).

The above comments show distinctly that facing the lack of contemporary Polish novelists interested in the issues of multiculturalism and immigra-
tion, Polish intellectuals used *White Teeth* and its marketable qualities to
initiate an important dialogue about Polish reality and future. No wonder,
then, that in 2004, upon Smith's visit to Poland for the launching of the
translation of *The Autograph Man*, Przemysław Czapliński informed the
writer in an interview that in Poland she had been recognized as "an almost
Polish writer." Incidentally, 2004 marked the beginning of Polish membership in the European Union and the resulting Polish mass emigration to
Great Britain. Under these new circumstances, the "Polishness" of *White
Teeth* resounds with new connotations. Czapliński attributes this "Polishness"

to the fact that the novel tells the story of "a community that has finally gained access to a better world."

In the light of the "Polish life" of *White Teeth*, the figures of mediation and translation pervading the novel acquire yet another meaning. Published in Great Britain in 2000, and focusing on immigrant experience in the world where even traditionally remote cultures have an increasing chance to interact, *White Teeth* seems to be a novel consciously designed for a global reader. "Calling" for translation, the novel is imbued with awareness that its new contexts of interpretation might be diverse to an extreme. Hence, the reliance on recycled images, the "common" language of television and other media, which takes the authority away from the author and places the responsibility for meaning largely in the hands of the reader/translator. As Smith clearly suggests in *White Teeth*'s conclusions, her tactic is not to "speed up the myth" of past tensions and future perfections but to encourage the judgment of the "onlookers" (448). Although this tactic carries with it a danger of commodification, Smith seems to adopt it with full consciousness that while a large group of "onlookers" will prefer to be entertained by "the getaway of a small brown rebel mouse," there will also be another group who will pay attention to "a bleeding man slumped across a table" (448).

## Notes

[ii] One of the problems of the novel, however, is that we do not receive much information on how Alsana feels about the separation from her son. With the exception of Irie Jones's character, we gain very little insight into the feelings and psyche of the characters who represent minority women. While Samad Iqbal's and Archie Jones's internal dilemmas receive a lot of attention, Alsana's and Clara's thoughts are often ignored. Even though we are told that Clara reads feminist books (Greer's *Female Eunuch*, Jong's *Fear of Flying*, de Beauvoir's *The Second Sex*) and later attends night classes in "Black Feminism," we never see her grow as a character in response to these books. In contrast, and perhaps as a way of re-visiting the portrayal of women in *White Teeth*, Zadie Smith's excellent third novel *On Beauty* depicts very strong women characters. One of the central themes of *On Beauty* is friendship between two black women of different generations, national backgrounds (Caribbean and the United States), and diverse views on the woman's role in the family. The unlikely friendship of Kiki Belsey and Carlene Kipps echoes or perhaps completes the vision of friendship represented by Archie and Samad in *White Teeth*.

[iii] My discussion in this section is influenced by the article "Historia zdetronizowana," written by Jerzy Jarniewicz and published in the Polish weekly *Tygodnik Powszechny*. Jarniewicz observes that the reality, which forms the focus of Smith's interest, is a processed, mediated

world, "framed in ready-made formulas and paradigms" (n.p.).

[iv] I am grateful to Dr. Kristin Dykstra for pointing this out.

[v] Gilroy's use of the term "culture industry" seems to be influenced by Adorno and Hork-heimer's approach, which treats cultural production as being driven entirely from the top down by organized capital. While I share Gilroy's critical attitude toward corporate misuse of multiculturalism, my own approach, as my further discussion will demonstrate, is closer to the views on cultural production represented by Simon During, Andrew Ross, and Janice Radway. These scholars synthesize Adorno and Horkheimer's theory *and* the ideas of Raymond Wil-liams, who poses cultural production as collective and popular, driven from the ground up. Overall, I understand cultural production as predominantly horizontal rather than vertical, and I recognize culture's multiple agents, which include both hegemonic and counterhegemonic forces.

# Contributors

**Matthew Walker Paproth** is currently a Marion L. Brittain Postdoctoral Fellow at the Georgia Institute of Technology. He received his PhD in May 2006 from Southern Illinois University Carbondale, and his dissertation is titled *"Modernist Authors, Postmodernist Writers: Joyce, Beckett, Rushdie."* He has published essays on Joyce and Beckett, and he is currently working on a project about narrative strategies in popular TV series.

**Urszula Terentowicz-Fotyga** is a Senior Lecturer in English at the Maria Curie-Skłodowska University in Lublin, Poland, where she teaches courses on nineteenth-and twentieth-century British literature. She has published on Virginia Woolf, the psychological novel, and contemporary British fiction. She is the author of a book on the semiotics of women space in Virginia Woolf's novels, *Semiotyka przestrzeni kobiecych w powie ciach Virginii Woolf* (UMCS, 2006). She is currently working on a book about the topos of the country house in contemporary British novels.

**Ulka Anjaria** is an Assistant Professor in the Department of English and American Literature at Brandeis University. She is currently working on a manuscript on the 1930s realist novel in India. She has published articles in the *Sarai Reader* and in *Economic and Political Weekly*.

**Maeve Tynan** is an Assistant Lecturer in Mary Immaculate College, University of Limerick, Ireland. Her research interests are Anglophone Caribbean poetry, postcolonial theory, and black British writing.

**Raphael Dalleo** is an Assistant Professor in the Department of English at Florida Atlantic University, where he teaches U.S. Latino/a, Caribbean, and postcolonial literatures and cultural studies. He serves on the international advisory board of the journal *Latino Studies*. His articles on Caribbean and U.S. Latino/a literature have appeared in *ARIEL, Anthurium, South Asian Review*, the *Journal of West Indian Literature, Latino Studies*, and *Small Axe*. He is coauthor of *The Latino/a Canon and the Emergence of Post-Sixties Literature* (Palgrave Macmillan, 2007), an analysis of the relationship of contemporary Latino/a literature to politics and the market.

**Lexi Stuckey** is a Master of Arts candidate at the University of Central Oklahoma. She is completing work on her thesis, which examines textual and historical revision in Rudyard Kipling's novel *Kim*, and recently published an article, "Teaching Conformity in 'Harrison Bergeron,'" in *Eureka Studies in Teaching Short Fiction*. Lexi plans to pursue doctoral studies in English literature, with a continuing emphasis on the Victorian and postcolonial.

**Kris Knauer** studied and taught at universities in Poland, California, and England. He obtained his PhD from the University of Silesia, Poland, for his work *Reciprocity and Multicultural Imagination* in 1999. He co-edited *Britishness and Cultural Studies: Continuity and Change in Narrating the Nation* (2000) with Simon Murray, and *Mobility and Identity* with Tadeusz Rachwal (2005). He also published many academic articles and essays in literary, postcolonial, cultural, and critical studies and wrote for the London-based *Drum* magazine. He is currently teaching part-time in adult education at Morley College, London, and independently finishing his book *Liquid City: New Predicaments and New Paradigms in Contemporary London Literature*. His next stop will possibly be Sierra Leone.

**Susan Alice Fischer** is Professor of English at Medgar Evers College of the City University of New York. She is co-Editor of *Changing English*, a Routledge journal, and book reviews editor of *Literary London: Interdisciplinary Studies in the Representation of London*. Recent essays and reviews have appeared in *The Swarming Streets: Twentieth Century Representations of London* (Amsterdam Rodopi, 2004), *Tulsa Studies in Women's Literature*, *The Women's Review of Books*, and elsewhere. She is completing a book about contemporary women's London narratives.

**Tracey L. Walters** is Associate Professor of Literature at Stony Brook University. She recently published *African American Women and the Classicist Tradition: From Wheatley to Morrison* (Palgrave, 2007). She has published numerous articles on black British literature including "Music and Metafiction: Aesthetic Strategies in Black Writing," "'We're All English Now Mate' Zadie Smith's *White Teeth* and the Question of Black/British Fiction." Walters also works in the area of *Classica Africana*. In her next project she will examine the representation of fashion in black literature.

**Sharon D. Raynor** is currently the Department Chair and an Assistant Professor in the Department of English and Foreign Languages at Johnson C. Smith University in Charlotte. She has written and directed two oral history projects sponsored by the North Carolina Humanities Council entitled "Breaking the Silence: The Unspoken Brotherhood of Vietnam Veterans," and "Soldier-to-Soldier: Men and Women Share Their Legacy of War." She has publications in *CLA Journal* (College Language Association), *Dos Passos Review, Who's Who in Contemporary Women's Writing, Encyclopedia of America Poetry: The Twentieth Century, From Around the World: Secular Authors and Biblical Perspectives, The Encyclopedia of African American Folklore,* and *The Encyclopedia of African American Literature.*

**Z. Esra Mirze** is Assistant Professor of English at the University of Tampa, where she teaches postcolonial literature and world literature. She is the author of articles on Orhan Pamuk and Fatih Akin. Her current project is on home and Muslim identity in postcolonial literature.

**Katarzyna Jakubiak** is an Assisant Professor of English at Millersville University of Pennsylvania. A native of Poland, Jakubiak worked as a freelance book scout and researcher for Zadie Smith's Polish publisher, Znak, in 2002-04. In December 2006 she completed her PhD in English at Illinois State University. Her dissertation, Performing Translation: Transnational Call-and-Response of African Diaspora Literature, focuses on the politics of translating African diaspora literature in various cultural contexts. She is also a translator. Her book of translations of Yusef Komunyakaa's poetry has received the 2005 New Voices in Translation award in Poland.